BILLY JOEL

Tempo
A Rowman & Littlefield Music Series on Rock, Pop, and Culture

Series Editor: Scott Calhoun

Tempo: A Rowman & Littlefield Music Series on Rock, Pop, and Culture offers titles that explore rock and popular music through the lens of social and cultural history, revealing the dynamic relationship between musicians, music, and their milieu. Like other major art forms, rock and pop music comment on their cultural, political, and even economic situation, reflecting the technological advances, psychological concerns, religious feelings, and artistic trends of their times. Contributions to the **Tempo** series are the ideal introduction to major pop and rock artists and genres.

BILLY JOEL

America's Piano Man

Joshua S. Duchan

ROWMAN & LITTLEFIELD
Lanham • Boulder • New York • London

Published by Rowman & Littlefield
A wholly owned subsidiary of The Rowman & Littlefield Publishing Group,
Inc.
4501 Forbes Boulevard, Suite 200, Lanham, Maryland 20706
www.rowman.com

Unit A, Whitacre Mews, 26-34 Stannary Street, London SE11 4AB

British Library Cataloguing in Publication Information Available

Library of Congress Cataloging-in-Publication Data

Names: Duchan, Joshua S.
Title: Billy Joel : America's Piano Man / Joshua S. Duchan.
Description: Lanham : Rowman & Littlefield, [2017] | Series: Tempo: a Rowman & Littlefield
    music series on rock, pop, and culture | Includes bibliographical references and index.
Identifiers: LCCN 2016042191 (print) | LCCN 2016043127 (ebook) | ISBN 9781442242050
    (cloth : alk. paper) | ISBN 9781442242067 (electronic)
Subjects: LCSH: Joel, Billy—Criticism and interpretation. | Rock music—United States—History
    and criticism.
Classification: LCC ML420.J72 D83 2017 (print) | LCC ML420.J72 (ebook) | DDC 782.42166092
    [B]—dc23 LC record available at https://lccn.loc.gov/2016042191

∞ ™ The paper used in this publication meets the minimum requirements of
American National Standard for Information Sciences Permanence of Paper
for Printed Library Materials, ANSI/NISO Z39.48-1992.

Printed in the United States of America

For Erin, Julia, and Mara

CONTENTS

SERIES EDITOR'S FOREWORD

As you go through your day with the music of American popular culture streaming around you through commercials, shows, films, shopping centers' in-store music players, or your own collected or suggested playlists of classics and contemporary covers, you are just as likely to hear a Billy Joel song as you are a song by the Beach Boys, Simon and Garfunkel, Bruce Springsteen, or Bob Dylan. His hits are still as popular as their hits, and his influence on younger artists is likewise as prevalent, particularly on those who approach composing popular music as both a craft and career. His complex yet accessible arrangements with solid, inviting melodies and harmonies serve storytelling lyrics, all of which have contributed to developing a popular culture that values music that connects us locally and nationally and helps us respond to the ups and downs of life.

Billy Joel's music does all of that and has long been awarded for its commercial appeal. Joel's intelligence and artistry have earned him critical acclaim as well—some of it quite prestigious—but perhaps a secret has been kept too well, such that outside of a few scholarly studies and college master classes at select schools and conservatories, he is still underappreciated for his indelible mark that has enriched American popular music. This contribution to the Tempo series by Joshua S. Duchan makes the case, convincingly so, that Joel's excellent songwriting is the engine that has driven the performer to a place of widespread cultural appeal and influence. Duchan has assembled the evidence and assessed its effect with a technician's skill but writes for everyone who is

curious to know more about Joel's music and why he matters to so
many.

Put simply and personally, I can get into the songs and the songs
continue to entertain me and speak to me as I move through life's
stages. They express a relatable emotion about a relatable story line, be
it joy, pride, hope, anger, grief, or resolve, and the circumstances Joel's
characters face feel similar to mine, my friends', and the strangers I see
often enough that they have become regulars in the scenes of my life.
Joel's music is personal but not insular. It often contains a wry observa-
tion wrapped in an upbeat line. The mood might be colored by melancholy, self-deprecation, or a devil-may-care joie de vivre, and in almost
every song, I hear a protest—either faintly or loudly—but it strikes me
as coming from a protestor who wants to be heard and included, not
abandoned. It's these complexities and tensions, which Joel takes great
interest in exploring in lyric and music, that make his work fit so well
into American culture and that almost necessitate for its fullest expression influences from jazz and classical traditions. This goes some way to
explaining what seemed like an incongruity in my younger life when I
picked through my father's record collection. He's a classical music guy
through and through, who also likes choral music, show tunes, and the
lighter jazz, ragtime, and operatic fare. On the record shelf, arranged to
the right of Bach, Beethoven, Chopin, Debussy, Grieg, Mozart, Satie,
and so many others, were the 1970s records of Billy Joel. Most of what
we think of as rock and roll and popular music has no appeal for my
father, but Billy Joel was the exception. I have to think he got on that
shelf with the classical artists because at the core of all their talents,
they were, first and foremost, piano men.

Scott Calhoun

TIMELINE

National and World Events	Billy Joel's Life and Career
	1922: Rosalind Nyman (later Joel) is born on February 22 in Brooklyn, New York, where the Nyman family had relocated from England in 1914.
	1923: Helmut (Howard) Joel is born on June 12 in Germany.
1939: World War II begins.	*1939*: Escaping the Nazis, the Joel family boards a cruise ship to sail from England to Cuba.
1941: The United States enters World War II following the Japanese attack on Pearl Harbor.	
	1942: The Joel family moves from Havana to New York City. Howard Joel and Rosalind Nyman meet in a production of Gilbert

and Sullivan's *The Pirates of Penzance* at the City College of New York.

1943:
Howard Joel is drafted into the U.S. Army and deployed to Europe.

1945:
World War II ends.

1946:
Howard Joel returns from Europe. He and Rosalind Nyman are married.

1947:
The first houses in Levittown, New York, go on sale, beginning an era of massive housing developments.

1949:
William Martin Joel (aka Billy Joel) is born on May 9 in the Bronx, New York City.

1950:
Korean War begins.

1950:
The Joel family moves from the Bronx to suburban Hicksville, New York.

1953:
Korean War ends.

1953:
Joel begins piano lessons with a local teacher, Frances Neiman.

1954:
Senator Joseph McCarthy (R-WI) holds hearings, the culmination of several years of accusations regarding Communist infiltration into the American government and armed forces.

1955:
Following the departure of
French troops from Vietnam after
the Battle of Dien Bien Phu the
previous year, the United States
organizes a U.S. Military
Assistance Advisory Group for the
country, the beginning of
American involvement there.

1957:
The Soviet Union launches the
first satellite, Sputnik, into space,
sparking the "space race."

1957:
Howard Joel leaves the family and
returns to Europe.

1960:
The film *The Magnificent Seven* is
released. The western's
soundtrack, by Elmer Bernstein,
influences Joel.

1961:
The city of Berlin is partitioned by
the construction of the Berlin
Wall, a symbol of the Cold War.

1962:
The Cuban Missile Crisis
transpires as Soviet missiles are
stationed in Cuba and later
withdrawn.

1963:
The Beatles release their first
album, *Please Please Me*.
Martin Luther King Jr. gives his "I
Have a Dream" speech in
Washington, D.C.
President John F. Kennedy is
assassinated.

1963:
Joel sees James Brown play at the
Apollo Theater in Harlem.
Joel joins his first band, the
Echoes (later known as the
Emeralds and the Lost Souls).

1964:
The Beatles come to the United States, starting "Beatlemania."

1964:
Joel sees The Beatles perform on the *Ed Sullivan Show* on February 9.

1967:
Joel joins The Hassles, recording two albums with the group, *The Hassles* and *Hour of the Wolf*.

1968:
The North Vietnamese Army launches the Tet Offensive, by some accounts a turning point in the Vietnam War.
Martin Luther King Jr. is assassinated.

1969:
The Apollo 11 mission successfully lands American astronauts on the moon.
President Richard Nixon signs Executive Order 11497, establishing the draft lottery.

1969:
Joel attends the Woodstock music festival in White Lake, New York, for one day. The festival would become a symbol for the countercultural movement.

1970:
Four students are shot by state troopers during an antiwar protest at Kent State University in Ohio.
The Beatles' final album, *Let It Be*, is released.

1970:
Joel starts Attila, a heavy metal group, with Jon Small, the drummer from The Hassles. They record one album, *Attila*.
Joel is briefly hospitalized after a failed suicide attempt.

1971:
Joel signs a record deal with Family Productions.
Cold Spring Harbor, produced by Artie Ripp, is released.

1972:
A recording of "Captain Jack" airs on Philadelphia radio station WMMR-FM, prompting multiple requests.
Joel plays at the Mar Y Sol festival in Puerto Rico, a turning point in the development of his skills as a performer.
Joel reunites with his father and learns of his half-brother, Charles Alexander Joel, who would become a successful classical pianist and conductor in Europe.
Joel moves to Los Angeles amid a contractual dispute with Family Records and performs in a local bar under the name Bill Martin.

1973:
Joel marries Elizabeth Weber Small.
Joel signs a new record deal with Columbia Records.
Piano Man, produced by Michael Stewart, is released.

1974:
President Richard Nixon resigns, ending the Watergate Scandal that began two years earlier. Gerald Ford assumes the presidency.

1974:
Streetlife Serenade, produced by Michael Stewart, is released.

1975:
New York City runs out of money and petitions the federal government for assistance. At first President Ford denies the request but later approves the city's bailout.

U.S. involvement in the conflict in Vietnam officially ends after the fall of Saigon.

1976:
Joel returns to live in New York. *Turnstiles*, produced by Joel, is released. Joel begins touring as a headliner.

1977:
The film *Star Wars* is released. It becomes the highest-grossing film of all time until *E.T. the Extra-Terrestrial* (1982).
A twenty-five-hour power failure in New York City results in looting and disorder.
Elvis Presley dies.

1977:
The Stranger, Joel's first album produced by Phil Ramone, is released. It remains Columbia Records' best-selling album until 1985. "Just the Way You Are" wins two Grammy Awards, Record of the Year, and Song of the Year.

1978:
Pope John Paul I succeeds Pope Paul VI as the 263rd Pope; he dies after thirty-three days and is succeeded by Pope John Paul II.

1978:
52nd Street, produced by Phil Ramone, is released. It wins Grammy Awards for Album of the Year and Best Pop Vocal Performance, Male. "Honesty" is nominated for the Grammy for Song of the Year.

1979:
After a revolution, Iran becomes an Islamic Republic. Radicals invade the American embassy and take hostages, demanding the return of the U.S.-backed Shah for trial.

1980:
Glass Houses, produced by Phil Ramone, is released. It wins the Grammy Award for Best Rock

Vocal Performance, Male, and is nominated for the Grammy for Album of the Year.

Joel and Elizabeth Weber separate.

Frank Weber, Elizabeth's brother, becomes Joel's manager.

1981:

Songs in the Attic, Joel's first live album, is released.

1982:
Time magazine replaces its annual "Person of the Year" cover story with "Machine of the Year," observing the rise of computing technology.

1982:

The Nylon Curtain, produced by Phil Ramone, is released. It is nominated for a Grammy Award for Album of the Year.

Joel's marriage to Elizabeth Weber ends.

1983:

An Innocent Man, produced by Phil Ramone, is released. It is nominated for a Grammy Award for Album of the Year. "Uptown Girl" is nominated for a Grammy for Best Pop Vocal Performance, Male.

Columbia Records reissues *Cold Spring Harbor,* correcting the tape-speed mistake that marred the original release.

1985:

Joel is nominated for a Grammy Award for Best Video Album for *Billy Joel: Live from Long Island.*

Joel marries Christie Brinkley. Their daughter, Alexa Ray, is born.

Greatest Hits, Vol. I & Vol. II are released.

1986:
The Bridge, produced by Phil Ramone, is released.

1987:
Joel becomes the first American rock musician to perform in the Soviet Union. A live album capturing the concerts, *Kohuept*, is released.

1989:
The Berlin Wall is dismantled. The first Gulf War begins.

1989:
Joel removes Frank Weber as his manager amid accusations of financial mismanagement.
Storm Front, produced with Mick Jones, is released. It is nominated for Grammy Awards for Best Pop Vocal Performance, Male, and Producer of the Year. "We Didn't Start the Fire" is nominated for Grammys for Record of the Year, Song of the Year, and Best Pop Vocal Performance, Male.

1991:
The Cold War ends as the Soviet Union is dissolved. The first Gulf War ends.

1991:
Joel is presented with the Grammy Legend Award. He also wins Grammys for Best Long Form Video (for *Live at Yankee Stadium*) and Best Short Form Video (for "When You Wish Upon A Star").

1993:
River of Dreams, produced by Joel, Danny Kortchmar, Joe Nicolo, and David Thoener, is

released. It is nominated for the Grammy Award for Album of the Year. "The River of Dreams" is nominated for Grammys for Record of the Year, Song of the Year, and Best Pop Vocal Performance, Male.
Joel and Christie Brinkley separate.

1994:
Joel's marriage to Christie Brinkley ends.
Joel receives the Billboard Century Award.

1996:
Joel launches a college lecture tour, "An Evening of Questions, Answers . . . and a Little Music," speaking at thirty-two schools.
Joel launches the Long Island Boat Company, building a powerboat named the Shelter Island Runabout.

1997:
Greatest Hits, Vol. III is released.
Joel is presented with the ASCAP Founder's Award for Lifetime Achievement.

1999:
Worldwide sales of Joel's records exceed 100 million units.
Joel is inducted into the Rock and Roll Hall of Fame by Ray Charles.

2000:
Joel is presented with the James Smithson Bicentennial Medal from the Smithsonian Institution. The live album, *2000 Years: The Millennium Concert*, is released, based on his December 31, 1999, concert at New York City's Madison Square Garden.

2001:
Al Qaeda terrorists attack New York City and the Pentagon and attempt to attack the White House.
The United States invades Afghanistan.

2001:
Fantasies & Delusions: Music for Solo Piano, produced by Steve Epstein, is released.
Joel is presented with the Johnny Mercer Award from the Songwriter's Hall of Fame.
Joel performs "New York State of Mind" on *America: A Tribute to Heroes*, broadcast on thirty-one networks following the 9/11 attacks.

2002:
Movin' Out, choreographed by Twyla Thorpe and featuring Joel's music, opens on Broadway. It is nominated for ten Tony Awards and wins two, Best Orchestrations and Best Choreography.
Joel is nominated for the Grammy Award for Best Pop Collaboration with Vocals for "New York State of Mind" with Tony Bennett.

2003:
The United States invades Iraq.

2004:
Joel marries Katie Lee.

2007:
The Great Recession begins.

2007:
Joel releases two singles, "All My Life" and "Christmas in Fallujah" (the latter sung by Cass Dillon), his first pop records since *River of Dreams*.

2008:
Joel plays two concerts closing Shea Stadium in New York City, which are later released as part of the musical documentary, *Last Play at Shea* (2010).

2009:
The Great Recession ends.

2009:
Joel's marriage to Katie Lee ends.

2010:
Joel opens 20th Century Cycles, a motorcycle shop, in Oyster Bay, New York.

2011:
Howard Joel dies on March 8.

2012:
Joel plays at *12.12.12 The Concert for Sandy Relief* following the devastation brought to the New York area by Hurricane Sandy.

2013:
Joel receives the 36th Annual Kennedy Center Honors.

2014:
Joel is awarded the Gershwin Prize for Popular Song from the Library of Congress.
Joel receives the ASCAP Centennial Award.
Rosalind Joel dies on July 13.

Joel begins the first "residency" at Madison Square Garden, performing monthly concerts.

2015:
Joel marries Alexis Roderick. Their daughter, Della Rose, is born.

ACKNOWLEDGMENTS

Since I've known Billy Joel's music for as long as I can remember, in a way it feels like I've been working on this book for my entire life. Therefore, I have a lifetime of family, friends, and colleagues to thank for their part in helping me as I've played, studied, analyzed, and written about Joel's music. But I'll keep it brief.

I am eternally grateful to Billy Joel, who kindly spoke with me directly, by phone and at his beautiful home, about his music, inspiration, and compositional process. This book is undoubtedly richer as a result. Thanks also to Keri Aylward and Claire Mercuri, whose assistance made my conversations with Mr. Joel possible.

I must acknowledge my debt to some of the biographers and scholars who wrote about Joel and his music before I did. Works by Mark Bego, Ken Bielen, Walter Everett, A. Morgan Jones, Christian Klein, Fred Schruers, Richard Scott, Bill Smith, and others proved invaluable as I wrote this monograph, as did countless newspaper and magazine articles. I would also like to thank Ashley Bradetich, Shannon Kennedy, and Scott Hawkins for their research assistance at various stages of this project, and Ryan Bañagale, Katherine Boas, Fiona Linn, Wendy Matthews, Thomas MacFarlane, and Emery Stephens for their support of and feedback on my ideas throughout the process. Additionally, members of the International Association for the Study of Popular Music (U.S. branch), the American Musicological Society, and the Society for Ethnomusicology provided helpful critiques and encouragement when I presented my preliminary work on Joel's music at their meetings, as did the anonymous reviewers who read my articles for *Rock Music Studies* and the *American Music Research Center Journal*. Editors Gary Burns and Thomas Riis (respectively), along with *The Cambridge Companion to the Singer-Songwriter* editors Katherine Williams and Justin Williams, also offered insightful suggestions for refining my ideas, for which I am most thankful.

I owe much gratitude to my colleagues at Wayne State University for their support as I worked on this research: Jon Anderson, Karl Braunschweig, Tinley Daniel, Norah Duncan, Walter Edwards, Sharon Lean, Mary Paquette-Abt, Matthew Seeger, John Vander Weg, and Mary Wischusen. I also thank Wayne State University's College of Fine, Performing, and Communication Arts for its generous support through a Faculty Creative/Research Grant and the Humanities Center for its assistance through its Resident Scholars and Working Group Grant programs. Additionally, thanks are due to the Rock and Roll Hall of Fame and Museum's Library and Archives, especially Jennie Thomas, for assisting me with archival materials. And I thank the folks at Rowman & Littlefield, Scott Calhoun, Bennett Graff, and Natalie Mandzuik, for helping me bring this book to fruition.

Finally, my sincerest thanks go to my family: my wife, Erin, and daughters, Julia and Mara; my parents, Lynn and Brian, and brothers, Peter and Evan; Jan and Bill; and Bob and Wendy. Your unwavering love and support mean the world to me.

INTRODUCTION

Billy Joel's music is perhaps best understood as a chronicle of the post–World War II generation, the baby boomers. It is their lives he sings about most of the time, relating the ways the world changed around them. They were born at a time of great promise, when the American Dream seemed to many people not only a possibility but a probability. Yet for many, that dream remained unfulfilled, a broken promise that engendered a measure of cynicism as the Soviet Union beat the United States to space with the launch of its Sputnik satellite in 1957, the civil rights movement of the 1960s made clear the deeply engrained discrimination widespread in American society, the Watergate scandal sapped the government's integrity in the early 1970s, the conflict in Vietnam became a real existential threat played out on television between scenes of carnage and a lottery in which lives literally hung in the balance, and economic shockwaves like the 1973 oil crisis proved the ability of far-off powers to drastically affect the daily lives of millions in the United States and other Western countries. One of Joel's talents is his ability to identify and translate large and complex trends like these, and their emotional impact, into concise and powerful musical statements. The first goal of this book is to help readers understand that translation.

On one hand, there are those who are familiar with and appreciate Joel's music. Perhaps they find its turns of phrase clever or its musical impact poignant. For many, it has served as a soundtrack to their lives, its characters and struggles relevant and instructive. On the other hand, there are those with merely a casual knowledge of Joel's music at best. These people might vaguely know "Piano Man," "Just the Way You Are," or "We Didn't Start the Fire," but have never dived deeper into his catalog. They may even adopt the (somewhat) snide attitude the press has (sometimes) taken to Joel's songs, such as an essay in *Slate* in which Ron Rosenbaum calls Joel "The Worst Pop Singer Ever" or a more recent story on the twenty-fifth anniversary of "We Didn't Start the Fire," which describes the song as "Billy Joel's awful, educational hit" (Fetters 2014). While the former group may embrace this book as it discusses many of Joel's songs (hits and deep album cuts), I hope the latter group finds this book interesting too, perhaps even gaining from it a new appreciation of Joel's songs.

I have always been in the first camp, the enthusiasts. Joel's music, which I first heard as a child riding in the back seat of my parents' car, has always "spoken" to me. The first time I was allowed to write a college term paper on a topic of my own choosing, I selected one of his albums. It was the most fun I had ever had in a music class, which means a lot coming from someone who took piano lessons for nearly fifteen years, majored in music in college, and eventually earned a doctorate in the subject. At one point I could play and sing through Joel's entire catalog. And although I admit that I faked my way through many of his songs, that experience in fact nicely parallels Joel's own musical training, where figuring out music by ear was his preferred working method.

But why study Joel's music? What makes it important? Its significance can be demonstrated in several ways. It has been tremendously successful commercially, as he remains one of the top-selling artists, with thirty-three Top 40 hits and most of his albums going multi-platinum; he has sold more than 150 million records worldwide and earned eight Grammy Awards and twenty-three nominations. It has also earned him numerous accolades, many of which are noted in this book's timeline.

Joel has been the subject of several biographies, some of which were important in providing background information for this book, including Mark Bego's *Billy Joel: The Biography*, Hank Bordowitz's *Billy Joel: The Life and Times of An Angry Young Man*, Fred Schruers's *Billy Joel: The Definitive Biography*, and Bill Smith's *I Go To Extremes: The Billy Joel Story*. Ken Bielen's book, *The Words and Music of Billy Joel*, was also informative as it examines every song in the composer's catalog with less emphasis on biography and more on sound and lyrical meaning. Moreover, there are countless interviews, profiles, and reviews published in newspapers and magazines that inform my work. And I was fortunate to interview Joel personally while writing this book, engaging the composer in several lengthy conversations about his working methods, his songs, their inspiration, and the meanings they hold for him.

Yet scholarship on Joel's music is scant, as more sustained musicological attention has been paid to other popular musicians of his generation whose work comments on society, such as Bruce Springsteen, Elton John, and Peter Gabriel. Moreover, popular music textbooks reference Joel mostly in passing. Thus, this book contributes to the small library of academic writing on Joel's music, which so far includes works like Scott Allsop's 2009 article on pedagogical uses of "We Didn't Start the Fire," Michael Borshuck's 2016 essay on Joel as a "professional singer-songwriter," Walter Everett's 2000 study of learned and vernacular styles in Joel's compositions, A. Morgan Jones's 2011 dissertation on Joel's songs and videos, and Christian Klein's 1991 sociological study of "Goodnight Saigon." A second purpose of this study, then, is to build on this literature in order to position Joel's music within twentieth-century American and popular music history.

Although biographical elements are used to understand Joel's songs and a brief sketch of his life and career appears in chapter 1, this book is not a biography. Rather, its chapters examine selected songs, grouped according to certain themes. Chapter 2 focuses on various places Joel addresses in his music, such as the American West, Los Angeles, New York, and suburbia. Chapter 3 examines Joel's songs that touch upon domestic and international politics. The next chapter looks at songs that offer glimpses of life in American working-class and middle-class culture, while the one that follows attends to many of Joel's songs about relationships and what they reveal about (changing) attitudes toward gender. Chapter 6 tackles Joel's relationship with the entertainment industry, analyzing the most significant critique of his music—that it lacked a style of its own—and examining the two strongest influences on his style, classical music and The Beatles. Chapter 7 argues that one of Joel's most distinctive qualities is the way (or rather, ways) he approaches history musically. The book concludes in chapter 8 with an assessment of Joel's lasting significance. Each chapter can be read as a stand-alone essay, but reading the later chapters after the earlier ones will enhance their impact.

Arranging this book thematically highlights the development of Joel's attitude, perspective, and compositional style. The dynamism it reveals resists the common temptation to view a single song as a representation of a static, unchanging perspective. Some of the chapters are organized chronologically, discussing several songs in the order they were composed. Others group songs by topic rather than their place on Joel's career timeline. Some songs show up in multiple chapters, while many songs in Joel's catalog are not mentioned at all.

In almost all cases, I write about the original studio recordings of Joel's songs, found on his albums (which can be purchased from most music retailers). Many bootleg and official concert performances can be found on the Internet, but for the sake of limiting the study and ensuring that all readers can refer to the same source material, I focus on the original recordings as the primary version of the musical text. Here I draw on a definition of "text" from the field of cultural studies, where it means anything that can be interpreted, including books, art, music, and so on (see Edgar and Sedgwick 1999, 415).

One could argue that recordings merely capture *a* performance and do not themselves represent "the work." Most classical music is like this—one orchestra's recording of a Beethoven symphony is not more "the symphony" than another's. But as philosopher Theodore Gracyk has argued, "Recordings are the primary link between the rock artist and the audience, and the primary object of critical attention. . . . The relevant work (the recording) frequently manifests another work, usually a song, without being a performance of that song" (1996, 18). Moreover, musical aspects that gain importance in rock music, such as guitar distortion, timbre or tone quality, and panning, are best captured on audio records and not in a notated musical score, the medium in which earlier popular and classical traditions were based. For convenience, I often use the word "song" to describe a piece of Joel's music, an object of analysis, when sometimes the word "recording" would also do. This wording accepts the notion that, in rock music, the recording is nonetheless taken not only as a *representation* of an underlying composition we might call a "song," but as the song itself.

Any piece of writing—musical, literary, scholarly—draws on its writer's perspective. This book is no different. While I point to events in American and world history, and aspects of Joel's biography and career, to contextualize Joel's songs, in the end many of the nuances I discuss result from my own interpretation, informed by my own listening, life experience, and scholarly training. The temptation to prioritize the songwriter's intended meaning for a piece of music—sometimes to the exclusion of other meanings ascribed to it—is great, especially in the case of singer-songwriters, like Joel, who are often described as "confessional" and whose music is often interpreted as pertaining directly to their own lives in a rather intimate way; as David R. Shumway puts it, their "confessional stance in their songs reveal[s] their interior selves and their private struggles" (2016, 11). But when placed within the broader contours of music history, we see that only some music has been interpreted like that. For example, a singer of Tin Pan Alley songs (the American popular music around the turn of the twentieth century) would not have been understood by audiences as singing about himself or herself, but instead simply embodying a character in song. Joel readily admits that some of his songs are autobiographical while others have little to do with his life. A third point of this book, then, is to argue that Joel's music succeeds because of the way many people could understand it in relation not to Joel's life necessarily (although that is important), but to their own lives, over which they did not always have complete control.

Of course, Joel's intended meanings for his songs are important. That is why, throughout this book, I incorporate into my analyses Joel's remarks, drawn from the media and my discussions with him. But a composer's ideas about his or her music do not always line up with the ideas that music inspires in listeners. Moreover, the meanings that listeners derive from music are valuable in the pursuit of understanding the music and its impact. Cultural critic Roland Barthes called this the "death of the author," refuting the idea that the writer of any text is the sole determiner of its meaning. To Barthes, the message of a text "lies not in its origin but in its destination" (1977, 148), which popular music scholar Keith Negus explains as "a shift in processes of interpretation: a move from an authoritative text to intertextual reference points; from an author's intentions to a reader's insights" (2011, 615). I hope that readers of this book will gain a better understanding of some of those reference points through the historical context my analyses provide, which will hopefully lead to greater insight into Joel's songs themselves.

Ultimately, as Allan F. Moore writes, while "popular songs create meanings in listeners," they do so because "the listeners create the meanings through listening to the songs" (2012, 2). In other words, both the music and its listeners have a role to play in the creation of musical meaning. The meaning-making process happens through listening, when any meaning thought to be embedded in the text is understood in light of the listener's own life experience. Because each listener's life experience is unique, "the meanings they find in their listening cannot be predetermined" (163–64). In the case of this book, readers may or may not agree with the meanings I make despite the experience and research on which they are based. So it is important to understand that "we can only specify a range of possibilities as to what [songs] might be thought to be about" (6), an analytical limitation that leaves plenty of room for varying interpretations.

There are some basic musical terms used in this book that should be defined from the outset. Many of these describe parts of a song's *form*, the sequence of sections that constitute the whole piece of music:

- A *verse* usually corresponds to one stanza of a song's lyrics, relaying its narrative and telling its story. Often there are several verses in a single song, all of which share the same essential musical elements in the accompaniment but contain different lyrics. Joel's "Piano Man," for example, has multiple verses describing the various patrons in a bar, all set to the same music.
- A song's *chorus* usually contains the same words and music each time it is played. The lyrics of the chorus ordinarily convey the main point of the poetry, so it is common—though not a hard-and-fast rule—for a song's title to be drawn from its chorus (as in "We Didn't Start the Fire").
- In some cases, the final line of each verse may be the same, in which case it is called a *refrain*. Refrains can be the song's title (as in "She's Always a Woman"), but this is not a requirement (see "Summer, Highland Falls"). Often, a song with a refrain will not have a separate chorus section.
- The *bridge* of a song provides contrast to the musical and lyrical material of the verses and chorus. It can embody a change of

perspective or mood and often either increases the song's tension (as in "Allentown") or releases it (as in "She's Right on Time").

- In songs employing *strophic form*, the musical structure contains only a series of verses without a chorus (as in "The Entertainer"). When a bridge is inserted between two verses in a strophic song, the form is called *modified strophic* (heard in "A Matter of Trust").

- Many songs also include an *introduction*, sometimes abbreviated as "intro," which refers to music at its beginning (usually not including vocals) that precedes the first line of sung text (as in "The Stranger"). Similarly, many songs have a *coda* or *outro*, indicating a section that sees the song to its end after all the verses, choruses, and bridges have finished (as in "Leningrad"). Codas or outros often include ad-lib vocal lines (repetitions of earlier lyrics or improvisations on them), instrumental solos, or both.

- Instrumental solos occur in many songs, where a melodic instrument plays but the vocal parts are absent. For example, "Just the Way You Are" features a saxophone solo, "I Go to Extremes" includes a keyboard solo, and "You May Be Right" splits the instrumental solo section between the electric guitar and the saxophone. The solo is sometimes based on melodic material sung earlier but may also be melodically different. In most cases, the musical material used in the accompaniment to an instrumental solo comes from one of the song's formal sections (verse, chorus, or bridge).

In addition to these formal terms, many of the analyses in this book consider the tonal aspects of the music. Most songs in Western popular music are written in a *key*, identified by the name of the pitch that is most important and upon which its scale is built. For example, a song in the key of C, such as "And So It Goes," will use the pitch C as its primary tone, called the *tonic*. Melodies are most satisfying when they end on the tonic, but denying that satisfaction is a potent technique for creating musical tension. A song's harmony, the combinations of pitches (usually forming *chords*) in the background that accompany the melody, is also most satisfying when it ends on a chord built on the tonic pitch, since the consonance of the tonic chord resolves the tension created by any preceding dissonances. Again, denying the satisfaction of a climactic *cadence* (the movement between chords at the end of a phrase) can be an effective means of creating tension and building expectations in listeners.

Chords normally contain three or four pitches at varying intervals but can be made more dissonant if nonchord tones are added, as Joel does in "And So It Goes." And while the harmony of much popular music rests on three basic chords—the first built on the tonic, a second on a pitch four steps higher in the scale, and a third on a pitch five steps above the tonic—there are plenty of examples of songs that utilize additional chords. "State of Grace," for example, employs a sequence of chords that lead listeners rather "far" from song's tonic (A) before returning. (See chapter 5 for more detailed analyses of "And So It Goes" and "State of Grace.") Moreover, some songs change keys (a device called *modulation*) partway through in order to signal an increase in excitement, energy, or intensity (as in "Movin' Out [Anthony's Song]").

Joel, who is sometimes described as a craftsman of songwriting, has a firm grasp of all of these musical elements and more. With the exception of "We Didn't Start the Fire" (see chapter 7), he always begins writing songs by composing a melody and accompanying harmony. Then he attempts to "decode" what the music is saying, creating and refining lyrics to match that musical message. Thus, there is a tight confluence—at least to Joel's ear—between the sonic and linguistic components of his songs, which helps to justify the close attention paid in this book not only to the lyrics but also to other musical properties, including melody, harmony, form, and aspects of the recording process such as sound effects, double-tracking, and panning. For rock music, the latter group is just as essential to compositional process as the former (Zak 2001).

The combinations of sounds and words we hear in Joel's song are not created in a vacuum, however. Instead, Joel reacts to the world around him. The ultimate goal of this book is to trace the economic, cultural, demographic, technological, and social forces at work in the world, as well as the world events—local, national, and international—that provided the context within which Joel composed. For the songs analyzed here, this book aims to explain not just what a song "means," but why that topic, those sounds, and those words would be relevant and meaningful for Joel and his listeners at the time that song was written.

I

"SOMEWHERE ALONG THE LINE"
Biography and Influences

Like all of us, Billy Joel is a product of his time. That time, the second half of the twentieth century and the beginning of the new millennium, is a crucial one because so much in the world changed. World War II, a conflict of truly global proportions, prompted massive shifts in American society. The Cold War, which quickly followed, seemed at some moments like it would lead to the end of the world amid dueling nuclear annihilations. Meanwhile, important developments like the civil rights movement, suburbanization, the conflict in Vietnam, and a seemingly fantastic parade of technological advances all affected and forever altered the way everyday people lived their everyday lives.

The world of music underwent a similar transformation. The popular music industry grappled with the last gasps of Tin Pan Alley, the increasing influence of black American genres, and the realization of the potential of music to cross racial boundaries. It witnessed an embrace of counterculture, a proliferation of new artistic sensibilities and technological capabilities, and the audience's evolving expectations of the musicians to whom they listen. Meanwhile, the classical world continued its search for an enduring tradition to succeed Romanticism through an embrace of technology, science, postmodernism, and other forces. In this cauldron of historical, economic, political, and musical change, Joel forged a career and legacy built on songwriting and the potential for music to capture and speak to people's most pressing concerns: their lives, their loves, their work, and their identity.

William Martin Joel was born on May 9, 1949, in the Bronx, New York City. His mother, Rosalind (née Nyman), came from a fairly well-off family of English Jews who had immigrated to the United States in 1914. His father, Howard (born Helmut) Joel, was from a family who was once successful in the German garment business but lost everything after the Nazis came to power, fleeing to Cuba in 1939 and making their way to New York three years later. Roz and Howard met during a 1942 production of Gilbert and Sullivan's *The Pirates of Penzance* at the City College of New York; Howard was drafted the following year and they married upon his return in 1946. Both came from families that appreciated music: Roz's father was an enthusiastic supporter of the arts, who would later take Billy to cultural events in the city, and Howard was a classically trained pianist despite his career as an engineer.

Soon after their son was born, the Joels moved out of the city to Hicksville, a new suburb on Long Island. Billy grew up in a house on Meeting Lane, in a community of tract housing known as a Levittown, filled with inexpensive, prefabricated homes intended to meet the surge in demand created by the many servicemen returning from war (see chapter 2). By 1953, he began music lessons with a local piano teacher, Frances Neiman, who put him on a steady diet of the classics. He would play these, but rather than pay close attention to the notes in the score, he would often improvise the études by ear—a skill that would serve him well as he expanded his repertory through avid listening. In a letter he wrote for inclusion in the press kit announcing the release of *Cold Spring Harbor* in 1971, he recalled: "I guess I started writing when I was about seven year[s] old. I was too lazy to read my Bach or Shubert, so I'd make up some of the parts to fake out my mother." The young Billy took in a wide variety of musical genres through the radio. Still, Howard did not approve of much popular music, a fact that Joel says only strengthened his motivation to play such songs on the family's piano: "It was almost forbidden—that's why I really got off on it" (qtd. in Elliott 1978, 111).

Howard Joel's career, which included employment at the Dumont television manufacturing company, RCA, and eventually General Electric, increasingly took him on the road, with more and more trips out of

the country. His frequent travels had a musical upside, as Billy benefitted from the "crazy Latin records" he brought back from South America (Elliott 1978, 111), but his absences were still hard on the family.
Roz's had sister died after giving birth to a daughter, Judy, in 1947, and
the little girl was eventually entrusted to Howard and Roz. So in a way,
Billy's cousin became his sister. Howard's outlook on life since arriving
in the United States was not especially rosy; Billy remembers clearly his
father's remark, "Life is a cesspool," when he was six years old (qtd. in
Schruers 2014, 24). By 1957, Howard left the family and returned to
Europe. Many of Billy's biographers have pointed to this departure as a
defining moment in the young musician's life. For example, Bill Smith
writes, one "aspect of Billy's life that is essential to understanding his
innermost being is the relationship, or more accurately the non-rela-
tionship, that Billy has had with his father Howard. That and its far
reaching emotional ramifications have left scars" (2007, 104). Ultimately, Billy grew up in a family that did not quite fit in: his father was gone,
his sister was not really his sister, and they were Jewish—albeit largely
nonpracticing—in a neighborhood of Gentiles.

A member of the class of 1967, Billy did not graduate from Hicksville High School. Not that he did not care for learning: his love of
reading is well documented, as is his deep fascination with history (see
chapter 7). Still, at the time he was more interested in music than class.
In 1963, he joined his first band, the Echoes, with Jim Bosse (later the
subject of the song "James"), Bill Zampino, and Howie Blauvelt. They
later called themselves the Lost Souls and played local gigs as well as a
statewide band competition in 1965.

But it was the night The Beatles played on the *Ed Sullivan Show*,
February 9, 1964, that solidified the fourteen-year-old Joel's desire to
play rock and roll music. Despite his interest in Elvis a few years earlier
and a trip to see James Brown play at the Apollo Theater in Harlem in
1963, the combination of the sounds The Beatles made and the images
of wildly excited girls screaming in response left an indelible impression. By 1967, as it became clear that the other members of the Lost
Souls were not as serious about pursuing careers in music as he, Joel
joined The Hassles, the resident band at My House, a nightclub in
Plainview, Long Island. The group included Jon Small on drums, Harry
Weber on keyboards, Richie McKenna on guitar, and "Little John"
Dizek on vocals. Small was married to Weber's sister, Elizabeth, and

they had a son together. There was some tension within the band, which led to Small seeking to replace Weber. That is where Joel came in, bringing Blauvelt, a bass player, with him. To Joel, after jobs on oyster boats and inking typewriter ribbons, the steady gig—and $250 per week—probably sounded really good.

The Hassles were signed by United Artists and managed by Irwin Mazur. They recorded two albums, *The Hassles* and *Hour of the Wolf*, which Joel finds unmemorable but nonetheless valuable experiences. And although he was initially hired as the keyboard player who occasionally sang backup, he eventually took over lead vocals from Little John. He also played on several other recordings, backing Chubby Checker and Shadow Morton, though he cannot recall with certainty whether his efforts made it into the final cuts or were just demo recordings.

Eventually, Joel and Small left The Hassles and refashioned themselves a heavy metal duo, with Small on guitars and Joel on keyboards and (screamed) vocals. They called themselves Attila and recorded one album, *Attila*, with Epic Records, which, like The Hassles' records, also flopped. As Joel later wrote, in his characteristic self-deprecating humor, the album received "rave reviews from two people . . . both of them our road managers. Exit 'Attila'" (Joel ca. 1971). Epic quickly dropped the band.

Although it became clear that Attila was a failure, Joel's friendship with Small endured. Still, it was not without tests. For a time, the two lived together with Small's wife, Elizabeth. Eventually, she took off with Joel, her husband's best friend, who assumed—incorrectly—that she had already broken things off with her husband. In the ensuing debacle, Elizabeth temporarily stayed away from both men as they awkwardly patched up their friendship. The emotional stress of the situation, plus the demise of Attila, was a new low for Joel, who one night in 1970 attempted suicide and woke up in a hospital after getting his stomach pumped (Small had found him). "I thought to myself, *Oh, great, I couldn't even do this right*," he recalled. "It was just another failure" (qtd. in Schruers 2014, 65). A few weeks later, after drinking a bottle of furniture polish in another attempt, he entered Meadowbrook Hospital. There he encountered people who had far worse (mental) problems than he, a sobering realization. Aside from a newfound appreciation for his own life, he also emerged with a new set of songs, which would serve as the backbone of his first solo album.

Cold Spring Harbor came about when Mazur connected Joel with Woodstock impresario Michael Lang, who passed along a demo of some of the songs to Artie Ripp. Family Productions, Ripp's company, soon made an offer. Considering how low Joel was feeling about his life and prospects, and his attempts to end his own life, Mazur did his best to have him sign quickly and raise his spirits. Ripp invited Joel to Los Angeles to make his debut album, named after a small Long Island town. It was an attempt to establish him musically as a singer-songwriter and accordingly featured his voice and piano, backed by a band of studio musicians. According to drummer Rhys Clark, the drummer on the album, Joel was optimistic about the album and looking forward to coming to Los Angeles to record it (qtd. in MacFarlane 2016).

Unfortunately, when it was released in early 1971, *Cold Spring Harbor* was marred by an error that resulted in Joel's voice sounding higher than it actually did in the studio. Joel later compared it to the effect behind the voices of Alvin and the Chipmunks. Thomas MacFarlane wonders whether it was an attempt to "brighten" the sound of the record by slowing down the tapes during the recording process (so they would play a little faster upon playback), which was a common practice at the time. Needless to say, while Joel did not enjoy the process of recording the album—Ripp asked for repeated takes, which he found wearing—he was certainly unhappy with the result. Nonetheless, Ripp sent him on the road to promote the album. The letter Joel wrote for the *Cold Spring Harbor* press kit was his effort to cut through what he calls the "jive superlatives and dull 'hep-cat' talk" of the industry. It concludes: "The record company gave me a piano so I'm writing a lot of new things. As you know, they'd like to present me as a dynamic electric personality. Well, onstage I get it on pretty well, but otherwise, I'm about as sparkling as warm beer. . . . I hope you like the album, but if you're not crazy about it, it makes a great frisbee" (Joel, letter, 2–3).

While on tour, Joel started to get the sense that something was not right with Family Productions. Copies of *Cold Spring Harbor* were scarce on record store shelves, the songs were seldom heard on the radio, and the band was not getting paid. This led to Joel, Elizabeth Weber, and her son moving to Los Angeles in an attempt to wait out his contract and figure out their next step (see chapter 2). There he took a gig at a local bar, the Executive Room, under the name Bill Martin; Weber worked there as a waitress. The experience led him to compose "Piano Man," which would anchor his next—and first successful—album and earn him his moniker.

Though dissatisfied with the *Cold Spring Harbor* recording, Joel was, at his core, a performer. One show in particular, at the 1972 Mar Y Sol Festival in Puerto Rico, is fabled as a turning point in this regard. The rain-soaked crowd was unenthusiastic when Joel took the stage, the story goes, but as he launched into a remarkably convincing impersonation of Joe Cocker—impersonations have always been part of his act—they started to come back out. Before an initially curious and increasingly engaged audience, Joel did his set, including a few more impersonations.

In the audience at Mar Y Sol was Clive Davis of Columbia Records, the company Joel had long set his sights on. (He once told his mother that he was not going to Columbia University, but to Columbia Records.) Davis had been intrigued when he heard about a new song, "Captain Jack," that was becoming something of an underground hit. Joel had recorded it earlier that year at a Philadelphia radio station, and after the broadcast, the requests started coming in. Listeners wanted to hear it again and again. Soon, copies of the tape were circulating in New York, where Columbia was headquartered. Davis had come to Puerto Rico to see what all the fuss was about.

It was worth it. Based in part on Joel's performance in Puerto Rico, an offer from Columbia was soon on the table. But Joel's existing contract with Family Productions added a wrinkle. Columbia eventually extricated Joel from his deal with Ripp, although the Family logo would continue to appear on—and the company would continue to receive a cut of—Joel's records going forward. Still, given the failure of *Cold Spring Harbor*, Joel was happy to move camp to Columbia in 1973.

The *Piano Man* album, featuring songs written around the time of Joel's move west and recorded in Los Angeles, was released by Columbia Records in November 1973. It climbed the *Billboard* Hot 100 and the Adult Contemporary charts, peaking at numbers twenty-five and four, respectively. *Rolling Stone* praised it for Joel's "new seriousness and musical flexibility" (Breschard 1974), and the subsequent tour met with some positive notices. But Joel reportedly earned less than eight thousand dollars on the album, leading him and Elizabeth to question where the rest of the money went. The answer, of course, was the royalty Ripp continued to collect on every record sold, a weight Joel would continue to bear for years to come.

Seeking greater control over the business of his music, Joel asked Elizabeth to become his manager, replacing Jon Troy, whose service is memorialized in "Say Goodbye to Hollywood." Columbia sought another album quickly, so Joel soon found himself back in the studio in Los Angeles with a group of session musicians, recording tracks that would become *Streetlife Serenade*. The process seemed rushed, and having been on the road with *Piano Man*, Joel had not had much time to come up with new material. The album was released in October 1974 to tepid reviews; critic Stephen Holden wrote, "Joel's keyboard abilities notwithstanding, he has nothing to say as a writer at present" (1974). Looking back, it is Joel's least favorite work: *"Streetlife*, to quote one of its lyrics [from "The Entertainer"], should be 'put in the back in the discount rack like another can of beans'" (qtd. in Schruers 2014, 107).

Following the disappointing performance of *Streetlife Serenade*, Joel looked for new creative support. An attempt at demos for what would become *Turnstiles* was recorded at Caribou Studios in Colorado, using Elton John's band under the direction of Jimmy Guerco. But Joel was unhappy with the results and missed the musical camaraderie of his road band, including drummer Rhys Clark and bassist Doug Stegmeyer, so the Caribou sessions were scrapped. He sought famed Beatles producer George Martin, who politely declined. Elizabeth moved their whole operation back to New York, securing a house along the Hudson River in the small town of Highland Falls and bringing her husband close enough to home to form a band of his own making, with Long Island musicians of his own choosing. Stegmeyer, himself originally from Long Island, stayed on while guitarists Howie Emerson and Russell Javors and drummer Liberty DeVitto entered the picture. Richie Cannata added saxophone, keyboards, and vocals. These musicians would form the core of Joel's band, in the studio and on the road, for many years. Meanwhile, old friend Dennis Arfa came on as booking agent and Jeff Schock joined up as road manager.

The tracks that became *Turnstiles* were ultimately recorded on Long Island, with Joel producing, and the album was released in May 1976. It received mixed reviews but, in hindsight, was a turning point in Joel's career and songwriting. With his own band and support team, he was finally able to pursue his work on his own terms. Musically, Joel started to shed his fascination with a western style (see chapter 2) and focus more on his own compositional voice, as heard in tracks like "Summer, Highland Falls," "New York State of Mind," and "Miami 2017 (Seen the Lights Go Out on Broadway)."

Despite getting the sound he wanted from the musicians he picked, Joel knew that a real producer was necessary for the next album. And considering that neither *Piano Man* nor *Streetlife Serenade* nor *Turnstiles* had really been hits, there was a measure of pressure from the record company to make something big happen. Thus, well-known and successful producer Phil Ramone—who had most recently won the Album of the Year Grammy Award for Paul Simon's *Still Crazy After All These Years* (1975)—was brought on board as work began on *The Stranger*, which would be released in September 1977.

The Stranger made Billy Joel a household name. It reached number two on the *Billboard* Hot 200, earned Grammys for Record of the Year and Song of the Year for "Just the Way You Are," and achieved platinum status. The singles charted well too: "Just the Way You Are" reached number three, "Movin' Out" hit number seventeen, "Only the Good Die Young" peaked at number twenty-four, and "She's Always a Woman" also topped out at number seventeen. Critical praise for the album was also forthcoming. Writing in *Rolling Stone*, Ira Mayer observed, "Joel has achieved a fluid sound occasionally sparked by a light soul touch" (1977). Timothy White later opined that *The Stranger*

> accentuated Joel's uniqueness in rock and roll—he'd successfully merged the vernaculars of Hollywood sound stages with those of Schubert and Tin Pan Alley, along with the warm ambiance of Sinatra saloon albums, 1950s car-radio pop, the sound of the Beatles-led British Invasion, and the rich melodicism of post-New Wave rock. It was a remarkable feat, making his piss-off, polyglot music the most widely accepted since the Beatles, yet completely his own. (1990, 561–62)

Ramone stayed for the next album, *52nd Street*, which was released in October 1978. Like the one before it, this record was wildly successful, hitting number one on the *Billboard* 200 and eventually going multiplatinum. The singles were hits too, with "My Life" reaching number three, "Big Shot" hitting fourteen, and "Honesty" climbing as high as number twenty-four. The album won two Grammys (Album of the Year and Best Pop Vocal Performance, Male), and "Honesty" was nominated for Song of the Year. *52nd Street* bears a distinctively jazz flavor, not only in the midtown Manhattan reference in its name, but also in the contributions of jazz trumpeter Freddie Hubbard to "Zanzibar." Yet despite its commercial success, the album prompted some of the most scathing reviews of Joel's work to that point (see Holden 1978), solidifying some of the lines of fire in the battles between the musician and his critics in the press (see chapter 6).

With two hit albums and a string of hit singles, Joel had hit his stride. On *Glass Houses*, released in March 1980, he once again changed his sound, this time from the jazz atmosphere of *52nd Street* to an edgier, more guitar-driven approach. Set against the emergence of styles such as punk and new wave, *Glass Houses* was somewhat baffling to the music press, whose critical reviews of the music and Joel's onstage performance irked the performer greatly (he would start tearing up reviews and insulting critics from the stage; see Nelson 1980). The album did not continue the "light soul touch" of some of his earlier work but instead looked back to the rock music of the mid-1960s. The new emphasis on the guitar, which benefitted from the efforts of guitarist David Brown, also added some bigger, louder numbers to the band's repertory—perfect for performance in ever larger venues. *Glass Houses* won the Grammy for Best Rock Vocal Performance, Male, and was nominated for Album of the Year.

Around this time, Joel and his wife-turned-manager, Elizabeth, began to show some strain on their relationship, which is expressed musically in songs like "Stiletto" (from *52nd Street*). By the end of 1980, she was replaced in her managerial duties by her brother, Frank Weber. The marriage would officially end in 1982.

Although Joel did not record an album of new songs in 1981, Columbia released a live album, *Songs in the Attic*, in September. Drawn from several years of performances in small clubs, the record revisits several songs from the early part of his career, including "Everybody Loves You Now" (from *Cold Spring Harbor*), "Los Angelenos" (from *Streetlife Serenade*), and "Captain Jack" (from *Piano Man*).

Joel's next studio effort was *The Nylon Curtain*, released in September 1982. A more musically ambitious album than his earlier records, it was explicitly inspired by The Beatles. The influence of the Fab Four can be heard in tracks like "Laura" and "Scandinavian Skies," but more significantly, their efforts to create a unified song cycle—perhaps best exemplified by the concept album *Sgt. Pepper's Lonely Hearts Club Band* (1967)—are reflected in the way *The Nylon Curtain* takes on the state of the American psyche in the Reagan era. Disappointment, frustration, and resignation are the predominant moods as the heightened possibilities engendered by postwar optimism were dragged down by Cold War realism. *The Nylon Curtain* was not as commercially successful as Joel's previous releases, but it earned him more critical praise than he previously enjoyed. Crispin Cioe called it Joel's "most serious and accomplished effort to date" (1982). And Holden remarked that the album "finds Billy Joel on higher artistic ground than ever before" due to its more socially conscious songs, such as "Allentown" and "Goodnight Saigon" (1982).

After the seriousness of *The Nylon Curtain*, Joel's next album marked a return to his roots. *An Innocent Man*, released in August 1983, featured a collection of 1960s styles, from the doo-wop of "The Longest Time" to the shades of Motown in "Tell Her About It." It climbed as high as number four on the *Billboard* 200. As singles, "Tell Her About It" topped the charts, "Uptown Girl" peaked at number three, and "An Innocent Man" reached number ten. "Uptown Girl" was nominated for the Grammy Award for Best Pop Vocal Performance, Male, but the album lost out on Album of the Year to Michael Jackson's *Thriller* (1982).

Recognizing demand and Joel's string of successes, Columbia issued Joel's *Greatest Hits, Vol. I & Vol. II* in September 1985. Beginning with *Piano Man*'s title track and proceeding through *An Innocent Man*'s "The Longest Time," the double-album also included two new songs, "You're Only Human (Second Wind)" and "While the Night Is Still Young." Also in 1985, aboard a yacht sailing around Manhattan Island, Joel married supermodel Christie Brinkley. Their daughter, Alexa Ray, was born in December of that year.

Now a father, Joel became enamored with his daughter and somewhat less focused on satisfying his record company's desire for more albums. Nonetheless, he recorded nine songs for *The Bridge*, though the compositional process was difficult and his in-studio relationship with Ramone had largely run its course. Looking back, Joel finds many of the tracks disappointing. But there were some highlights, the brightest of which was his collaboration with his idol, Ray Charles, on "Baby Grand" (Schruers 2014, 182–85). Steve Winwood also appeared on "Getting Closer" and Cindy Lauper co-wrote and added vocals to "Code of Silence."

The Bridge was released in July 1986, and although the album did not climb the charts, three of its singles fared well: "A Matter of Trust" and "Modern Woman" (the latter also featured on the soundtrack to the film *Ruthless People*) both reached number ten, while "This Is the Time" peaked at number eighteen. Critic Anthony DeCurtis was ultimately pleased with what he heard, calling it "a smart, sophisticated collection of songs that seemingly brings us closer to Billy Joel than we've ever been before" (1986, "The Bridge"). The album became the last to include Ramone as well as band members Stegmeyer and Javors. It also has the distinction of being Joel's final album to bear the Family Productions logo.

The late 1980s were a challenging time for Joel financially. He ended his business relationship with former brother-in-law Frank Weber, who stood accused in a series of lawsuits of financial mismanagement on a grand scale that ultimately left Joel with little of what he had earned. The legal wrangling would last into the next decade and leave a mark on Joel (as heard in *River of Dreams'* "The Great Wall of China"), whose view of the music industry has never been especially bright (see chapter 6).

Still, there were good moments. Joel largely self-financed a 1987 tour of the Soviet Union, a historic undertaking that made him the first American rock musician to perform in the Red Empire. While playing concerts in Moscow and Leningrad, Joel took his rock performance to an audience that was, by all accounts, eager to see and hear it but uncomfortable under the watchful eye of Communist Party minders. The shows were filmed for a documentary (and a live album from the tour, *Kohuept*—Russian for "concert"—was released the same year), but under the glare of the lights needed for filming, Soviet fans were noticeably hesitant to let loose. Joel's demands for the lights to be turned off included behavior the press would later call a "tantrum," coverage of which eclipsed that of the tour's musical diplomacy.

When it came time for the next album, Mick Jones was brought in as producer and mandated with finding a new sound for Joel. Those efforts bore fruit on *Storm Front*, released in October 1989, as many of the songs capture a new, raw energy. The record's biggest hit was "We Didn't Start the Fire," Joel's second number one (discussed at length in chapter 7). The album peaked at number one on the *Billboard* 200, and the other singles performed well too: "I Go to Extremes" hit number six, "And So It Goes" thirty-seven, "The Downeaster 'Alexa'" fifty-seven, and "That's Not Her Style" seventy-seven. "We Didn't Start the Fire" was nominated for three Grammys: Song of the Year, Record of the Year, and Best Pop Vocal Performance, Male. And the album itself was nominated for two: Best Pop Vocal Performance, Male and Producer of the Year. Joel included numbers from the album in a historic performance at Yankee Stadium—the park's first-ever rock concert—in June 1990.

Joel's final studio album of pop songs was *River of Dreams*, released in August 1993. Again a new producer, Danny Kortchmar, was brought in, along with new musicians. The concept album traces a path from anger and disillusionment toward redemption and serenity. It also met with commercial and critical success, as it was nominated for the Grammy for Album of the Year while its title track was nominated for Song of the Year, Record of the Year, and Best Pop Vocal Performance, Male. *Rolling Stone*'s Kara Manning called it "compelling" as "Joel pushes forward with faith in the future, faith in love, faith in hard-earned, if frustrated, wisdom" (1993).

"Famous Last Words," the last track on *River of Dreams*, proved prophetic, as Joel largely abandoned pop songwriting after his twelfth studio album. He continued performing, launching the highly successful "Face-to-Face" tours with Elton John in 1994. And he continued composing but not pop songs. Instead, he focused on classical, especially Romantic, styles. By the turn of the century, he was ready to share them. Pianist Richard Joo played ten of Joel's compositions on *Fantasies & Delusions: Music For Solo Piano*, released in October 2001 (see chapter 6). The album did remarkably well, topping the classical charts.

Joel's songs reached new audiences when *Movin' Out* opened on Broadway in October 2002. Choreographed by Twyla Thorpe, the show traces the story of Brenda and Eddie (characters from *The Stranger*'s "Scenes from an Italian Restaurant") and the experiences of a generation coming of age on Long Island in the 1960s. The score is drawn entirely from Joel's catalog, performed by an on-stage cover band. The show ran until December 2005 for a total of 1,303 performances, winning Tony Awards for Best Choreography for Thorpe and for Best Orchestrations for Joel and Stuart Malina. It received eight additional Tony nominations.

To date, Joel has continued performing while also giving lectures and master classes at schools, colleges, and universities. Columbia released a third volume of *Greatest Hits* in 1997, as well as some boxed sets (such as *My Lives* in 2005) and live albums (*2000 Years: The Millennium Concert* in 2000 and *12 Gardens Live* in 2006). In 2008, he played the final concerts at New York City's Shea Stadium, where The Beatles had famously performed, a two-night event that was captured in the musical documentary, *The Last Play at Shea* (2010). His marriage to Brinkley ended in 1994; he was married to Katie Lee from 2004 to 2009 and wed Alexis Roderick in 2015 (their daughter, Della Rose, was born later that year). He released two songs, "All My Life" and "Christmas in Fallujah," in 2007 but otherwise stayed out of the songwriting business.

Joel's list of awards is lengthy but includes some significant accolades, such as his induction into the Rock and Roll Hall of Fame in 1999, the Kennedy Center Honors in 2013, and the Gershwin Prize for Popular Song from the Library of Congress in 2014. He began a historic "residency" at New York's Madison Square Garden in 2014—the arena's first—with the promise to play monthly concerts for as long as demand allows. As of this writing, the open-ended gig is ongoing.

As remarkable as Billy Joel's biography is, the heart of his story is found in his songs. There, he observes, reflects, and comments on the world around him. He responds to the ways it has changed and fondly recalls the way it used to be. He does not retreat into a rose-tinted landscape of nostalgia but recognizes that, as he sings in "Keeping the Faith" (from *An Innocent Man*), "the good old days weren't always good and tomorrow ain't as bad as it seems." So while one could read Joel's career as an epic tale of challenge and eventual triumph, there is more to the story than just one man's journey. Indeed, the songs tell us not just about Joel—although many do that—but also about ourselves. Aside from his musical gifts, one of Joel's greatest talents is his ability to see the big picture, the forces that affect our lives in ways we cannot always perceive. The rest of this book aims to illuminate that perspective.

2

"NEW YORK STATE OF MIND"

Geography, Places, and Spaces

Ever the balladeer, Billy Joel often uses his songs to document and comment on the world around him. He has written songs about various places in his life, including New York, California, and suburbia. In true singer-songwriter fashion, his portrayals typically reflect his personal experience with respect to each locale. After all, his life story is one that is framed, in part, by his movement to and through various places and spaces. His relocation to California in 1972 after the commercial failure of *Cold Spring Harbor* is a defining feature of the early part of his career, one that shapes the topics he sings about and the sounds he uses to illustrate them. His later return to New York is similarly heralded in song.

Music has been used to evoke a sense of place for centuries. A European fascination with Turkish music in the seventeenth and eighteenth centuries, for example, shaped pieces like the famous closing movement of Wolfgang Amadeus Mozart's Piano Sonata No. 11, "Alla Turca" (1783), while Antonín Dvořák's interest in late-nineteenth-century America can be heard in his Symphony No. 9, *From the New World* (1893). The tradition of linking music and place is also strong in American popular and classical music, from the 1894 Tin Pan Alley favorite "The Sidewalks of New York," by Charles B. Lawlor and James W. Blake, to Charles Ives's orchestral set *Three Places in New England* (1908–1914).

More recent thinking about the relationship between music and place has highlighted the way the former invokes and evokes the latter while anchoring social, cultural, and political beliefs. Music can powerfully illustrate the bonds that bring people together as well as the differences that set them apart. Martin Stokes argues that "music is socially meaningful not entirely but largely because it provides means by which people recognise identities and places, and the boundaries which separate them." Importantly, music is not only made *in* particular places or "social spaces"; it *transforms* them (1994, 4–5). While listening to Joel's "Say Goodbye to Hollywood," for example, listeners across the country could find their homes aurally reconstructed by the historical and sonic referents to Los Angeles in the song's musical fabric. No matter where the actual act of listening happens, the sonic amalgam of that song recalls a famous rock-and-roll sound particular to a distinct (and perhaps distant) time and place. Joel thereby continues this tradition of music and place, conjuring geography and space and delimiting boundaries, through both his music and lyrics.

"'CAUSE IT GETS ROUGH ALONG THE WAY": BILLY JOEL VENTURES WEST

As a debut album, *Cold Spring Harbor*, named after a town on New York's Long Island, not far from Oyster Bay and Hicksville, had good potential. Critic Stephen Erlewine called it "a minor gem of the sensitive singer/songwriter era." But its success was stymied by a catastrophic technical error—corrected in the 1983 reissue—giving Joel's voice a chipmunk-like quality. Meanwhile, Joel was realizing that the terms of his record deal with Artie Ripp and Family Productions were less than favorable and the promotional tour was growing tiresome. To make matters worse, *Cold Spring Harbor* was getting neither airplay nor space on record shelves (Weitzman 1974). "I knew I'd got screwed" in the deal, he later recalled. "The people who did it were in L.A. I figured that was a good base of operation for me to try to get out of [the record] deal. And that they weren't going to look for me right under their noses" (qtd. in Sheff and Sheff 1982). So Joel moved to Los Angeles and took a regular gig playing cocktail piano at the Executive Room, a local bar just south of Hollywood. He played under the name Bill Martin.

The distance from New York gave him space to clear his head and an opportunity to refine his skills and begin writing new material.

Joel's next album, *Piano Man*, was released in 1973 while he was in California. In many ways, it captures the optimism Joel might have felt upon leaving the debacles of his solo debut behind and traveling west. Appropriately, the album opens with a number called "Travelin' Prayer," which, although delivered in the form of a plea for the Lord to look after his "baby" amid her travels, carries an infectious rhythm and country-western instrumentation that immediately puts the listener on notice: this is not just another album of piano ballads and love songs, although it includes both. While it is not clear whether Joel is singing as himself or as a character, his "baby" is clearly far away ("across the sea") and on the move, and he requests that the road beneath her feet be made softer and the ground she may have to sleep on be warm and dry. The snare drum, the first sound we hear, keeps up a busy pattern, forward-moving but not aggressive. Each piano chord strikes quickly, holds onto its notes, and then disappears with a flurry. Later, other instruments join in: a fast-picking banjo, a fiddle, and a jaw harp, adding a bounce to the song's instrumental fade-out. Joel describes it as "very bluegrass country" (personal interview).

Aside from the fact that the song "Piano Man" is set in the Executive Room, there is little on the album *Piano Man* that situates it specifically in Los Angeles. Instead, it is an album about the West more generally. This locale, and the sounds associated with it, inspired Joel because it was all so new to him:

> I was fascinated with this, because this wasn't music that I'd heard growing up in New York. You don't hear a lot of country-western music, you don't hear a lot of cowboy music, you don't hear a lot of bluegrass [in New York]. The closest you'd hear to a country-western song would be, maybe, a Johnny Cash hit record. This is kind of weird music to hear in New York. It doesn't fit. But it was interesting to me. I got out there [to Los Angeles] and all of a sudden you had these artists like the Eagles, Jackson Browne, J. D. Souther, Linda Ronstadt, who were echoing country music even in the pop tunes that they were doing and even in the rock and roll. . . . It was a different kind of instrumentation, a different kind of songwriting. And I kind of dove into that for a while. I wanted to see what it was like to write like that. (personal interview)

One example is *Piano Man*'s "The Ballad of Billy the Kid," in which Joel weaves a yarn of Wild West thievery and justice. To reinforce the western setting, strings play in a style reminiscent of American classical composer Aaron Copland and western films (which Joel admires), while Joel uses the piano, some horse clops, and a harmonica to create the desired effect. When it really gets going, the rest of the band brings in the electric guitar, bass, and drums to emphasize the expansive nature of the narrative in an almost cinematic style. ("The Ballad of Billy the Kid" is discussed in more detail in chapter 7.)

Later on the album, "Stop in Nevada" tells the tale of a woman seeking escape from a failing marriage by making her way to California via the Silver State. The strings from "The Ballad of Billy the Kid" return here (though not in Coplandesque fashion), joined by the pedal steel, an instrument closely linked with the country and western genres. The pedal steel also shows up on "Somewhere Along the Line." Thus, in several of the tracks on *Piano Man*, Joel uses both lyrical and musical devices to convey a sense of travel, escape, and optimism associated with geographic distance and the West, as well as rather different places and spaces from New York.

But California, Joel's ultimate destination, never really agreed with him. Some of his most biting criticism can be heard on his next album, *Streetlife Serenade*, which, unlike *Piano Man*, was written while he actually lived in Los Angeles, justifying a deeper examination of how its sounds reveal Joel's attitude toward the city. For example, "Los Angelenos" tears into the people and lifestyle of the city. This straight-ahead rock song features a strong backbeat, a punchy electric bass, and a distorted electric guitar supporting Joel as he pounds on his Wurlitzer D-40 keyboard. The verses, alternating between only two chords (D-minor and C-major), recite a litany of the city's personages: "Midwestern ladies," "New York cowboys," "electric babies," and "hot sweet schoolgirls." The bridge expands the song musically as Joel describes the pointless activities of the city's residents, from retreats into nearby mountains and canyons to seemingly endless driving ("going nowhere on the streets with the Spanish names"). No one really comes from Los Angeles, Joel argues; the place has no culture of its own. "Los Angelenos all come from somewhere," yet their stay in the city amounts to a "funky exile." These opening lyrics clearly spell out the sense of distance he observes: he describes them but is not one of them, and there is little binding them to each other or to the city. Later, the song's concluding lines start with the same first phrase but end more pointedly: "It's so familiar, their foreign faces."

For some, Joel's words and attitude were a little too much. Writing in *Rolling Stone*, Stephen Holden labeled "Los Angelenos" "a hackneyed picture postcard of L.A. as sexual wasteland" (1974). Ultimately, it is a song about insincerity and deception, the familiar and the foreign, and (a lack of) place. While the West Coast was a place for Joel to regroup and perhaps right a few wrongs, such a diversion was not in his original plan. It was the result of failure, not success, especially as he compared himself to other emerging and established singer-songwriters like James Taylor, Joni Mitchell, and Paul Simon (DeMain 1996). A life of hard work in New York was all Joel had known, so the culture of leisure he found in California—"makin' love with the natives in their Hollywood places"—was anathema to him. And while the city's drug culture was widespread—"tanning out at the beaches with their Mexican reefers"—it did not appeal much to this straight-laced New Yorker.

The melody of "Los Angelenos" emphasizes the themes of place, familiarity amid foreignness, and disconnect. Each verse begins with an upward leap to the highest pitch of the song, an A. Because this is near the top of Joel's vocal range, he ends up almost screaming whichever lyric falls on that note. Twice it is the first syllable of the word "Angelenos," giving it an emphasis that seems to convey a sense of frustration; the second time, toward the end of the track, he holds the note for an extra few beats as if to drive this point home. In other instances, the high A lands on adjectives describing, with an unmistakably mocking tone, what Joel sees around him: "*sleek* new sports cars," "such *hot* sweet schoolgirls," "it's *all* so easy," "it's *so* familiar."

Although early in the song he takes a jab at transplants from the Midwest, Joel most clearly points to Los Angeles's large Latino (specifically Mexican) population and its influence. He even rolls his *r*'s while singing a few lyrics as if effecting a Spanish accent. "Yeah, every street had a Spanish name and at first I didn't even know how to pronounce most of them," Joel recalls. "It was new to me, it was foreign, it was exotic in its own way" (personal interview).

Part of the Latino influence can be explained historically, as Joel points out. California was largely settled in the eighteenth century by the Spanish in an attempt to Christianize and otherwise displace a number of Native American tribes living in the region. Upon gaining independence from Spain in 1821, it became a part of the new nation of Mexico. After a series of revolts in the 1830s and 1840s, including a brief period as the independent "California Republic," it officially became an American state on September 9, 1850, following the conclusion of the Mexican-American War two years earlier.

While Joel was living there, the Latino population of Los Angeles was experiencing a significant growth spurt. Census data show that it more than doubled from 1960 to 1970, increasing from 582,309 to 1,288,716. It nearly doubled again by the next census, rising to 2,071,530 in 1980. Moreover, as a percentage of the total population in the county, Latinos grew considerably: 9.6 percent in 1960, 18.3 percent in 1970, and 27.6 percent in 1980. In fact, a 2001 report found that "the growth of Los Angeles County since 1960 is almost entirely the work of non-White and non-Black groups," and while the city's Asian population (the other racial group the report tracked) also grew rapidly over the same period, neither its actual number of persons nor its proportion of the city's total population were as large as those of the Latino population (Ethington, Frey, and Myers 2001).

A person's outlook on life is undoubtedly shaped by the environment in which he or she is raised. In terms of both history and population, California and Los Angeles differed greatly from New York and Long Island. The Dutch initially settled there among the Algonquin- and Iroquoian-speaking Native Americans in the early seventeenth century until the British annexed the colony in 1664. Moreover, during Joel's childhood on Long Island in the 1950s and 1960s, the Latino population was neither as numerically significant nor as strong an influence as it would later become. In 1950, less than 0.1 percent of the population of the State of New York was identified as "other race," and by 1960 it had risen to only 0.1 percent. (The U.S. Census did not start asking questions about Hispanic origin, as it was initially called, until 1970. See Gibson and Jung 2002; Schmidley and Cresce 2007.) Therefore, the move to Los Angeles placed Joel not only in a new city with a new culture dominated by new faces, but also one that bore little resemblance to those in which he grew up. "You see that in the architecture, you see it in the names of the streets, you see it in Mexican *food*, which we [did not] have in New York," Joel says (personal interview). Ultimately, as biographer Richard Scott concludes, "Los Angelenos" is evidence of Joel's "increasing dissatisfaction with California culture and [his] desire to return home" to New York. After all, he believed his "art was being diluted by the California ambiance" (2000, 25–26).

"I KNOW WHAT I'M NEEDING": RETURN TO THE EMPIRE STATE

Joel's return to New York in 1976 shows up musically in thoroughly positive ways. Even just a glance at the cover of *Turnstiles*, released that year, portrays Joel and his band at the turnstiles of a New York City subway station, dressed in costumes corresponding to characters from the album's songs. It is clear that this record is, if nothing else, Joel's New York album. The opening track, "Say Goodbye to Hollywood," announces his departure from Los Angeles in no uncertain terms while featuring a recording technique associated with that city. Later, "New York State of Mind" offers a through-and-through love song for the Empire State, invoking two of its musical hallmarks, jazz and Tin Pan Alley. By employing these styles, Joel reinforces the geographical focus of each song's lyrics.

"Say Goodbye to Hollywood" begins with a kick and snare pattern on Liberty DeVitto's drums that immediately sets the pace and signals that this song has a sense of movement, deliberate and forward going. After two bars, the band enters and we hear, alongside Joel's piano and Doug Stegmeyer's bass, the added sound of a castanet—reflecting the Spanish influence in Los Angeles—that appears a split-second before each snare hit. The modified strophic song contains four verses, each of which ends with a refrain that includes its title. The lyrics describe Bobby and Johnny, friends whom the unnamed protagonist is sadly leaving behind. The bridge, played after the second and third verses, carries the crux of the song's message: "Movin' on is a chance you have to take anytime you try to stay together," yet if you merely say "a word out of line," you may discover that your friends have permanently disappeared. Although the song's narrator appears to say "goodbye" throughout each refrain, the last verse concludes that among the "many faces in and out of my life," some will remain constant while others will prove occasional. "Life is a series of hellos and goodbyes," Joel sings, and now it is time for the latter. "It was a bittersweet farewell," he explains (personal interview). Sorrowful as the lyrics read, the tone of Joel's voice is not sad. The vocal track has a quick delay effect on it that gives the number a punchy, percussive quality, which stands in direct contrast to the vocal track on *Streetlife Serenade*'s "Souvenir," for example, a sad song whose lead vocal is bathed in melancholic reverb but features no delay.

On "Say Goodbye to Hollywood," Joel attempts to emulate the sound Phil Spector produced in such recordings as the Crystals' "Then He Kissed Me" (1963) and the Righteous Brothers' "You've Lost that Lovin' Feelin'" (1965) (Bego 2007, 99–101; Bielen 2011, 33; Holden 1978). In his words: "I did it in a Phil Spector style. I was thinking of [Spector's wife] Ronnie Spector and the Ronettes when I did it" (qtd. in Bego 2007, 86). Spector's signature technique is known as the "wall of sound." To create it, he used a large rhythm section with a studio orchestra, employed multitrack recording techniques to create many layers of sound, and applied a strong echo effect to the result. This amalgam, which also included a version of the mix played through a loudspeaker in a converted bathroom and then re-recorded by another microphone, results in what musicologist Albin Zak calls an "extravagant use of ambiance" that "became part of rock's recording lexicon" (2001, 78). Spector described records made this way as "symphonies for the kids" (Thomson, "Phil(ip Harvey) Spector.").

Joel's song follows Spector's formula. Not only do we hear the band from the song's introduction throughout the track, but Joel also adds new layers along the way. Backup singers join him on the refrains. During the repetition of the bridge and the final verse, they harmonize with his lead. And strings enter on the second verse and grow more prominent during and after the first bridge, although they move out of the way for Richie Cannata's saxophone solo. Whether Joel's efforts to harness Spector's effect ultimately succeed is a matter of debate, however. Biographer Mark Bego writes that the wall of sound "was totally the sound that Billy achieved on 'Say Goodbye to Hollywood'" (2007, 100), while Holden claims that the song "failed to build a mighty enough wall of sound" (1978). But Ronnie Spector was certainly impressed. She recorded her own version of the song, accompanied by Bruce Springsteen's band, which was released as a single in 1977.

Joel is clear about the connection between "Say Goodbye to Hollywood" and Spector's production style, remarking: "I would imagine that would be pretty obvious to anyone who knows the history of pop music, that you would be hearing the Phil Spector drum-beat introduction with the big wall-of-sound echo" (personal interview). He has also explicitly linked it with his departure from Los Angeles, calling it a "celebratory song."

> Some people think that the lyrics are somewhat sneering and that was not my intention at all. I quite appreciated my time in Los Angeles. But I was a New Yorker so I wanted to celebrate my time there [in Los Angeles] but also my return to New York. So it wasn't a look backwards in bitterness or anger or sneering in any way; it was sort of a "thank you." (personal interview)

Still, the connection between the use of Spector's production style and the subject of Los Angeles as a place in "Say Goodbye to Hollywood" often remains implicit. Yet it bears emphasis, for at least two reasons.

First, Spector's sound was distinctive and indelibly associated with Los Angeles, where it was originally developed at the city's Gold Star studio with a group of session musicians known as The Wrecking Crew. Although it was becoming more national in orientation, at that time the American music industry was still somewhat regionally oriented, with individual cities serving as anchors of regional markets, within which many independent studios and labels could successfully operate and, through local disc jockeys, reach their audiences (Ennis 1978). Among the many locally owned record labels, often called "independents," New York had Atlantic, Chicago had Chess, Detroit had Motown, Memphis had Sun and Stax, and Los Angeles had Spector's Philles (see Gillett 1996).

Second, an earlier attempt to record the songs that would end up on *Turnstiles*, with producer James William Guercio and Elton John's band at Caribou Studios in Colorado, left Joel musically dissatisfied. He subsequently assembled his own band of Long Island–based musicians (with whom he would later tour and make subsequent albums) and re-recorded the album, producing it himself, in New York. So it would not be entirely accurate to describe "Say Goodbye to Hollywood" as having a genuine wall of sound, but it would be right to call it a carefully and consciously crafted emulation, homage, or tribute (personal interview). Thus, despite the fact that the song overtly celebrates Joel's departure from Los Angeles, it nonetheless simultaneously conjures one of the most distinctive features of that city's popular music soundscape.

The day he arrived back in New York, Joel was so overcome with emotion that he immediately wrote the song that would become "New York State of Mind." In fact, he began writing the lyrics while on a bus making its way up route 9W from LaGuardia Airport toward his new home in Highland Falls, on the Hudson River near West Point. "I got off the Greyhound bus and walked into the new house and sat down at the piano and wrote," he later recalled. "That's how I was feeling: glad to be home in New York" (qtd. in Sheff and Sheff 1982). Now one of his most well-known numbers, "New York State of Mind" is filled with geographic and cultural references to the Empire State, from the Hudson River to the city's newspapers and neighborhoods. He acknowledges that some might find other places more appealing, but when it "comes down to reality," what he really needs is New York.

In the mid-1970s, New York City was not exactly paradise, however. As the post–World War II industrial boom receded, many of the country's manufacturing industries faced increasing difficulties stemming from foreign competition, increasing pension costs, rising fuel prices, and other sources. The trend known as "white flight," in which white residents left urban centers for the suburbs in response to rising crime rates and a growing population of racial minorities and the poor, affected many American cities, including New York (see Boustan 2010; Bradford and Kelejian 1973; Guterbock 1976; Frey 1979; Marshall 1979; Grubb 1982; Mills and Price 1984; and Mieszkowski and Mills 1993). Troubled city finances only added to the problem. By April 1975, the municipal government had run out of money and was unable to raise more, as its huge deficit hampered any attempt to secure credit (see Dunstan 1995). Mayor Abraham Beame petitioned President Gerald Ford, whose refusal to consider a federal loan prompted the famous *Daily News* headline, "Ford to City: Drop Dead" (Van Riper 1975). Although Ford never actually uttered those exact words and did, in fact, change his mind and support federal assistance by November, the image of a hardened, unwelcoming city in decline was indelibly etched (Roberts 2006). It was a far cry from the cleaned-up, Disneyfied, tourist magnet of Times Square that would emerge twenty years later (see Bell 1998; Rossi 1998; Sussman 1998; Wasko 2001; and Wollman 2002).

None of that bothers Joel in "New York State of Mind." To a large degree, it was because the city's image was getting beat up that Joel returned in the first place. "When the New York financial crisis started happening, there was a lot of anti-New York sentiment in L.A. from former New Yorkers and I got pissed off," he said. "I woke up one day and just said, 'I'm going back'" (qtd. in Marsh 1978). The city's troubles lend it character, in contrast to the singer's former residence in California. On the West Coast, it was "so easy living day by day, out of touch." New York may not be an "easy" place to live, but, Joel seems to imply, it is more genuine. As the lyrics suggest, it is "the rhythm and blues."

Musically, however, "New York State of Mind" is not only rhythm and blues, although the song's rhythmic aspects and vocal delivery certainly draw on that style. Joel himself "saw it as more of a standard, a 1940s- or 1950s-style blues song, in the manner of 'Georgia on My Mind,'" according to Schruers (2014, 115). Joel's piano is front and center, maintaining a leisurely pace in support of the lead vocal. In an analysis of the song, Robert Schultz points to influences from both the classical and blues spheres: the "motivic unity," or musical ideas that tie it together, is transformed and given a blues inflection (2005, 43–46). Most strikingly, however, the piano's decorative figures lend the song a jazz flavor. In fact, before playing the song at the Bottom Line, a New York club, in June 1976, Joel even instructed the audience to picture themselves after several drinks in a "sleazy jazz club" in New York at about three o'clock in the morning (Frederick S. Boros Audio Recordings 1976). The song's very first notes and chords include, in quick succession, chromatic cascades and rich collections of pitches well outside the key in which the song is written, C-major. And the bridge travels through the keys of G, F, and A-major. Joel rarely uses such a full melodic and harmonic palette; none of the other songs discussed in this chapter even comes close. But jazz does.

Joel's evocation of jazz in "New York State of Mind" is appropriate, given his description of the song's intended purpose as "a standard" and New York City's position as an important site in the history of the quintessentially American genre (see, for example, Charters and Kunstadt 1962; Chevigny 1991; Fletcher 2009; Giddens and DeVeaux 2009; Jackson 2012; and Stewart 2007). The story of jazz usually begins in New Orleans with Louis Armstrong and Jelly Roll Morton, travels north to Chicago with King Oliver and Armstrong, and then lands in the Big

Apple with Duke Ellington where swing, bebop, and later styles emerge. (Other important locales such as St. Louis and Kansas City are usually mentioned along the way.) "Though pared down to a small fraction of the Swing Era's scale," writes musicologist Richard Crawford, "New York's modern jazz scene [in the middle of the twentieth century] blossomed: uptown in Harlem, downtown in Greenwich Village, but most of all in the heart of midtown, on 52nd Street between Fifth and Sixth Avenues" (2001, 760). Indeed, "New York has a kind of jazz influence on me," Joel told Susan Elliott (1978, 113). According to Thomas MacFarlane, one of Joel's "most important contributions" to pop-rock music was his ability to integrate "jazz-derived elements" (2016). Joel would return to the theme of New York jazz two years later on his aptly titled album *52nd Street*.

Beyond its jazz sonority, "New York State of Mind" also alludes to another musical genre: Tin Pan Alley. So named because the cacophonous sound of cheap pianos coming from the offices of several music publishers all on the same block seemed a bit like banging on tin cookware, Tin Pan Alley has come to signify both the American popular music business between about the 1890s and the 1930s and a specific form of music. Most importantly, Tin Pan Alley—the actual place—was located in New York City, on 28th Street. Indeed, early Tin Pan Alley songs have been dubbed "the first distinctly New York product" (Hamm 1983, 341) and helped to establish the basic musical framework of much of the popular music that followed. Many Tin Pan Alley songs later became jazz standards.

Typically, Tin Pan Alley songs were made up of alternating verses and choruses containing the song's title, or a series of verses each ending with a refrain that included the title. These formal sections were usually made up of four phrases, often using one of two patterns: AABA, meaning the opening musical idea is repeated, then a new idea is presented before the first one returns; or ABAC, in which the opening idea returns in the third phrase, but the second and fourth are different (sometimes called "two halves"). Like much later popular music, many Tin Pan Alley songs were about people, such as Chauncey Olcott's "Sweet Rosie O'Grady" (1899), and places, such as Lawlor and Blake's "The Sidewalks of New York" from five years earlier.

As a genre, Tin Pan Alley songs reveal much about what was on people's minds around and just after the turn of the twentieth century, as their lyrics used common, colloquial language to address current issues and events, from popular ethnic stereotypes to the First World War. As "Sweet Rosie O'Grady" demonstrates, Irish stereotypes were common, as were Asian and Hawaiian subjects (see Garrett 2008, 121–214). Changing attitudes toward American involvement in World War I can be traced in song from Alfred Bryan and Al Piantadosi's "I Didn't Raise My Son to Be a Soldier" (1915) to George M. Cohan's "Over There" (1917). Thus, "especially after 1900," writes Nicholas Tawa, "the overly pathetic sentimental ballad" popular in the nineteenth century "had given way to a newer song of feeling that was more cognizant of contemporary conditions" (1990, 199).

Also a "song of feeling" that is unabashedly sentimental, Joel's "New York State of Mind" shares many features with the Tin Pan Alley genre, although the fit is not perfect; Michael Borshuk observes that while Joel "avoided Tin Pan Alley's musical forms," that avoidance was nonetheless informed by his keen awareness of those forms, which he embraced in spirit if not exactly in form (2016, 94). "New York State of Mind" includes four verses that roughly fit the ABAC pattern and finish with the title lyrics. Consider the first verse: The initial melodic phrase (beginning with "some folks like to get away") descends two steps, quickly rises back up to the starting pitch, repeats the gesture, and then finishes with a descent. The second phrase ("hop a flight to Miami Beach") repeats the same descending-ascending-descending shape one time but moves all the pitches higher. The third ("but I'm taking a Greyhound") starts out similar to the first phrase, on the same pitch and with the same downward motion, but descends farther before rising to end on the same pitch as the first phrase did. And the fourth ("I'm in a New York state of mind") starts with a leap upward followed by a descent back to its starting pitch. The other verses basically follow the same pattern. So while clearly inspired by the four-phrase, two-halves design, the first and third melodic phrases are similar but not, as the archetype would suggest, exactly the same.

While lacking a repeated chorus, "New York State of Mind" does contain a bridge ("it was so easy . . . ") that provides contrast with the rest of the piece, a common feature in both jazz and popular music. The melody is lower in Joel's vocal range than in the verses, and the harmony uses a new pattern of chords that take the music in a different tonal direction. The lyrics strike a more nostalgic mood and are delivered in an almost speech-like manner, with short bursts listing the things he missed about the Big Apple, such as the *New York Times* and the *Daily News*. Finally, like Tin Pan Alley, the lyrics of "New York State of Mind" are largely colloquial and reveal something that may have been on the minds of many New Yorkers, an enduring loyalty through both good times and bad.

Joel's celebratory return to New York is therefore conveyed on several levels simultaneously. The lyrics include enough references to life in the city that both residents and nonresidents would know exactly what he is singing about; the mixture of joy and nostalgia is clear. But beyond the words, Joel's use of musical style is purposeful. "I wanted to see if I could write what they call a 'standard,' which could be a timeless sort of melody although it hints at the golden age of the songwriters from the '20s to the '60s," he explains. "So it would have some jazz in the chordings" (personal interview). Both jazz and Tin Pan Alley contributed prominently to the repertory of standards, so it would make sense for Joel to draw on them while composing "New York State of Mind." And both are genres whose histories are inextricably linked to the city that never sleeps.

SHOWDOWN IN "NO MAN'S LAND"

If Joel's ode to New York comes across like a love song for a city, there is no mistaking his attitude toward the places and spaces just beyond its limits. Throughout his career, Joel has taken a rather dim view of suburbia as a land of bland inconsequence, of mind-numbing commercialism, and with a complete lack of identity. From the boredom of *Piano Man's* "Captain Jack" to *Streetlife Serenade's* "The Great Suburban Showdown" to the seething anger of *River of Dreams'* "No Man's Land," he has been consistent in using his music to rail against the emptiness and excess of suburban life.

The modern concept of suburbia emerged in the wake of World War II, as a booming economy in the United States provided a foundation on which the middle class could build. In order to meet the needs of returning veterans and their growing families, whole neighborhoods were constructed of "tract housing," long rows of inexpensive and nearly identical homes (Kelly 1993). Joel grew up in one of the first such developments, not far from the original Levittown, so named because William Levitt and his company, Levitt & Sons, built the homes there. (Hicksville, Joel's actual hometown, is a couple of miles north.) The explosion of suburbia is related to the phenomenon of "white flight" mentioned earlier, as many of those leaving the city found suburban enclaves appealing. The resulting communities were more homogeneous than the city and presented amenities the urban center could not, including better schools and relatively spacious yards for the kids. Suburban towns offered a sense of safety due to the distance from the city and its problems yet easy access to its cultural attractions thanks to a new interstate highway system.

Despite all their promise and the high expectations of a better life, many people found the prefab suburbs like Levittown underwhelming. The monotony of the landscape, with its identical houses later pictured on the cover of Joel's album, *The Nylon Curtain*, was matched by the character of the people. Hicksville, writes Dave Marsh, was "a haven for people who left the city to find something better, only to find that their neighbors were only the cream of what they'd just left." The result, according to Joel, was a kind of identity crisis: "You're a nothing, you're a zero in the suburbs. You're mundane, you're common. You have 2.4 children, you have a quarter acre plot of land, you have a Ford Wagoneer. Who gives a damn about you?" (qtd. in Marsh 1978). He later remarked that suburbia

> was supposed to be a safe place for kids, and a place for kids to play, away from the tenements of the city. . . . We were bored out of our minds! We played city games. We were all city people living in this kind of half-country, half-city place, not sure, "Well, what do we do with this?" "What is it? Where are we? Who are we? What are we?" All the houses were cookie-cutter, and everybody tried to make their house look different, which was kind of charming in a way but also kind of sad. (personal interview)

"Captain Jack" captures this suburban identity crisis. The song was a small hit even before it was recorded in the studio; while on tour promoting *Cold Spring Harbor* in 1972, Joel played it at the Philadelphia radio station WMMR-FM after being recruited by music director Dennis Wilen (Weitzman 1974); Ed Sciaky was the DJ (*Root Beer Rag* 1988). Months later, listeners were still calling in requests for the song.

When stations in New York City got a hold of the tapes and started playing them on air, two things happened quickly: Joel developed a small "cult" following and executives at Columbia Records became interested in this new, young voice (Bego 2007, 61). In a way, then, "Captain Jack" helped build momentum for Joel's career back east while he was busy out west.

What was so appealing about the song? For one thing, the lyrics describe a sense of boredom, even amid comfort and pleasure, to which many suburban listeners could relate. The song's narrator makes several attempts at excitement—a trip to Greenwich Village, listening to music, even a turn at masturbation—but ends up resorting to drugs (in the song, Captain Jack is the dealer; in reality, it was a street name for heroin). Life is so easy that it is tragic: "You've got everything, but nothing's cool. They just found your father in the swimming pool." There is no escape, just a relentlessly nagging feeling that there must be more but, even with a new car, no way to get it.

The song's introduction begins with an organ, as if recalling a staid mainline church. Joel's vocal delivery during the verses, detailing this sense of insatiable yearning, is dynamically flat, reinforcing the dull sentiment portrayed in the lyrics. Only the piano, bass, and a sparse drum pattern accompany the singing. The slight echo on the vocal line is almost taunting. When the chorus, and Captain Jack, arrives, the musical excitement is palpable: a distorted electric guitar roars in, the organ returns with fast repeated notes, and the drums are noticeably busier with a lot of cymbal crashes. The musical interlude following the chorus brings the energy back down a notch. The guitar is no longer distorted, the organ plays slower sustained chords, and the drums adopt a simpler pattern. By the time the next verse arrives, the instrumentation is pared down once again, letting Joel's languid piano move the song along as the organ lingers in the background, a reminder of the high of the chorus.

Joel has called "Captain Jack" a "look out the window song," written when he was living in an apartment near a housing project and could literally see, from his window, suburban kids pull up in their cars and buy drugs from someone who lived there. Joel's middle- and lower-middle-class suburban upbringing left him ill-equipped to understand why affluent suburban kids would need to turn to drugs for excitement. "What's so horrible about an affluent young white teenager's life that he's got to shoot heroin? It's really a song about what I consider to be a pathetic loser kind of lifestyle" (qtd. in Bego 2007, 71).

In "The Great Suburban Showdown," Joel is less concerned with the excitement of the suburbs—or complete lack thereof—than with the banality he finds there. After all, now he has been living in Los Angeles, experiencing life outside his hometown bubble. The song's narrator (perhaps Joel himself?) is on a flight from the West Coast, headed east. Four verses detail his destination, his childhood home where his family awaits him. The images are pleasant but mundane. There will be a lot of sitting around, retelling old stories as the television plays in the background. Food will be cooking on the barbeque in the meticulously manicured backyard. He will be so "bored to death" that he might just have to "hide out" in his old bedroom, as usual. "I know it should be fun," he sings, "but I think I should've packed my gun." The mythical Wild West clearly trumps safe and boring eastern suburbia. "I hear a lot of ennui in the music," Joel says. "There's kind of a lazy summer afternoon feeling to it. . . . There's a banal mood to it, and a lot of the suburbs, I think, are banal. That's the way of life; I mean, it's not the hustle-bustle of the city and it's not the pastoral peace of the countryside. It's neither-nor" (personal interview).

A meandering synthesizer line introduces the track, and it takes a few seconds before it feels like this opening melody has any sort of direction. Of course, that is Joel's point. As this opening melody arrives at the start of the first verse, Joel's voice enters and the piano takes over the accompaniment. Unlike "Captain Jack," the lead vocal in "The Great Suburban Showdown" is mixed dry, discarding the taunting echo for a more plaintive affect. Later in the verse, the pedal steel arrives in the background, further contributing to what Ken Bielen calls the song's "languorous atmosphere" (2011, 31) and reinforcing the song's West Coast perspective.

During the bridge, Joel fills in the picture a bit. He has "been gone for a while." Now, with his horizons proverbially expanded, this old hometown seems monochromatic; "the streets all look the same." Yet he knows well the ritual of the visit and he has to "play the game" by taking part in what now seem like quaint family activities, the "ceremonies of suburbia" (Bielen 2011, 31). The last verse reveals the final twist: he is "only coming home to say goodbye" and plans never to return again. "It wasn't specifically about me," Joel explains, "but it was about that experience of going back to visit with the family in a place where you couldn't wait to get out of" (personal interview). While the eastbound trip fits Joel's timeline, the song diverges from his biography as he has embraced his East Coast roots.

"No Man's Land," released almost twenty years later, reveals that suburbia is still on Joel's mind—and that the resignation of "Captain Jack" and "The Great Suburban Showdown" has been replaced by cynicism and anger. The introduction illustrates this with its distorted electric guitar, incessantly repeated notes on the rhythm guitar, and Joel's clavinet, whose sharp, metallic timbre seems antithetic to the soothing (and absent) sound of acoustic piano. Despite the fact that the verses begin low in Joel's vocal range and at a quieter dynamic, they are filled with a seething potential energy, as if each line might end in an explosion. It does not take long for that explosion to arrive, as the third line of each verse sees the melody jump up an octave, where the pitches are as much screamed as sung. Two lines later, as the musical buildup to the chorus begins, Joel sings in a sarcastic, sardonic tone, listing all the things that suburbanites might find exciting but that really illustrate their superficiality: the "big business," the "sports franchise," the "real thing." Translation: modern suburban life actually offers nothing of real value.

Joel's imagery is in particularly good form on "No Man's Land." The suburban reverence for big-box commercialism is wrapped in a potent mock-religiosity that pairs capitalism with primitivism: "Give us this day our daily discount outlet merchandise," he sings. "Raise up a multiplex and we will make a sacrifice." Looking back, he says,

> What's happening is rampant consumerism. . . . We have destroyed a lot of the physical aspects of the country, and the spiritual aspects. It's this ongoing development of suburbia [that] for so many years we're all programmed to think we want, that everybody wants. . . . Everything is pretty on the surface, but underneath it's corrupt. The whole thing is built on crap. (qtd. in Schruers 2014, 222)

On one hand, Joel's lyrics and comments reflect a growing national trend in the late twentieth century, in which retail chains simultaneously expanded the number of stores they operated and the number of products sold at each store. One study of American retailers argues that, between 1977 and 2007,

> because of the interaction of economies of scale on the cost side with a demand for one-stop shopping, any innovation that directly increases the number of stores a general-merchandise chain operates also induces the chain to expand the range of products it sells. On the cost side, as a chain adds stores—increasing sales volume—economies of scale cause the marginal cost of the product to fall. Lower marginal cost induces the chain to increase its range of product offerings, drawing in more customers who take advantage of its "one-stop" offering. The combination of more products and more customers at each store increases store profit, prompting the retail chain to add even more stores. (Basker, Klimek, and Van 2012, 543)

On the other hand, Joel's observations of the religiosity of the shopping experience align with theories about how that experience, in those places, fulfills a basic human need in ways similar to religion. In many cultures, the design elements of religious spaces model the world in order to provide a sense of physical and existential center. Crosses and four corners recall the four compass points; domed structures mimic the sky and the cyclic circularity of seasons and celestial bodies. Thus, "the geometric designs in the mall," writes Ira Zepp, "tell a story about how we ultimately understand the world to be; they are a replication of the larger planet. We have said by this paradigmatic structure that our experience of the world is one of balance and harmony. We have traveled to the 'center' and discovered unity" (1997, 34). So Joel's take on the American suburban centrality of shopping, of its communal and spiritual appeal, was right on the mark.

At the same time, in "No Man's Land," Joel slams suburbia's insubstantiality, continuing the argument from decades prior in "Captain Jack." The teenagers of the earlier song are now the grown-ups, even if their attitude and behavior are unchanged. An incessant focus on yuppie gossip replaces old-fashioned neighborly concern, as the highlight of a suburbanite's day is the revelation that a neighbor has been busted for cocaine. A line about "Lolita and suburban lust" presumably references Amy Fisher, known as the "Long Island Lolita," a seventeen-year-old whose affair with a married man ended when she shot his wife in May 1992. The story made national news and provided tabloid fodder for months. In this vapid and debauched environment, children do not stand a chance (witness "their boredom and their vacant stares"), which leads to Joel's concern for the future: "God help us all if we're to blame for their unanswered prayers."

"Instead of feeling sarcastic about the suburbs, I was feeling very protective of Long Island. It was disappearing" as development ("*over-development*" in his words) stretched across the island all the way to the Hamptons. "My daughter [Alexa Ray] was seven or eight years old at that time. And I used to tell her stories about [how] we grew up near a farm, or where I grew up this place was all fishing community—they were disappearing." In their place, Joel saw the proverbial "gold statue. 'Give us this day our daily discount outlet merchandise.' Who ever heard of a discount outlet out in the sticks?! You know, there was a *general store!* And now, it's 'Generica' [a play on "generic" and "America"]. And you're seeing the whole thing being paved over. And all the original families are leaving, and the kids can't afford to stay because the whole thing's being suburbanized" (personal interview).

That "protective" reaction to the changes surrounding him is borne out in the fervor with which Joel sings "No Man's Land." The chorus, which nostalgically pleads for the memories of some mythologized pre-suburban times ("who remembers when it all began, out here in No Man's Land?"), presents his strained voice, yelling over the distorted grinding of the band and backed by a choir of voices holding long chords on the syllable "ah" before joining in on the refrain. Those words are sung with harsh attacks on "out" and "here" and accents emphasizing the *short-long-long* rhythm of the words "no man's land." It is almost a (religious?) chant, delivered with great volume and requiring great energy. The third and final time he repeats the title, the band and backup singers cut out, leaving just Joel's voice and its taunting echo to drive the point home. Clearly, Joel's passion for the topic has reached fever pitch. Unlike the placement of "Captain Jack" at the end of *Piano Man* or "The Great Suburban Showdown" buried in the second half of *Streetlife Serenade*, "No Man's Land" is the opening track on *River of Dreams*. Joel wants listeners to think about this first. Unchecked, the song ultimately argues, suburbia can destroy social fabric.

Although their topics and meanings are varied, one conclusion to be drawn from this sample of Joel's songs on places and spaces is that they strongly influence how he—and we—see the world around us. And while this perception is often portrayed in negative terms, from "Los Angelenos" to "No Man's Land," it does not always have to be so, as

"New York State of Mind" demonstrates. Moreover, Joel's work, especially "Say Goodbye to Hollywood," reveals how music need not even be about a particular place as much as movement from, through, or between places. Indeed, our connections to places and spaces define us and integrate our experience of the world with that of other people, and Joel's songs accomplish just that. Importantly, the ease with which we can change our sense of place—through physical movement or the evocation of place through music—means our (musical) experience of the world is that much richer.

3

"WHERE'S THE ORCHESTRA?"

Domestic and International Politics

Like many of his singer-songwriter peers, Billy Joel has sometimes addressed political topics in his music. While songs from the beginning of his career focus mostly on personal matters and relationships, in its middle and later stages, he began to turn to more overtly political topics, especially after *The Stranger* secured his place among the top popular musicians of the day. The term "politics" often refers to the affairs of government and those who are part of it or wish to be. In essence, politics are about power—who has it (and who does not) and what they choose to do with it. The songs discussed in this chapter share a concern with the ways people or institutions in power exert control over others. Indeed, this is a significant theme in Joel's music generally, as the next chapter considers the politics of class and the subsequent one addresses the politics found within personal relationships. Here, however, the focus remains on songs that observe, address, and comment on national and international politics in a traditional sense, including "Miami 2017 (Seen the Lights Go Out on Broadway)" (from *Turnstiles*), "Goodnight Saigon" and "Where's the Orchestra?" (from *The Nylon Curtain*), and "Leningrad" (from *Storm Front*). While some are more explicit than others, they all bear traces of the effects of politics on individuals.

"JUST SURVIVING IS A NOBLE FIGHT": NATIONAL POLITICS

While Joel's first three solo albums are generally not concerned with political matters, such concerns start to appear on his fourth, *Turnstiles*, in two tracks, "Prelude/Angry Young Man" and "Miami 2017 (Seen the Lights Go Out on Broadway)." Both adopt the perspective of outside-looking-in. In the first song, Joel sings as a narrator describing the title character, his struggles, and their emotional toll. The story he tells is of class-based politics or, better put, class-based political rage (and is therefore discussed in detail in chapter 4). In the second, he assumes the role of a refugee looking back on the cataclysmic fate of New York City. With the exception of the bridge of "Angry Young Man," when Joel shifts to a first-person perspective, the rhetorical performance of distance heard in both songs helps to convey a sense of us-versus-them—a balance (or imbalance) of power one might feel when experiencing the blunt end of political force.

National and local politics are at the heart of "Miami 2017." While the devastation to New York City described in the lyrics is hyperbolic, the city itself was in a downward spiral in the 1970s, as discussed in the previous chapter. As the Big Apple failed financially and begged the federal government for a bailout, anti–New York sentiment was on the rise throughout the rest of the country, since many believed the city's troubles were of its own making. "The city was on the verge of bankruptcy and they thought it might default," Joel told Bill DeMain. "A lot of people in Los Angeles," where Joel was living, "were kind of gleeful about that: 'Ha, ha, New York's going down the tubes.' I got very defensive" (qtd. in Bego 2007, 103). It was easy to imagine a panicked dystopian metropolis without law enforcement, sanitation, power, or other basic services. Would the rest of the United States simply give up on New York City and cut it loose?

This is the "apocalyptic vision" Joel explores in "Miami 2017," sung from the perspective of a New York City refugee just over forty years later. He reminisces about seeing the iconic bright lights of Broadway go dark, a macabre concert in Brooklyn from which attendees witness the explosion of the bridges leading in and out of Manhattan Island, an evacuation attempt thwarted by a union work stoppage, and the arrival of an aircraft carrier from the naval base in Norfolk, Virginia, to assist amid the mayhem. The ultimate irony is found in the nonchalance of the narrator's descriptions. Although the city's theater district lies in ruins, the debris looked so similar to the pre-bankruptcy scene on 42nd Street that most New Yorkers "almost didn't notice it." And although churches were burning in Harlem, that too was hardly different from the normal state of things, as "they always burned up there before." The scene brings to mind the "natives" of New York City, who, as E. B. White described in 1949, lend the place "solidity and continuity," even in the face of extermination from a prophetic "single flight of planes no bigger than a wedge of geese," whose impact "can quickly end this island fantasy, burn the towers, crumble the bridges, turn the underground passages into lethal chambers, cremate the millions" (698, 710). There was no way for White to know about the September 11, 2001, terrorist attacks on New York City, of course. But echoes of his sentiments resonated with Joel as he performed "Miami 2017" during the *Concert for New York City*, a star-studded, televised production that included musicians, actors, and politicians honoring first responders from the city's police and fire departments, on October 20 that year.

During the *Concert for New York City*, Joel called "Miami 2017" a "science fiction song." The track begins with a gradual fade-in featuring an edgy, distorted Moog synthesizer sliding between two chords while a siren—a sonic symbol of crisis—alternates between two notes, which slowly drop in pitch as it moves off into the distance. The sounds are all harsh, and there is no bass line to offer a musical foundation. Yet the picture is clear: something is wrong. Joel's piano enters after about fifteen seconds while the Moog's buzzing is still fading away. Quick, broken chords played in a high octave counter the lower-pitched, darker tones of the synthesizer and siren. The piano's pitch and melody signal something different from the earlier, harsher sounds as it transports the listener to Florida, where the narrative begins.

After the piano melody drops down toward the middle of the instrument's range and cadences, resting for a moment on the tonic chord, the story begins calmly as the first verse opens with the parenthetical phrase of the song's title. Joel's voice delivers the facts straightforwardly, describing the abandonment of New York while establishing the retrospective nature of the story: "They all bought Cadillacs and left there long ago." The quick echo on the vocal track portends the disturbance that will soon be revealed and perhaps contributes to the song's "science fiction" quality. The accompaniment is provided by Joel's piano and faintly heard strings. But as he reaches the lyric, "They turned our power down and drove us underground," the band enters with cymbal crashes and a guitar line that parallels the bass, rising as the tension of the story reaches a breaking point: "But we went right on with the show." The calm of the first verse is gone, and the show, it seems, is no longer just a memory of the past. It is happening here, in the present; we are reliving the destruction. With the band in full swing, the song's aggressive rock drive takes over, propelling its apocalyptic description.

In the final verse (at about 3:45), the band drops out again as Joel's character returns to a reflective posture, lamenting how few New Yorkers remain. The mood is calm, but as the final lines are sung, the band reenters in a last-ditch effort, once again crashing cymbals and offering a rising bass line, as if resolving to resist fading away: "They say a handful still survive . . . to keep the memory alive." After Joel's voice holds out the final lyric and the sound of the band decays, the piano returns, repeating the broken chords from the introduction as the track fades into oblivion. Like "The Ballad of Billy the Kid" (from *Piano Man*) discussed in chapters 2 and 7, Joel intended for "Miami 2017" to be "couched in dramatic," even cinematic, "terms" (personal interview).

One of the cleverest aspects of "Miami 2017" is the way its description accesses politics on multiple levels. The most obvious is the drama, played out on the national stage, between the city and federal governments, in which the latter held all the power. "*They* turned our power down," Joel sings angrily, taking the New Yorkers' side. The aircraft carrier, too, stands as a symbol of national power. Yet for much of the city's financial crisis, federal power was exercised through indifference rather than action. "During the chaos in New York and despite the devastating effect its collapse would have on national and world commerce," writes historian George J. Lankevich, "there was an almost surrealistic unconcern in Washington." Fifteen mayors from around the country lobbied for a bailout, but the feds held fast. Even the West German chancellor, Helmut Schmidt, expressed concern that New York's disarray was disturbing business in Zurich and Frankfurt. But the White House stood firm. As the Thanksgiving holiday drew closer, the crisis intensified the potential damage a bankruptcy could inflict on the national economy. Polling data showed the American people's disapproval of Ford's hard-line refusal, while the city made a clear effort to raise revenues through layoffs and transit fare hikes. Ford finally relented. The resulting bailout ultimately cost taxpayers nothing, and the U.S. Treasury made millions in profit (Lankevich 2002, 218–20).

On another level, "Miami 2017" reveals political tensions *within* the City of New York. Unlike many cities in the United States, New York is composed of five separate counties, known as boroughs, stitched together into one municipality. Joel's lyrics mention four of the five, but not all are treated equally in the song's narrative, a distinction that reveals a split within the city itself. Two boroughs are explicitly destroyed: Manhattan, home of many of the city's landmarks, is sunk at sea while the Bronx is "blown away," perhaps with firepower from the warship. In contrast, Brooklyn and Queens, which share the westernmost end of Long Island, are largely spared, as the former lasts at least long enough to host the aforementioned concert and the residents of the latter are told that they "could stay." (Staten Island is left out completely, though one can imagine if Manhattan were to sink, it might be underwater too.) The differences between the ways the boroughs are treated imply political power and choice. For example, consider the use of military force in the song: the carrier saves some and destroys others. It is a distinction that brings to mind military theorist Carl Phillip von Clausewitz's famous aphorism, "War is the continuation of politics by other means" (1989, 87).

In actuality, differences between the boroughs can be traced all the way back to the founding of the city, when in 1898 various towns and counties were joined in what was called "consolidation." Joanne Reitano describes how "mock funeral services were held in parts of Brooklyn and Queens where Consolidation threatened to bring more taxes, immigrants, crime, and corruption. By contrast, Manhattan hailed Consolidation as a milestone akin to the Erie Canal and the Brooklyn Bridge" (2006, 83–84). In the 1970s, interborough differences were no less apparent as even basic services were provided unevenly. For example, a February 1970 snowstorm was followed by quick plowing in Manhattan while the outer boroughs waited a week to be cleared. "City Hall's indifference to their plight," Lankevich writes, "left many citizens furious" (2002, 207). Manhattan continued as a center of global commerce and finance, exemplified by the 1972 completion of the gleaming Twin Towers of the World Trade Center near the island's southern tip. But other boroughs, with less wealth and political clout, were hemorrhaging. "Between 1970 and 1975, the South Bronx alone lost 16 percent of all its housing (43,000 apartments) as four square blocks were lost weekly to physical decay and fire. An accelerated exodus from the devastation was the inevitable result" (209).

While Joel's connection to New York City is firmly rooted in his biography, the effects of national politics can be heard in several of his other songs. For example, both "Allentown" (from *The Nylon Curtain*) and "The Downeaster 'Alexa'" (from *Storm Front*), discussed in detail in the next chapter, can be understood as musical responses to such political forces. In the first, globalization and the erosion of American manufacturing exacerbated the class differences between management and blue-collar workers, exposing a politics of class whose effects would be felt well beyond the Pennsylvania city named in the song's title. In the second, the repeated failure of state legislatures and executives to cooperate on and coordinate commercial fishing regulation contributed to a confusing patchwork of laws that placed a great burden on those whose livelihoods depended upon their catch. Subsequent legislative efforts to ban certain fish outright threatened, in the eyes of some, to extinguish a way of life entirely. Both songs thus engage with politically fraught issues while focusing, like "Miami 2017," not on those who make policy but on those affected by it.

"WE WATCHED THE POWER FALL": INTERNATIONAL POLITICS

As his career developed through the 1980s, Joel also used his music to comment on issues of international politics. Critic Stephen Holden observed in *Rolling Stone* that it was on *The Nylon Curtain* when Joel most decisively shifted his gaze away from his hometown. "Until this album, Joel's socially acute songs have been set mostly on his home turf; 'Captain Jack,' 'Piano Man' and 'Scenes from an Italian Restaurant' defined the New York suburban milieu in bold, if occasionally awkward, strokes. On *The Nylon Curtain*, [we] find Joel tackling subjects farther from home and larger than his own neighborhood" (1982). The album's title references the "iron curtain," the symbolic separation of Western Europe and its allies from Eastern Europe and the Soviet Union, from the end of World War II until the end of the Cold War in 1991. "Nylon" invokes the fabric's widespread use during this period. Initially intended as a replacement for silk in military supplies during World War II, it was introduced into consumer goods after the conflict's end. The material's synthetic character—it does not appear in nature—renders it akin to the long rows of identical, inexpensive, prefabricated tract housing available for soldiers returning from the war, pictured on the album's cover silhouetted against the orange hues of a setting sun. There, in the "lifeless conformity of Levittown-style housing," the suburban "good life" such developments seemed to promise actually amounted to little more than indistinguishable, empty shells (Everett 2000, 116). As Joel explains: "When I think of the West, I think of a nylon curtain. It's soft, but still a barrier . . . sort of a rose-colored isolation" (qtd. in Smith 2007, 181).

One of the tracks on *The Nylon Curtain* is "Goodnight Saigon," which Holden describes as "starkly descriptive" and the album's "stunner" (1982). The song offers a retrospective tale of American military involvement in Vietnam, told from the perspective of an enlisted soldier (a perspective he returns to in "Christmas in Fallujah" in 2007) and evokes feelings of fatalism, futility, and naïveté along with brotherhood and unity. According to Christian Klein's sociological study, the fact that Joel never served in Vietnam did not have a significant impact on the song's reception, which was positive among veterans and nonvets alike. Importantly, this emotional centerpiece of the album is rooted in a conflict largely viewed as a proxy for the larger ideological divergence between American democracy and Soviet Communism, the same split demarcated by the iron curtain.

The first sounds in "Goodnight Saigon" are of insects on a quiet Vietnamese countryside. Slowly, the reverberations of helicopter rotors grow closer and louder until Joel's piano begins playing the song's distinctive, rising four-chord figure. That motive repeats over a descending bass line, similar to the broken chords of "Miami 2017." As the chopper and piano fade, Joel's protagonist enters, singing reminiscently about basic training on Parris Island, the site of a Marine Corps Recruit Depot off the coast of South Carolina. A lone acoustic guitar offers accompaniment. Then the scene shifts to the Vietnamese countryside, where young soldiers feel little connection to home while nervously eyeing the landscape for the enemy. Joel's voice is "tight, wound-up [and] higher and tenser than usual" (Holden 1982). Additional instrumental layers are added until the entire band is playing by the third verse. The terror of war, symbolized by the darkness of night—mentioned four times in the lyrics—forges bonds between the soldiers as they sing together in the song's chorus, "We said we'd all go down together." It also drives many of them mad, a fact Joel shares in the song's opening lines ("we left as inmates from an asylum"). While the first verse is sung quietly, by the song's midsection, Joel is screaming at the top of his range. After the choir of soldiers sings the final chorus, the fade-out begins. The piano repeats the opening four-chord sequence. Then the helicopter returns and heads off into the distance, leaving a full thirty seconds of nighttime sounds to end the track.

"Goodnight Saigon" stands at the intersection of both national and international politics, as the Vietnam War it describes had both foreign and domestic ramifications. Historian Robert Buzzanco writes:

> *Vietnam was a transformative event, with the war and opposition to it reshaping American life.* Vietnam generated the largest mass protest movement in US history; it exposed the limits of liberal reform; the war forestalled anti-poverty and civil rights progress and radicalized movements associated with those issues; helped bring other movements into existence, like Women's Liberation or the Counterculture; and provoked a backlash that continues to influence American politics and society to this day. (1999, 6, italics in the original)

The conflict's origins lay in Vietnamese resistance to French colonial authority, which erupted in the First Indochina War (1946–1954) and culminated in the French defeat at the battle of Dien Bien Phu (an event also mentioned in Joel's later song "We Didn't Start the Fire," discussed in chapter 7). Following the French exit, the United States became the chief supporter of the South Vietnamese government against Communist North Vietnam, which was backed by the Soviet Union and China. The first American military "advisors" were sent to the country as early as 1950, but troop numbers rose quickly in the 1960s as the American policy emphasizing the "containment" of Communism pushed Presidents Kennedy and Johnson to escalate American involvement.

The war became a hot topic in national politics, especially during the 1960s, as young men were increasingly sent to fight overseas. During the first half of the decade, the tone of the rhetoric from the military and the government was optimistic, and the public believed it. William Westmoreland, the four-star army general who commanded U.S. forces in Vietnam, 1964–1968, and served as the army's Chief of Staff, 1968–1972, was *Time* magazine's Man of the Year in 1965, described as "the sinewy personification of the American fighting man" ("Man of the Year" 1966). He declared in 1967 that the war had reached a point "where the end comes into view" (Berman 1991, 116). It would officially end eight years later.

Things began to change after the Tet Offensive, a large-scale attack by the North Vietnamese Army on cities and towns across Vietnam beginning on January 30, 1968. The Americans and South Vietnamese were able to repel the attack, and historians generally agree that it was a military victory for the U.S. forces and their allies. But its scope and the fact that it took Westmoreland's forces largely by surprise drastically shook public confidence in the general, the military, and the White House. Trusted *CBS Evening News* anchorman Walter Cronkite delivered a major story on the battle and its aftermath, famously concluding, "It seems now more certain than ever that the bloody experience of Vietnam is to end in stalemate." President Lyndon B. Johnson reportedly responded, "If I've lost Cronkite, I've lost middle America" (see Willibanks 2007, 68–69). The enemy troops were clearly, as Joel sings, "sharp as knives."

Subsequent requests for additional troops and the resulting expansion of the draft further stoked the antiwar movement and riled an increasingly skeptical American populace. The method by which young men were conscripted was seen as particularly suspect, as a disproportionate number were minorities while nearly all members of local draft boards were white (Anderson 2007, 250–51). Moreover, earlier exemptions for college students were revised, making students with lower grade point averages eligible for conscription. Then on November 26, 1969, President Nixon signed executive order 11497, which established the "draft lottery" held on December 1 and broadcast by all major television and radio networks. Through this lottery, the Selective Service System determined the order in which men born between 1944 and 1950 would be called for military service in 1970. A similar lottery was held on July 1, 1970, for men born in 1951, and additional drawings were held annually until 1975, although the draft numbers issued in 1972 and later were never used.

One reason the draft was so scary was because the images from Vietnam broadcast on the nightly news showed the brutality of war in ways Americans had never before experienced. When the Tet Offensive reached the U.S. embassy in Saigon, news cameras captured the footage, which quickly reached American living rooms where people could plainly see "widespread bloodshed and devastation," which resulted in many soldiers coming home, as Joel describes, "in plastic" body bags (Willibanks 2007, 69). The contrast between these images and the tone of the news briefings coming from Washington fueled the public's distrust. Indeed, in what was dubbed "Maximum Candor," in 1964 the American government reversed its earlier policy of providing as little information as possible to journalists covering the conflict. Instead, reporters were given increased access to military personnel and battles and provided with much more information about troops and operations. As a result, Clarence Wyatt concludes, the press "depended on the government for information concerning the war and, consequently, allowed the government to shape the news" (2007, 280).

And although many Americans did not support the increasingly common student protests, disapproval of the war continued to rise during Richard Nixon's presidency, especially after he ordered the invasion of Cambodia, an expansion of the war that contradicted his earlier promises to end the conflict. Thus, the revelations wrought by the media coverage of the Tet Offensive and the Cambodia incursion, combined with the draft and the heavy-handed response to student protests—exemplified by the shooting of four students by state troopers at Ohio's Kent State University on May 4, 1970—invigorated the antiwar movement (see Anderson 2007; Fry 2007).

David E. James identifies "Goodnight Saigon" as one of several popular songs that convey a "synthesis of sympathy for the soldier with recognition of his trauma" through lyrics containing images as much "derived from a decade of cultural exploitation of deranged vets, especially from films of the late 70s, as from any actual experience." This "model" of the GI, James concludes, "made him a pawn of 80s' political exploitations of the war, much as he had been a victim of the war itself" (1991, 246–47). As Joel sings, "Who was wrong? And who was right?"

Ultimately, Joel's ode to young American soldiers highlights the way circumstances were largely beyond their control. He lists the comforts they did and did not have, from the significant to the mundane: they lacked a home front and soft soap but were given *Playboy* magazine to read and comedian Bob Hope to watch. They indulged in music (cassette tapes of the band the Doors) and drugs as distractions from the terror of combat. What they could not do, however, was exert much influence over their own fate, an omnipresent fact that motivated a sense of collective fatalism. If they were going to go down, they would "all go down together."

As musical compositions, the parallels between "Goodnight Saigon" and "Miami 2017" are striking. Both employ a fade-in to the introduction and a fade-out at its conclusion, musically suggesting that the song is an excerpt from a larger experience. Both address some kind of devastation, whether to the cityscape and spirit of New York or the minds, bodies, and spirits of American soldiers in Southeast Asia. They do this largely in the past tense as a story told by a scarred survivor. And in both, the dramatic arc of the story is conveyed through both the instrumentation, which accumulates as the song gets going and then dissipates as it approaches its end, and the intensity of Joel's voice, which begins calmly, ratchets up with tension in the middle, and then calms back down.

There are differences, of course. The devastation of "Miami 2017" was (mostly) hypothetical, while that of "Goodnight Saigon" was surely not. And while "Goodnight Saigon" uses the choir to symbolize the soldiers' collectivity and brotherhood, "Miami 2017" includes only Joel's voice. Considering the story of the songs, however, such a choice makes sense. "Goodnight Saigon" accesses a historical moment of collectivity; men were drafted in groups, soldiers acted in groups, and protests were staged in groups. In "Miami 2017," as Joel sings, only a "handful still survive."

While Joel's formula for retrospective songs of catastrophe seems clear, that does not mean either song was formulaic to the point of banality. In fact, both had demonstrable impact. The inclusion of "Miami 2017" on Joel's live recording *Songs in the Attic*, in the post-9/11 *Concert for New York City*, and in the December 12, 2012 *Concert for Sandy Relief* benefit held at New York City's Madison Square Garden for the victims of Hurricane Sandy (during which several lyrics were

changed to emphasize the storm's damage to various New York neighborhoods) demonstrates that song's staying power. "Goodnight Saigon,"
in turn, is credited with helping to convince Senator Barbara Boxer (D-
CA) to sponsor federal legislation compensating Vietnam veterans for
disabilities traced to the use of Agent Orange (a toxic herbicide widely
used to destroy the landscape under which the North Vietnamese
forces took cover) on the battlefield (Bordowitz 2005, 145; Smith 2007,
182).

The conflict in Vietnam was only one front in the larger Cold War
between the United States and the Soviet Union. It is considered "cold"
because no direct, large-scale military action was taken by one side
against the other, despite proxy wars like the one in Vietnam. Nonetheless, it had a profound effect on global politics as well as politics within
many counties. It also indelibly shaped the worldview of those who
grew up at the time, including Joel. "You have to understand," Joel
explains, "this is the defining political aspect of my life and everyone
else who grew up in the Baby Boom; the Cold War was almost our
whole life. We all thought we were gonna, you know, blow up, in a
hydrogen bomb explosion. And then this war ended for me . . . and
that's really what this song is about" (qtd. in Joel, *Greatest Hits Volume
III: The Video*).

The influence of the Cold War on Joel's music is perhaps best exemplified by "Leningrad," a song partly set in the Soviet Union, in a city
whose name memorialized Vladimir Lenin, one of the philosophical
architects of Communism (see Ruble 1990; Arthur L. George 2003). It
traces two life stories, Joel's and that of a Russian man, Viktor. Importantly, the narrative and musical climax brings listeners into a present
where the clear distinctions of the Cold War are blurring. What were
once perceived as insurmountable differences are, ultimately, swept
away as Joel realizes their similarities.

The track begins with a solo piano introduction. Stately chords
played with dotted rhythms (*long–short–long–short*) suggest the seriousness of a national anthem—specifically, a Russian one: though the
opening sonority is major, the second instance of the opening motive is
presented in a minor key, evoking a more somber mood. These chords
give way two measures later to a melody, played and harmonized in the
right hand, which is balanced by a bass line played in octaves in the left.
One gets the impression that each key on the piano's keyboard is played

with power and precision, much the way the Soviet anthem projected the country's military might musically (at least to Americans, as seen in films like 1990's *The Hunt for Red October*).

The first verse starts with Viktor's beginnings. Born in the mid-1940s, the boy's father was killed, probably a casualty of the Siege of Leningrad by the Germans from 1941 to 1944. Thus, Viktor is "a child of sacrifice, a child of war." The second verse repeats the melody of the first, as Joel describes how Viktor fell in line with his comrades, serving the State and drinking vodka. "A Russian life was very sad," he sings, "but such was life in Leningrad."

The song uses modified strophic form. The first two verses sit low in Joel's range, enabling him to sing in a syllabic, declamatory style that comes across matter-of-factly. Then Joel moves to the bridge, where the harmony switches abruptly to a minor chord and the melody leaps up an octave, lending Joel's voice a more effortful timbre. The story moves from bleak Leningrad to hardened America.

"I was born in '49," Joel sings of himself. He identifies as a "Cold War kid" and describes the McCarthy-era mentality with which he was schooled. It was a period, beginning at the close of World War I and reaching fever pitch in the early 1950s, when American political leaders, such as Senator Joseph McCarthy (R-WI), and ordinary citizens grew increasingly suspicious of alleged Communist activity or sympathizers within the United States. Prominent entertainers, artists, and intellectuals were among those targeted by McCarthy's House Un-American Activities Committee (see Morgan 2004; Schrecker 1994).

"Stop 'em at the 38th parallel, blast those yellow reds to hell," Joel continues, making reference to the circle of latitude that served as the border between North and South Korea. It was seen as a line-in-the-sand beyond which the United States and its allies would prevent Communist expansion, exemplified by the Korean War (1950–1953), another Cold War proxy conflict. The combination of racial and ideological epithets Joel uses was typical of colloquial language at the time, in which the enemy (Communist North Koreans) was often described in popular culture in derogatory terms.

This was the world of Joel's earliest, formative years, a time of great fear and vulnerability. School-age kids routinely practiced hiding under their desks in the event of a Soviet air raid. Joel asks, "Haven't they heard we won the war?"—World War II—"What do they keep on fighting for?" These lyrics "are particularly striking," A. Morgan Jones observes, "in that they show Americans in a position of weakness and confusion" (2011, 143). For young children, it was easy to learn hateful stereotypes of Koreans or Russians. But to understand the causes of conflicts like the Korean War (on the other side of the world) and McCarthy's congressional hearings (much closer to home) required asking some questions to which the answers were sometimes less than clear.

As "Leningrad" continues with another verse, Joel returns to Viktor. After serving in the Soviet army, he retired and became a circus clown, deriving joy from the happiness he would bring to Russian kids. In a clever turn of phrase, Joel then uses "children" to pivot into a second bridge, where he once again sings of Americans. This time they are kids in Levittown, whose youth includes the terrifying experience of bomb shelters, underground rooms where people were meant to ride out an air attack and its possible nuclear aftermath. This seemed especially likely when, for thirteen days in October 1962, the Soviet Union stationed ballistic missiles and bombers capable of carrying nuclear warheads on the island of Cuba, a Soviet ally roughly ninety miles off the coast of Florida. The resulting spike in tensions—many historians consider the incident the closest the Cold War ever came to turning hot—forced the American public to face the very real threat of imminent and fiery annihilation (Dobbs 2008; Alice L. George 2003).

The song's final verse brings listeners into the present, as Joel and his daughter, Alexa, visit the Soviet Union. They meet Viktor, who elicits giggles from the young girl. Joel concludes, "We never knew what friends we had until we came to Leningrad." The song then closes with a forty-five-second instrumental coda featuring a repetition of the opening piano melody, shifted up five steps to a new key and expanded to include drums, strings, and a choir. The final cadence brings the track to a satisfying end.

Joel did, in fact, make a well-publicized journey to the USSR in July 1987 to perform shows in Moscow and Leningrad; he was the first American rock star to do so. (The performances were captured on his live album *Kohuept*.) But the Soviet authorities were not pleased when one night Joel threw what was later called a "tantrum" on stage, flipping over an electric piano after the venue's staff refused to turn off the house lights. The lighting was necessary for the film crews on site, though Joel argued that the audience could not relax and enjoy the show due to the blinding glare. The media obsessed over the flap: an Associated Press story on the incident showed up as "Billy Joel Blows His Cool, Upsets Piano in Moscow" in the *Los Angeles Times* on July 27 and as "Billy Joel Has a Tantrum" in *The New York Times* the next day. Joel described his behavior as a defensive move—"I have to protect my shows. The people in the audience want to be in the dark; they want to cut loose"—while also observing that similar antics on American tours went largely unnoticed: "I've thrown [a] piano twenty times in the states and no one ever said a thing. All of a sudden I do it in Russia and it's an international incident" (qtd. in Smith 2007, 204–5). Clearly, rock music can be political.

Yet for all the song might be interpreted to say about international politics, Joel strives to keep the focus on individuals. This choice stands in contrast to other Cold War songs like "Russians," by his British contemporary Sting, where the lyrics speak in greater generalities even while touching on similar themes: "What might save us, me and you, is if the Russians love their children too." Joel's and Viktor's lives, "Leningrad" ultimately suggests, are more similar than they are different. Each is marked by the indelible impact of international politics, yet both men are still, at their core, human beings who recognize the power of a child's smile.

Both "Leningrad" and "Goodnight Saigon" are notable for the way Joel treats political conflict. The songs certainly share some similarities, including sparse introductions, gradually thickening texture, and the use of background vocal ensembles. The choral aspect, in particular, is one that Joel hears in a lot of his music, rooted deeply in his childhood musical experiences.

> I went to church when I was a little boy and I loved singing hymns. I didn't really like the whole religion shit. But I loved the singing and the harmony. . . . And I used to sing with buddies, back in the '60s, on the street corner, doo-wop and a cappella. And the fact that these four working-class kids could all of a sudden come up with this harmony, out of nowhere, it was *fabulous*. I was enchanted with it. . . . So there is a great deal of choral capacity in the music that I write. I've always been aware of it. Massed voices are a wonderful thing. (personal interview)

The differences between "Goodnight Saigon" and "Leningrad" are also striking. For example, while "Goodnight Saigon" is sung entirely in the first person, "Leningrad" makes extensive (but not exclusive) use of the third person, rhetorically separating parts of the narrative from Joel's own point of view. Moreover, unlike the solidarity communicated by the choir of soldiers in "Goodnight Saigon," Joel uses the choir from "Leningrad" (voiced by students from Hicksville High School, under the direction of Joel's former music teacher, Chuck Arnold) more as a "vocal chorus," a subtle but important difference supported by the way they are listed in the album's liner notes. In the coda to "Leningrad," the voices double not Joel's vocal line (as they did in "Goodnight Saigon") but the piano melody, which helps to reinforce the song's anthemic quality (Jones 2011, 135–36, 146).

Unlike "Goodnight Saigon," "Leningrad" tells two stories, Viktor's and Joel's. Importantly, the Russian experience precedes Joel's American one. This choice is echoed musically by the compositional styles of the introduction, verses, bridges, and coda. The rhythms of the introduction and coda, evoking a march, make it "possible to feel an affinity between this opening melody and that of the Soviet national anthem," as both share "crisp," "martial" qualities. Meanwhile, Joel's bridges tend "towards rock idioms" (Jones 2011, 139–41).

"THE CURTAIN FALLS" IN "WHERE'S THE ORCHESTRA?"

Joel's focus in "Leningrad" on the individual in the face of massive geopolitical forces was presaged significantly on *The Nylon Curtain*, an album on which all of the tracks are sung almost entirely in the singular or plural first person ("I" or "we"). Writing about individual people or characters was a conscious choice. In Joel's words:

> My ethic in writing songs throughout that era [around *The Nylon Curtain*] was always to be talking about *people*, whether it's a love song, a song about a relationship, or a friend, or a barfly—it's always got to be about a particular person. If you try to write for an audience or to a *concept*, I don't think you're really writing for anybody. But if you're writing for a specific person and a specific situation, a lot of people might be able to identify with that. (qtd. in Schruers 2014, 151)

On "Where's the Orchestra?," the album's closing number, Joel sings as a protagonist who takes in a night of theater but is confounded by its lack of musical accompaniment: "Wasn't this supposed to be a musical? Here I am in the balcony. How the hell could I have missed the overture?" He is confused when the expectations raised by his environment are unmet. Joel sings two verses calmly, describing the scene and his perplexed response to it. The end of the second verse transitions into the bridge, where he more confidently remarks how this was his "big night on the town." With a dramatic crescendo, the accompanying music swells as the melody reaches new heights. But the bridge ends sadly: "I assumed that a show would have a song, so I was wrong." The concluding verse shows his resignation, as he "at least" understands the actors' roles and the playwright's message. But the production's conclusion is still dissatisfying, and after the final curtain call, he is left asking the same question he started with, "Where's the orchestra?" The instrumental coda fades slowly toward an empty silence.

The lyrics of "Where's the Orchestra?" exemplify the overall mood of *The Nylon Curtain* and, in fact, many of Joel's political songs: disappointment, frustration, and resignation (see Duchan 2015). His use of the lyric "hell" reveals his frustration despite the even, resigned tone to the vocal line. Joel's character admits to having "absolutely no idea at all what is being said, despite the dialogue," a line that may be interpreted metaphorically as a reflection of society's vague understanding of historical events despite seemingly clear communication from authorities, such as the seemingly disconnected reports on the Vietnam War (at least before Tet) or Nixon's involvement in the Watergate scandal despite very public insistence that he was "not a crook," which consumed American politics for much of the first half of the 1970s.

The theatrical setting of "Where's the Orchestra?" is also reflected in the song's instrumentation and harmony. While Joel's piano holds the accompaniment together, the rest of the band is missing. Instead, listeners hear a string quartet along with passages of clarinet, saxophone, harmonica, and accordion. The use of a small ensemble of orchestral instruments fits the song's setting and supports the narrative in ways Joel's usual ensemble could not. Yet the instruments are, in dramatic terms, "nondiegetic," meaning the protagonist cannot hear them; after all, the show is not a musical. Instead, they accompany his "vocal persona," the expression of his thoughts, from and with a sense of distance (Cone 1974).

Because many of the instruments play individual solo lines, they seem to connote isolation, solitude, or loneliness. The clarinet and saxophone appear to tap into the film noir trope of the dark, lonely city. After all, the narrator's theater is likely located in such a place, probably New York City. The harmonica may convey a feeling of loneliness in outdoor, open spaces, just as Joel did in "The Ballad of Billy the Kid," where he evoked a solitary cowboy. Here he substitutes the canyons of the cityscape for those of the Western landscape.

Harmonically, "Where's the Orchestra?" draws on compositional devices familiar to musical theater. The song is composed in the key of C, the simplest and most straightforward of keys on the piano (owing to the fact that a C-major scale requires only white notes and no black ones), perhaps suggesting the way life's events appear simple, at least on the surface, even when they are not. The bridge modulates, changing keys from C-major to E-flat-major (foreshadowed in the song's introduction), which calls renewed attention to the song's melody and message. This kind of modulation has been much discussed in literature on musical theater as a device that can be used to heighten a song's emotional intensity, as it does here (see Buchler 2008).

Additionally, the reappearance of the melody from *The Nylon Curtain*'s opening number, "Allentown," played by the clarinet and harmonica during the coda of "Where's the Orchestra?," is reminiscent of a reprise, a common musical theater device where previously heard music is repeated later in the show. According to theater historian Joseph Swain, the "reprise operates, in the best instances, by revealing the dramatic relevance of an earlier expression to a new dramatic context" (2002, 322). Thus, the "Allentown" theme is recontextualized not only harmonically (now in a new key) but also dramatically, linking the emotional drama of the two songs that bookend the album and implying a unity within the work as a whole akin to the song cycles of Joel's classical idols (Duchan 2015, 170–71).

As the coda begins, Joel sings the final lyric, a repetition of the song's title. The melody of the phrase traces a pleasing descent, with "orchestra" landing on the song's tonic pitch, C, in a perfect authentic cadence (when the bass moves from the fifth pitch in the scale, G, to the first, C, as the melody ends on the same pitch). One would think that such a moment would bring about a sense of relief, as the musical and lyrical tensions of the song are resolved—perfect authentic candences are supposed to do that. Yet the resolution is weakened when the first chord of the coda, heard under "orchestra," turns out to be not a C-major chord, but a C-major-*seventh* chord. This combination of pitches includes not only the major triad, C–E–G, but also the seventh note of the scale, B, which clashes against the neighboring C. Thus, even at the moment of seemingly satisfying, ultimate conclusion, Joel musically indicates that not all loose ends are neatly tied up. "I didn't want it to be too pleasant," Joel explains. "This guy's going through something and he realizes, life is not a musical. It's a drama. And there's no singing all the time, and there's no happy chorus dancing" (personal interview). We hear the same inquiry with which the song began. Without the satisfaction of an answer, it seems the question alone must suffice.

Finally, Joel uses a panning effect, created by manipulating sounds across the two-channel, left-to-right stereo spectrum, to reinforce a sense of distance and space. Albin Zak describes the result as the evocation of a "panoramic soundstage across which elements can be positioned and moved about. . . . The more unique the space is, the less it represents experiences of sound in the natural world and the more the record takes on the quality of a dramatic stage" (2001, 145)—exactly what Joel is going for. Throughout the track, his voice is positioned far left while the instruments sound off to the right. Brief instrumental interjections, like the saxophone and clarinet, are farther right than the strings and piano. Although the instruments are in the song (listeners can hear them), the narrator, Joel, cannot. This effect heightens listeners' awareness of spatial distance, as focusing on the melody line may lead them to feel as if they are put in a corner, or stuck up "in the balcony" looking down upon events from the outside, insignificant, unable to affect the world around them.

What's so political about "Where's the Orchestra?" On the face of it, nothing. It is just a sad song about a guy disappointed by his choice of theater. But when considered metaphorically, its meaning emerges in new ways. Joel described it to Chuck Klosterman in personal terms, as a realization that he has "only felt content a few times in [his] life, and it never lasted" (2002; see also Klosterman 2004). Yet as the final statement on *The Nylon Curtain*, Joel's most political album, "Where's the Orchestra?" may be interpreted as the expression of the effect wrought by crushing political forces on individuals with no ability to control them. It also takes the collective frustration voiced on the album's earlier songs and recasts them in an individual, personal light. To Joel, the disappointment, frustration, and resignation the song conveys are the emotional responses to the impact of myriad political forces on people's lives. So while the song may not be "political" when interpreted literally, it nonetheless embodies a response to politics. As Joel put it, "Life isn't a Broadway musical; it's a Greek tragedy" (qtd. in Klosterman 2002).

4

"PRESSURE"

Living in American Culture

One of Billy Joel's gifts is his ability to perceive aspects of American culture and translate them into compelling musical narratives, as he does in his songs about the pressures incumbent in working- and middle-class life. His musical choices reflect his abiding concerns, changes in perspective, and continued development as a composer. This chapter examines six songs that span his catalog: "Ain't No Crime" (from *Piano Man*), "Prelude/Angry Young Man" (from *Turnstiles*), "Allentown" and "Pressure" (from *The Nylon Curtain*), "Running on Ice" (from *The Bridge*), and "The Downeaster 'Alexa'" (from *Storm Front*). If anything, the compositional variety of Joel's work illustrates how adeptly he uses musical features to communicate his observations of American culture and its effects on its men and women.

"I came from a blue-collar area," Joel explained in a 2007 interview. "You know, some people think that because I came from the suburbs I lived in a privileged area, very hoity-toity. Well, it wasn't. It was a working-class town" (qtd. in Righi 2007). After his father left, he says, "we were blue-collar poor people, which is different from *poor* poor people. You don't go to welfare when you're blue-collar poor. You somehow work. . . . You never ask for a handout. You would die first" (qtd. in Sheff and Sheff 1982). Even after critical and commercial success catapulted him to stardom, Joel continued to describe himself in similar terms. Just before his wedding to supermodel Christie Brinkley, he said, "We don't think of ourselves as royalty. We happen to be working people" (qtd. in Smith 2007, 195).

Throughout Joel's catalog, one finds pieces that engage with the difficulties of both working- and middle-class life from a variety of angles. His approach includes songs in which he sings as a distanced narrator describing working-class life (such as "Ain't No Crime" and parts of "Allentown") or as a working-class protagonist (as in parts of "Allentown" and "The Downeaster 'Alexa'"). Occasionally, he also conflates songs about the working class with attempts to write folk music (Jones 2011, 211–12). His songs about more general middle-class situations express cynical advice for the future ("Pressure") and anxiety at the pace of change in daily life in the present ("Running on Ice").

For example, "Angry Young Man" can be heard as an early, combative expression of class-based politics (although "Ain't No Crime," discussed below, appears earlier in Joel's catalog). As the title suggests, fury is everywhere in the music. "Prelude," the long instrumental introduction that precedes the song, begins with rapid, blistering strikes on the piano keyboard's central key, middle C. The idea was inspired by the rhythm of The Surfaris' 1963 instrumental, "Wipe Out" (personal interview). Quick staccato stabs at pairs of other pitches outline the harmony. As the phrase repeats, the band joins in, sustaining chords that support Joel's pianistic acrobatics while adding intensity through Liberty DeVitto's matching hi-hat rhythm. Suddenly, the piano's machine-gun Cs cease-fire and give way to a sequence of chords, played with the rest of the instruments and punctuated with cymbal crashes. In the third section, about thirty seconds in, the band backs off as Joel's piano offers a lighter melody made up of broken chords. Next, the first true melody appears, played by the piano, guitar, and (later) harmonica. DeVitto's drum pattern is sparse but heavy on the snare, an indication of the potential energy coiled up in the musical texture. Things heat up again as the piano trades back-and-forth phrases with the distorted guitar. At about a minute and a half into the track, after a repetition of the opening musical material, Joel again pounds C on the piano, this time in octaves, while the bass and the rest of the band offer a rhythmically syncopated counterpoint. The whole performance is loud, fast, and aggressive. When "Angry Young Man" begins (around the 1:50 mark), the dynamics come down and a strumming acoustic guitar joins the accompaniment as the focus shifts to Joel's voice.

The lyrics of "Angry Young Man" move quickly and rhythmically as they describe a man whose "working-class ties" and history of scars gained from battles lost has left him inflexible ("he refuses to bend, he refuses to crawl") and paranoid ("he sits in a room with a lock on the door"). Joel's melody consists of phrases that rise before falling slightly, a shape that repeats six times in each verse, once for each line of lyrics. But the melodic contour's descent does not quite match its ascent, so the repetitions of each phrase—especially when transposed up, as happens several times—impart a feeling of increasing poetic frustration and musical tension. In fact, the only moment of musical resolution, when the melody's fall brings Joel's voice all the way back down to its original tonic pitch, is at the final word of the refrain that ends each verse: "and he likes to be known as the angry young man."

Joel explains "Prelude/Angry Young Man" more narrowly. The title character refers to one of his tour managers, whom Fred Schruers identifies as Bob Romaine (2014, 78), a man so profoundly affected by his experience fighting in Vietnam that he was unable to perform his duties as part of Joel's organization.

> I had to let him go because he was killing the business we were trying to do. He was making enemies where we didn't need to have them and he was causing tension among the band and the crew. And I had to let him go: "Look, I have to let you go." He goes, "So you're like Pontius Pilate; you're washing your hands of me." And what struck me about that statement was, "Well, if I'm Pontius Pilate, that means you think you're Jesus Christ." And that was the essence of the song; that's where it came from. (personal interview)

The "Prelude," then, is supposed to represent both the conflict between Joel and his employee as well as the employee's inflated sense of self. "There's all this tension; there's all this conflict. There's this . . . manufactured nobility of the guy who feels like he's victimized," which is expressed through "grandiose" chords and musical gestures (personal interview). Thus, "Angry Young Man" expresses the frustration of an average Joe, whose aspirations were quashed by reality's limitations.

Of course, there are many more songs about both working- and middle-class culture in Joel's oeuvre—including "Piano Man" (from *Piano Man*) and "Movin' Out (Anthony's Song)" (from *The Stranger*)—but the examples considered here offer a glimpse of the multiplicity of approaches Joel has adopted while singing about a world beyond our control.

"AIN'T NO CRIME": EVOKING THE AFRICAN AMERICAN WORKING CLASS THROUGH BLUES AND GOSPEL

"You got to open your eyes in the morning," begins "Ain't No Crime." "Nine o'clock coming without any warning and you gotta get ready to go." This statement immediately sets the scene: between work and the occasional diversion of drunken revelry ("did a lot of drinkin', come home stinkin'"), there is little else in this song's protagonist's life. Every morning a "nine-to-five" job awaits, but not before a good upbraiding from a disapproving wife ("your lady . . . starts into weepin' 'bout the hours you've been keepin'"). The previous night's overindulgence was an enjoyable distraction but ultimately only that: "Just as surely as the wind keeps blowin', the grass keeps growin'," the song concludes, "you gotta keep goin' and the Lord have mercy on your soul."

"Ain't No Crime," which Joel describes as "really a working-class song" (personal interview), espouses that perspective through both lyrical and musical hints at blues and gospel styles, whose associations with the working class—especially the African American working class—run deep. Work, according to David Evans, is a subject often addressed by blues songs (2006, 85). Moreover, many forms of the blues in the twentieth century have been described as sites for "African-American working class self-understandings in the modern world" (Hunter 1997, 169). The association also extends to musicians, as David Grazian's ethnographic study finds that "most successful Chicago blues musicians are expected to comport themselves as working-class black men who have lived a life of hard labor" (2004, 145). Meanwhile, Jerma Jackson describes how both blues and gospel musicians "were rooted in rural communities and working-class urban enclaves" (2004, 23).

In "Ain't No Crime," the lyrical narrative, about a person with little sway over his circumstances yet still including glimmers of hope, recalls the spirit of many blues songs while the religious sensibility of the concluding line suggests a gospel approach. Then there is the music. In the archetypal blues, the harmonic progression that accompanies the melody basically centers on two chords whose roots are four steps apart;

a third chord, five steps away from the first, appears briefly near the end of a blues strain. Similarly, "Ain't No Crime" emphasizes two chords, four steps apart: in the key of C-major, a C chord and an F chord. Finally, the melody centers on the flattened third step of the scale, which is one of the common "blue" notes. It can be heard in nearly every one of the song's phrases, sometimes multiple times. "*Nine o'clock* coming, with*out* any warning," Joel sings in the second verse. The chorus includes: "Ain't No Crime, *say every*body gets that way some time." Finally, Joel's mixture of singing and speaking would be at home in blues and gospel.

Because of a few features, however, "Ain't No Crime" does not fit perfectly in the blues style. The archetypical blues consists of three four-bar phrases (hence the common name, "twelve-bar blues"), but the two verses in "Ain't No Crime" contain three six-bar phrases. The chorus comprises three four-bar phrases, but they also do not follow the blues chord progression. Thus, in "Ain't No Crime," Joel does not entirely commit to the blues genre but adopts enough generic markers to make the allusion clear.

Joel's piano is at the center of "Ain't No Crime," and the end of each phrase during the verses features a quick, three-beat melodic figure played solo on the instrument. Along with the rest of the rock band's rhythm section, the song also features an organ, whose presence suggests a church setting, home of the gospel style. During much of the melody, a mixed choir sings with or behind Joel's lead, exhibiting several of that style's typical features, including a wide vibrato and high levels of intensity and volume.

Using the choir was not Joel's idea:

> Early on . . . I depended on the producer [for *Piano Man*, Michael Stewart] to, you know, flesh these things out. I wasn't always crucial to what the arrangements of things were. I would come up with the rhythm. I would come up with the chords and the melody and the words. And then I would turn it over to the producer: "Well, you figure out how to make this work as a recording." I was more interested in the rhythm section and the band. I was always part of the band. (personal interview)

Joel's emphasis on being "part of the band," in which several different-sounding instruments work together to create one cohesive piece of music, meshes nicely with the musical connotations of the choral sound: group solidarity. "I was in chorus in elementary school, I was in chorus in junior high school, I was in chorus in high school," Joel explains. "I remember walking out of performances with the chorus and everybody being so psyched up—thrilled—we made that noise, we made that sound. . . . So I never thought of myself as a singer, but I always thought of myself as part of a singing *ensemble*" (personal interview).

The creation of community through the act of singing is an important component of many genres. Aaron A. Fox observes that in working-class music, "vocalization performs . . . an intertwining of self and other, and an aesthetic and ethical projection of the self into the experience of the other that is the basis for sociality" (2004, 321). The use of blues and gospel styles in "Ain't No Crime" thus presents a combination of voices evoking a sense of community. Still, they draw no conclusion other than that, despite any entertaining distractions, one must always return to the routine of work.

"ALLENTOWN": A SONG OF INDUSTRIAL DECLINE

"Allentown," the first track of *The Nylon Curtain*, opens with a steam whistle signaling the start of a factory shift—appropriate, since the Pennsylvania city for which the song is named was an important part of the American industrial boom following World War II. But in this song, Joel does not celebrate this industrial icon, rather he angrily bemoans its later decline, declaring right away that "they're closing all the factories down." Those factories belong to one of the country's largest steel producers, Bethlehem Steel, which was actually based in the nearby city of Bethlehem (Joel found the name "Allentown" easier to rhyme with and better sounding based on the rhythm). Faced with increasing foreign competition and rising retiree pension and health-care costs, this industrial giant became emblematic of the broader decline in American manufacturing in the 1970s despite having contributed directly to American landmarks like the George Washington Bridge and the Hoover Dam. By the time of *The Nylon Curtain*'s release, the company reported an annual loss of $1.5 billion and accelerated its factory closures. Joel notes that the song's melody and harmony were composed "probably in the '70s," but he "didn't write the song"—presumably referring to the lyrics—"until '82" (qtd. in Righi 2007), a time-line that fits the general industrial decline described here.

"Allentown" focuses less on the company's plight and more on how it affected rank-and-file blue-collar workers. With lines like, "It's getting very hard to stay," the song expresses their frustration and sense of helplessness. But more than that, Joel's lyrics convey a bitter sense of betrayal. After all, many steelworkers of the 1970s were Baby Boomers, born in the wake of World War II and taught to believe that "if we worked hard, if we behaved," they could expect a better life, a steady job, and decent working conditions safeguarded by robust unions. Yet this promise amounted to little when compared with "what was real: iron and coke, chromium steel," the economics of what was now an international industry in which American companies were flailing. Moreover, when the going got tough, "the union people crawled away," as Joel sings, spitting the *p*'s with disgust and holding onto the last word as if to draw out the retreat.

With this song, the scope of Joel's perspective on working-class life expands beyond just a story of one man's paranoid frustrations in "Pre-lude/Angry Young Man" or a hungover youth in "Ain't No Crime." For Joel, "Allentown" is about more than just the history of and problems faced by laid-off steelworkers of one Pennsylvania city; it represents those of a broader slice of Americans. Just the name "Allentown" sig-nifies something quintessentially American; Joel called it a "heartland name" (qtd. in Righi 2007).

> We used to play in the Lehigh Valley a lot, which is where Allentown
> is, Bethlehem, and those places, and I remember thinking: "Boy, this
> is really different than New York. This is *real* America, here." This
> was during the Reagan era and the horizons were starting to shrink.
> My generation, we thought, "We'll at least have what our parents
> had. Maybe things will be even *more* expanded than that." [But] the
> potential of that was starting to diminish. Kids didn't have the same
> job that their parents had because the steel mills were closing down.
> And I mean all you had to do was pick up a newspaper and you could
> read about it. (personal interview)

Indeed, the song's bridge describes how each child had "a pretty good shot" to at least match, if not exceed, his or her parents' socioeconomic status. But when that goal proved elusive, Joel notes how "they threw an

American flag in our face," a line that he told Timothy White references the distinction between World War II ("the wonderful war to make the world safe for democracy and hot homemade pie") and Vietnam ("ugliness, where the issues weren't cut and dried"). "That was the monkey wrench tossed into the mechanism of our spirit as a nation. They threw the American flag in our faces, saying 'Well, it's time for *you* guys to take up guns and go to war'" (1990, 565).

As with "Prelude/Angry Young Man" and "Ain't No Crime," Joel's piano serves as a musical anchor, with its steady, pounding chords lending the track a sense of forward motion, suggestive of an assembly line. But compositionally, the song remains uncertain; sometimes it seems like it is in the key of C, while at other points it sounds like it is in G. There are also passages implying D and F. Even when playing straightforward major chords, Joel includes pitches that are not "in" the triad: to the C-major chord, which includes C, E, and G, he adds a D. "These coloristic clusters," writes Thomas MacFarlane, "suggest the rich complexity of the lives of the workers who run the factory machines," which in turn challenge "the dehumanizing logic of a profit-driven society" (2016). Joel put it this way: "There's always a discordant note. There's always a rub and an unresolved suspension. . . . People may not even realize: 'Why am I feeling anxiety?'" (personal interview). In music theory terms, that anxiety is the result of hearing the dissonance, the unresolved a nonchord tone in a chord that is expected to be consonant. Of course, anxiety also fits the song's mood.

This anxiety and ambiguity extend to the lyrics as well, as the title appears at the beginning of some phrases and the end of others. Thus, as Robert Schultz writes, "the intricate search for identity with regards to tonal and lyrical structure in 'Allentown' very effectively embodies the struggle for personal identity in small town, blue-collar America portrayed in the lyrics" (2005, 46–51). The struggle evoked in "Allentown" is also illustrated by the imagery of *The Nylon Curtain*'s cover art, which pictures a row of identical houses—a reference to the suburban tract housing in which he grew up—as black silhouettes against a foreboding orange and black sky. The indistinguishable nature of the homes matches Joel's views on the monotony of suburban life, which made it all the more difficult to distinguish oneself or find one's bearings (this theme played into Joel's songs about suburbia, discussed in chapter 2).

Meanwhile, Joel's no-nonsense delivery imparts a persona that has little use for fancy vocalizing. Unlike in "Ain't No Crime," Joel sings alone, his solitary voice sounding against the clanging of factory machinery and a fuller band, comprising electric guitar, electric bass, and drums emphasizing the backbeat. The short delay applied to the vocal track creates an unnatural, cold, and mechanistic quality, enhancing the anger in the lyrics. Although the first and second verses use the pronoun "we," implying a sense community for which the protagonist sings, after the fury of the bridge the final verse adopts the first person "I," suggesting resignation and isolation (Jones 2011, 157). He is, in the end, a narrator at some distance from the action.

Thus, in "Allentown," several musical features line up to support a narrative—of anger, frustration, loss, and loneliness in an increasingly mechanized, globalized, and postindustrial world—that would seem at home in the tradition of American folk music stretching back through Bob Dylan to Pete Seeger and Woody Guthrie. Indeed, in the music video for "Allentown," Joel is seen observing the action, strumming an acoustic guitar while wearing a faded plaid shirt and a beat-up fedora. Yet, as A. Morgan Jones points out, these signifiers of folk are at odds with the video's professionally choreographed dance—during the guitar solo, six figures swirl gracefully around the stage, bowing to an American flag in lights—and the music's rock instrumentation and style (Jones 2011, 166, 211–12).

From the song's opening whistle to the metallic clanks of the fadeout, the sounds of "Allentown" make its gritty, industrial setting plain while letting Joel once again appear to fight for the little guy. The song's success—it spent six weeks on the *Billboard* Hot 100 chart, peaking at number seventeen—suggests that its sounds and message found a wide, receptive audience.

"THE DOWNEASTER 'ALEXA'": A BAYMAN'S SHANTY

While "Allentown" dealt with industrial decline in the American rust belt, "The Downeaster 'Alexa,'" released seven years later, sets its sights on the fishing industry off the coast of Long Island and New England, closer to Joel's home. The lyrics are peppered with geographic and nautical references; one could sail to the Block Island Sound, Gardiners

Bay, Martha's Vineyard, Montauk, and Nantucket while completing maritime tasks like charting a course, taking on diesel fuel, and working "with the rod and the reel." Right away, then, it is clear that this is a song about work on the water.

Joel sings as a lonely, beleaguered fisherman, who finds himself sailing ever greater distances in search of fish. The work is grueling, but he continues out of a strong sense of obligation; he has "bills to pay and children who need clothes." He comes from a long line of fisherman, but the nature of the work has changed and the future looks grim "for a man who works the sea." (His boat's name gives the song its title and also references Joel's older daughter.)

Whereas "Allentown" could serve as a metaphor for American industry in general, "The Downeaster 'Alexa'" is different. It offers no nostalgic reflection on "glory days," like the earlier song's "weekends on the Jersey shore" (Jones 2011, 182). Instead, there is nothing but stark reality. Another difference is the specificity with which "The Downeaster 'Alexa'" points to the sources of the fisherman's woes: increasing regulation of the fishing industry and the changing demographics of Long Island. Thus, to understand the song, it is helpful to know a bit about what inspired Joel to write it in the early 1990s—the changing conditions out on the water as well as on land—before examining how these conditions are expressed musically.

"They told me I can't sell no stripers," Joel sings, referring to the Atlantic striped bass (*morone saxatilis*), which have had a profound impact on Long Island's culture since at least colonial times. They spawn in East Coast rivers, mature in tributaries, and live most of their adult lives migrating up and down the eastern seaboard. They were once so numerous that they were used as agricultural fertilizer and so valuable that one of the first American public schools (in the Plymouth colony, 1670) was supported by income from its fisheries (see National Oceanic and Atmospheric Association; Massachusetts State Office of Energy and Environmental Affairs, Department of Fish and Game). But in the middle of the twentieth century, the population declined rapidly: between 1973 and 1984, catches dropped by nearly 90 percent (Wright 1984). The cause, many claimed, was overfishing.

In response, the Atlantic States Marine Fisheries Commission (ASMFC), with representatives from thirteen states from Maine to North Carolina, was formed to study the issue. In 1981, it suggested stricter limitations on the number and size of stripers that could be caught as well as closures of certain areas to commercial and recreational fishing (ASMFC 1981). But these suggestions went largely unheeded. As author Michael Crocker put it more recently, "From the start, the commission was crippled by the parochial interests of its members, whose constituents all vied for a cut of the migration" (2014). Moreover, the ASMFC's recommendations carried no legal weight, so there was no penalty if a state declined to update its policies accordingly. In 1984, the U.S. Congress intervened by passing the Atlantic Striped Bass Conservation Act, which allowed for actual penalties if a state failed to comply. As a result, Joel's character must travel "more and more miles from shore every year" just to find enough fish to make ends meet.

While the situation in the Chesapeake Bay was grim, the story was different and more complicated in New York. The striper population in the Hudson River was much stronger and more stable but out of reach due to the effects of pollution. Beginning in the 1920s, the Monsanto Chemical Corporation manufactured compounds containing PCBs (polychlorinated biphenyl), which were then sold to companies such as General Electric, whose facilities disposed of wastewater in the Hudson. (PCBs were later found to be highly toxic and were banned by Congress in 1979.) The striped bass would ingest the polluted water, so to prevent the carcinogens from reaching humans, the State of New York banned fishing for stripers north of New York City's George Washington Bridge in 1976 (see Rather 1985). Long Island's fishing industry was spared, but only for a time, as the 1984 act of Congress and a 1986 ban by the State of New York struck the island directly and, combined with the ban in Maryland, effectively ended all commercial striped bass fishing in the eastern United States.

The effect of the regulations and fishing bans was devastating—no wonder "The Downeaster 'Alexa'" begins on a minor chord. In 1985, Arnold Leo, secretary of the East Hampton Town Baymen's Association, told the *New York Times*, "You are looking at practically the end of baymen system on Long Island" (qtd. in Rather 1985). Some families, Leo said the following year, "have been fishing for many generations, and suddenly the younger generation is confronted with the fact that they cannot do what their fathers have done," a realization that tears at the "social fabric" of the three-hundred-year-old community (qtd. in Knudson 1986).

While the situation at sea was deteriorating, Long Island, especially the East End, was changing. As the dust from World War II settled and Levittowns were built in Nassau County, closer to New York City, the farther-out Suffolk County found itself host to new sets of visitors. At first it was artists and their ilk, but soon the affluence created by Wall Street, the "expanding highway and commuter rail systems, increased leisure time, and growing public desires for 'consuming nature'" converted the East End's "summer colony . . . into a 'weekend' and 'summer tourist' community" (Dolgon 2005, 39). Attracting this new money were the perceptions that the Hamptons and other nearby communities offered a slower, more peaceful lifestyle, yet also one where power and wealth could be exhibited (Gaines 1988).

Eastern Long Island's growth was widely distributed between the fabulously rich and the less so. Between 1950 and 1970, as other parts of Long Island experienced significant growth, East Hampton's population boomed. And between 1970 and 1980, as historian Corey Dolgon points out, "the greatest number of housing starts occurred in the traditionally working- and middle-class communities" (2005, 55). Many of those living in these new communities were not only doing so on weekends and during the summer but year-round. As a result, commercial infrastructure—shopping malls—grew, as did transportation, schools, and municipal governments.

But during the 1980s, population growth in eastern Long Island leaned more toward the wealthy, who benefited from improvements in telecommunications that allowed them to continue working on Wall Street while spending more time at the other end of the Long Island Expressway. Some found employment in the industries expanding in the middle of the island, such as Brookhaven National Laboratories and Grumman Allied Industries; their commute was even shorter. Thus, over the course of a few decades, and at the same time the striper population was crashing, the demographic profile of eastern Long Island shifted as new groups altered the population's mix and as the area's perceived allure drove up the cost of land. For many, the resulting financial pressure was difficult. For some, it was too much to bear. "Like all the locals here," Joel sings, firmly positioning his character among those with long-standing ties to the area, "I've had to sell my home."

Dolgon suggests that each wave of immigrants to the East End sought to tie their identity to their new home, to establish what felt like authentic roots in the area. Such efforts can be seen through musical and artistic renditions of "traditional" life in the Hamptons:

> From John Howarn Payne's "Home Sweet Home" (Payne's family was from East Hampton) to Whitman's "From Montauk Point" to Thomas Moran's "A Midsummer Day, East Hampton" to Irving Ramsey Wiles's "Scallop Boats, Peconic," artists have imbued East End landscapes with what the historian Helen Harrison called an "antique rural charm." Writers and painters tried to capture the land and sea as they saw them in an attempt to represent what was natural and authentic about both the physical environment and human nature. But such conceptions of what is *natural* and *authentic* always represented a culturally imposed view of nature juxtaposed with the growing pervasiveness of a rationalized industrial development and the seeming chaos of the city. And these artistic renderings were always intended for a bourgeoisie that sought cultural legitimation for its eastward migration and its physical conquest of the land. (Dolgon 2005, 67; see also Harrison and Denne 2002)

Joel's attention to the "natural" landscape can be heard in "The Downeaster 'Alexa'" as the melody soars, as if to stretch vast distances, and he sings about the "giants out there in the canyons."

It is this search for the "natural" and "authentic" that led to the region's many environmentalist and preservationist groups, which were often funded by the very people whose land use permanently altered the natural environment and changed the character of the area. Among them one finds Joel, whose 1990 *Concert for the Bays and Baymen*, in conjunction with the release of "The Downeaster 'Alexa'" the previous year, solidified his support—as an artist and as a (wealthy) local resident—for the baymen, whom he describes using the discourse of authenticity: "These guys represent something unique," he is quoted as saying. "They are the real Long Island, the Long Island that keeps disappearing. . . . They are living history" (qtd. in Wick 1992, 42; qtd. in Dolgon 2005, 71). (Joel's comments reveal an additional tension between commercial fishermen, the baymen, and recreational fishermen, the anglers, who were not subject to the same regulatory restrictions.) Baymen's Association president Arnold Leo described his flock as the "fabric of American culture," who "live simply, work hard, help thy neighbor," and wish to be "at one with one's fellow man and with God, to be a part of nature" (qtd. in Dolgon 2005, 72). Dolgon concludes: "History, ecology, and theology all come together as the baymen's story becomes a kind of regional jeremiad for newcomers to admire, lament, and ultimately adopt as their own story" (72). Against this backdrop, Joel sings, "there ain't no island left for Islanders like me."

"The Downeaster 'Alexa'" is a strophic ballad. In fact, there is a relationship between the narrative perspective Joel adopts in the lyrics and the particular chords he uses to accompany them. The introduction begins in A-minor, setting a dark tone for the song to follow. The first half of each verse then describes the forward-looking present using slightly more cheerful, C-major harmonies ("well, I'm on the Downeaster 'Alexa'"). The second half of the verse emphasizes a different chord, F-major (four steps higher), while looking backward to the past ("we took on diesel"). And later instrumental passages shift back to the minor sonority of the introduction, gently rocking between two chords, A-minor and C-major, as if a fishing rig bobbing on ocean waves.

In "The Downeaster 'Alexa,'" Joel aligns narrative and musical style more closely than in his earlier songs that describe working-class characters. Indeed, the song includes more folk elements than the cinematic grandiosity of "Prelude/Angry Young Man," the blues and gospel of "Ain't No Crime," or the driving rock of "Allentown." Three folk elements are especially pertinent: the meter, the instrumentation, and the vocal texture. Metrically, the song emphasizes the first and third beats of each measure—*one* two *three* four. This stands in contrast to the backbeat—one *two* three *four*—of the pieces discussed earlier in this chapter, as well as most of Joel's catalog in general. In "most rock and roll," Joel told *Entertainment Weekly*, "the beat is on the two and four. But we decided" to shift the accent to "the 1 and 3, which is very Celtic. All of a sudden the song made sense! It sounded like a real folk song" (qtd. in O'Donnell 2015).

The accompanying instruments are different in "The Downeaster 'Alexa'" too. For example, the piano is completely absent. While an electric guitar is present, it is more ornamental and atmospheric than melodic or harmonic. It plays distorted, descending slurs, a gesture suggestive of a lament, a genre with a long history in many folk music genres in which descending melodies signified mourning—an appropriate emotion given this song's subject matter. (Laments are also used in opera, especially during the Baroque period, but none of the phrases in "The Downeaster 'Alexa'" fits the typical lament as it was used in that genre because the bass lines in Joel's composition use different patterns.)

A more prominent instrument is the accordion, which carries strong folk connotations in both Europe and North America (see Keil and Keil 1992; Simonett 2012). Historically, the sense of authenticity carried by its sound has sometimes been harnessed in order to lend popular songs, which are not always seen as particularly authentic, a touch of gravitas. According to Marion Jacobson, "the traditions of the accordion are seen as cultural remedies for the shallowness of American popular music." Its status as a "low-tech, antipostmodern antidote to synthesizer saturation" was especially strong during its revival in the 1970s and 1980s— when Joel was writing "The Downeaster 'Alexa'"—as it was often used, in Jacobson's words, to "humanize" rock music and harmonize "working-class sensibilities" with the rock aesthetic (2012, 211).

At times, Joel's vocal delivery is also influenced by folk music. In the second half of the third verse, Joel sings "yah-yoh," accompanied by an improvisatory fiddle (played by an uncredited Itzhak Perlman). Both reappear after the final verse, but the vocal figure is expanded and reminiscent of a sea shanty: "yah-yah-yah-yoh" over a repeating motive in the accompaniment similar to the song's introduction. Jones points to these features, plus sound effects evoking sea gulls, as reinforcing the song's folk qualities and its sense of authenticity (2011, 186, 188–89). "There's an inherent *political statement* in folk music," Joel says. "There are people who are struggling, there's working-class stuff; you know, heroic things are going on. But it's subtle in how it's done" (personal interview).

The sea shanty is an ancient vocal style of folk music, usually sung by sailors while performing manual labor such as rowing oars or hauling rope. As a child, Joel would often thumb through his mother's copy of Margaret Bradford Boni's *Fireside Book of Folk Songs*, first published in 1947, which contains eleven shanties in its section of work songs, including "Yeo, Heave Ho!" and "Haul Away, Joe." The experience helped to shape his sense of what a folk song sounds like: "I took them all in," he recalls (personal interview). Like many work songs, sea shanties were often sung in call-and-response fashion. A leader, or "shantyman," would sing, and the rest of the men would respond using a few words or syllables, such as "ya-oh" (Palmer).

In "The Downeaster 'Alexa,'" however, we hear only one part of this two-part, back-and-forth vocal texture. The absence of the other voices helps convey the sense of loneliness the mariner feels, with the crying gulls his only companions. "I was just trying to evoke a man's voice above the waves," he says. "A single voice, a solitary voice, but trying to evoke the sea also. It's him *against* the sea; it's him *with* the sea" (personal interview). The image pictured on the cover of the song's single release sends the same message: bundled in a dark coat against a dark sky, Joel stares, stolid and unsmiling, past the viewer and into the distance. Aside from a single seagull soaring over his shoulder, he stands alone against a cold world.

"Prelude/Angry Young Man," "Ain't No Crime," "Allentown," and "The Downeaster 'Alexa'" illustrate how, despite varied musical styles, Joel sings as, for, and about hard-working people whose circumstances are worsening and who have little control over the forces that affect their lives. Over the course of his career, Joel's working-class songs grow darker and more resigned even as they achieve greater consistency in their lyrical and musical techniques. "Prelude/Angry Young Man" explores one man's paranoia and frustration using dramatic cinematic music; "Ain't No Crime" describes a night of fun while drawing on the stylistic markers of blues and gospel without wholly adopting either; "Allentown" mentions weekend getaways while expressing intense frustration and simultaneously portraying Joel as witness to and bearer of the folk tradition, all to an accompaniment consisting of mainstream rock instrumentation; and "The Downeaster 'Alexa'" offers little optimism but employs folk signifiers most thoughtfully in its meter, instrumentation, and texture. Ultimately, then, Joel's songs about the working class examine, comment on, and allow him to vocally embody parts of society and the historical and economic forces at work in people's lives.

DEALING WITH "PRESSURE"

Other songs in Joel's catalog embrace a more general or middle-class perspective in their evocations and descriptions of life in twentieth-century American culture. Still Joel continues to sing as, for, and about people and their struggles, an effort that links Joel's songs with those of other singer-songwriters of his day, such as Bruce Springsteen, many of whose songs are widely seen as adopting a similar perspective (Deardorff 2014). This sense of singing for and representing others also fits nicely with musicologist Allan Moore's concept of "authenticity of execution," or "third person authenticity," in which "a performer succeeds in conveying the impression of accurately representing the ideas of another, embedded within a tradition of performance" (2002, 218). The final sections of the chapter examine two such recorded performances, "Pressure" and "Running on Ice."

On "Pressure," the third track on *The Nylon Curtain*, Joel's voice addresses an unspecified subject, whom listeners quickly discover is an idealist who relies on faith and "some cosmic rationale" to face life's challenges. Adopting a seemingly wiser and more experienced perspective, Joel sternly warns of loneliness, high-pressure situations, potential violence, and generally tougher times ahead, repeatedly returning to the one-word refrain, "pressure." Like "Allentown," the song reflects the anxiety and anger of a generation in the clutches of realizing the fallacies of its youthful (American) dreams. It was initially inspired by a bout of writer's block. Yet, in the moment, that in itself signified to Joel a great challenge.

> I was kind of stuck for an idea for the next song during [the] album-writing process. And the person who was my assistant at the time said, "You look like you're under a lot of pressure," and I said, "Thank you!" I was feeling a lot of anxiety and [the song] just kind of came out of that. But I didn't write it until somebody said the word. (personal interview)

If certain aspects of the song's lyrics are rather vague, indicating neither whom Joel is singing to nor the exact challenges the future may hold, others situate "Pressure" more specifically. For example, the lyric, "All your life is channel 13, *Sesame Street*, what does it mean?" does so in two ways. On one hand, it locates the song geographically, as channel 13 is the public television broadcasting station in the New York City area. On the other, it places the song at a particular time—not surprisingly, somewhere in the 1970s or early 1980s—since the famed children's television show *Sesame Street* began airing in late 1969 on PBS.

None of this makes "Pressure" a song that is sung about, for, or to the working class. Instead, on offer is a more general sense of the mid- to late-century American experience, filled with equal parts pop-culture ephemera and arresting anxiety. Two of the song's lines illustrate a perspective rooted firmly in popular culture especially well; one addresses a well-known children's story and the other a popular dance. In the first, Joel's remark about "Peter Pan advice," and the mockingly delivered "all grown up and no place to go," references the title character from J. M. Barrie's 1904 story, *Peter Pan; or, the Boy Who Wouldn't Grow Up* (written first as a play but published as a book in 1911). Of course, by 1982, the character and story were accessible through several other incarnations that adults and children of the mid-twentieth century would likely have known. There were several stage productions, the most significant of which premiered on Broadway in 1924, with music by Jerome Kern, and 1954, directed by Jerome Robbins. The story was also famously made into film by Walt Disney Productions in 1953. In each of these versions, Peter Pan is an arrogant boy from a fantasy island, Neverland, whose inhabitants not only do not age; they steadfastly refuse to do so. It is an appropriate fantasy for the subject of "Pressure," who, having violated Pan's promise never to grow up, must now face the trials of adult life.

Pop-culture references continue in the song's second verse as Joel sings of a tap dance turned into a "crusade," a lighthearted entertainment into a serious campaign. As a style of dance, tap is historically rooted in a combination of Irish folk dance and blackface minstrelsy, a nineteenth-century form of American musical theater in which actors and musicians would blacken their faces and adopt crude stereotypes of African American characters and slave dances. As minstrelsy waned in the early twentieth century, tap evolved, absorbing elements from social dances such as the cakewalk and moving to vaudeville and Broadway stages. From there it was incorporated into the Hollywood movie musical as well (Hill 2010).

If the characters in "Pressure" are New Yorkers, they could have known tap dance through its many uses on Broadway. If not, they would likely still have known tap dance through film and television. Joel fondly recalls trips to the Hicksville movie theater with his maternal grandfather, Philip Nyman, in the early 1960s (Schruers 2014, 24). Famous for their on-screen dances, Hollywood duo Fred Astaire and Ginger

Rogers performed together in ten films between 1933 (*Flying Down to Rio*) and 1949 (*The Barkleys of Broadway*), most of which included one or more tap numbers. Their pictures were nominated for numerous Academy Awards (though none for Astaire and Rogers specifically), and as late as 2011, *The New York Times* called Astaire "a surpassing tap stylist" (Macaulay 2011). Most of Astaire's and Rogers's films together, and many of those from their solo careers, were box office successes, an indication of the large audience they reached.

Movie musicals, many of which included elaborate tap dance numbers, formed an important part of the core repertory of television programming right at the time when Joel was growing up, as major networks launched weekly broadcasts of older feature films. For example, *Monday Night at the Movies*, on NBC, aired *Kiss Me Kate* (a 1953 film adaptation of Cole Porter's 1948 Broadway show) and *Singin' in the Rain* (1952), within the span of two weeks around New Year's 1964. In addition, tap was featured on television programs, such as those hosted by Astaire and Gene Kelly, as well as variety shows like the *Ed Sullivan Show*, *The Johnny Carson Show*, and *The Lawrence Welk Show* (Hill 2010, 207–9).

The impact of tap dancing on the American social landscape was great and long-lasting. A 1941 article on Astaire in *Life* magazine declared, the "ability to tap had become a social asset" (Barnett 1941, 78). In 1961, Maria Beale Fletcher's tap skills were credited with helping her win the Miss America pageant ("The New Miss, Near Misses" 1961). On January 16, 1966, NBC aired "The Song and Dance Man," a musical history of tap dancing, on *The Bell Telephone Hour* (Hill 2010, 208). And the 1970s and 1980s saw the production of three important tap documentaries, covering legendary dancers from throughout the century: *Great Feats of Feet: A Video Portrait on Jazz and Tap Dance* (1977), *No Maps on my Taps: The Art of Jazz Tap Dancing* (1979), and *Jazz Hoofer: The Legendary Baby Laurence* (1986). For much of his childhood, Joel's house did not have a working TV, a fact that probably contributed to his love for books and also prompted his mother to expose him and his sister to cultural events (Connelly 1982). But the pervasiveness of tap on stage, film, and television makes it likely that Joel and his audience encountered this American choreographic form, implicitly understanding its association with lighthearted entertainment.

The smiles on the faces of Astaire and Rogers as they tapped their way into mid-century popular culture, as well as the blissful ignorance of Peter Pan as he flies and crows about Neverland, seem far removed from the world Joel's character inhabits in "Pressure" but very much akin to the person the song addresses. If nothing else, "Pressure" is a call to wake up and face a reality starkly different from the one depicted in movies and musicals. Indeed, as discussed in the previous chapter—and as would be made clear in the next song on *The Nylon Curtain*, which depicts the Vietnam War—the world was an increasingly dangerous place.

That certainty and the sort of fatalistic confidence it inspires are reflected clearly in the music Joel writes for "Pressure." Unlike the tonal ambiguity of "Allentown," this song remains firmly in one key area, moving back and forth between D-minor and its related major key, F-major. Joel reflects, "I like the interplay between going from the major back to minor. It's like, there is no solution, there is no resolve. You're always going to be trapped in this gerbil cage, you know? Running on the spinning wheel" (personal interview). The synthesizer melody, delivered in octaves, harmonized in thirds, and repeated before and after each verse, creates a striking dissonance against the steady drone-like D in the bass, amplifying the angst; Joel calls it his "foray into Tchaikovsky." Finally, the vocal line grows increasingly intense as the song progresses, utilizing a double-tracking effect on Joel's voice that creates a menacing urgency. This vocal intensity reaches the point where the "pressure" refrain is more shouted than sung. By its end, the relentlessness of the music, the apprehensiveness of the lyrics, and the forcefulness of Joel's delivery make "Pressure" an explosion of anxiety and, no doubt, an accurate summation of the American psyche in the mid-1980s.

"THE CULMINATION OF TECHNOLOGY AND CIVILIZED EXPERIENCE" IN "RUNNING ON ICE"

Anxiety also propels "Running on Ice." The song's title itself serves as a metaphor: while running on a sheet of ice, you find your legs working hard but your feet fail to move you forward, and the risk of falling down is great. Joel sings as an upper-middle-class urban man, "a cosmopolitan sophisticate of culture and intelligence." Yet despite these qualities, his life is lacking. He feels the "weight of all the useless junk" that "accumulates" on the shoulders of a "modern man." His efforts at advancement seem stymied, as each attempt to "climb" is met with a "new disaster." In the final verse, he describes his situation: "a bad waste, a sad case, a rat race." He feels immobile and helpless, a sentiment shared broadly with many of the characters in the songs explored in this chapter.

On one level, the frustration these lyrics describe may be drawn from Joel's own career woes. As noted in earlier chapters, his climb to stardom was neither direct nor easy. His business relationships often overlapped with personal ones—his first wife, Elizabeth Weber, was once his manager—which, not surprisingly, made things complicated. While recording *The Bridge*, Joel was served notice by the IRS that he owed millions in back taxes, an early indication of the financial mess that would explode later that decade, after the album's release, and prompt changes to both band personnel and production staff for the subsequent album, *Storm Front*, as well as an extended tour aimed at recouping his financial losses (Smith 2007, 206–29).

On another level, however, "Running on Ice" also captures a more general anxiety widespread in American society in the 1980s. The song offers a glimpse of three trends contributing to this sentiment: growth in typically urban industries and declines in others, the fast pace of technological innovation leading to significant changes in the American workforce (a theme presaged in "Allentown"), and a sense of changing gender norms.

"Running on Ice" is set in a city, which is described as an oppressive environment filled with tension. "There was a kind of frenetic urban thing to it," Joel told Schruers. "I was living in the city and I was feeling the pressure" (2014, 183). He specifically refers to "city life anxiety" stemming from a "world of high rise ambition," cleverly turning tall skyscrapers into lyrical metaphors for corporate greed. Indeed, cities were frequently the places where large corporations were headquartered, and New York hosted many of the financial world's big players, such as banks and stockbrokers. These institutions grew considerably in the 1980s. Of the twenty fastest growing job categories during the period 1979–1989, many were financial: mortgage bankers and brokers were number four on the list, growing 138.8 percent; business credit institutions were number six, up 122.2 percent; security brokers and dealers were number thirteen, increasing 104.3 percent; and "miscellaneous business services" and "accounting, auditing, and bookkeeping" were numbers seventeen and nineteen, rising 76.6 percent and 74.0 percent respectively. By contrast, industries traditionally based in rural areas, such as agriculture, saw significant losses over the same period (Plunkert 1990, 10–11). Thus, the city could seem a growing, important, and increasingly corporatized place. No wonder Joel complains of feeling "like a statistic in a system." The system in which he was raised twenty years earlier—using slide rules rather than calculators, typewriters rather than word processors, and promoting the suburban American family as a working father, stay-at-home mother, two kids, and a picket fence—left many ill-prepared for the realities of the 1980s workplace.

Joel's character in "Running on Ice" is the "culmination of technology," a telling turn of phrase. Technological innovation is perhaps best summed up by looking at the development of the computer, a seemingly ubiquitous device today that nonetheless had a profound impact on American lives in the late twentieth century. While early twentieth-century computers were often developed for military purposes—the 1946 Electronic Numerical Investigator and Computer ("ENIAC") at the University of Pennsylvania ran calculations for the U.S. Army's Ballistic Research Laboratory and studied the feasibility of the hydrogen bomb—rapid developments and refinements in components and programming languages led to an explosion of business, corporate, and consumer computing machines (McCartney 1999). As the devices grew smaller, faster, and more easily programmable, the computer transitioned from business applications, like IBM's 1400 series of mainframes (released in 1961), to personal devices, such as Steve Wozniak and Steve Jobs's Apple-1 in 1976 (and the more commercially successful Apple II the following year) and IBM's personal computer in 1981.

The incredible growth in technology, the industry supporting it, and the industries using it did not go unnoticed. In 1983 *Time* magazine famously abandoned its annual "Person of the Year" cover story for one on the "Machine of the Year," recognizing the arrival of technology that was greatly changing lives. Roger Rosenblatt's accompanying essay, which reads like a sales pitch yet drips with a sarcastic overabundance of American pride, describes the machines as the ultimate time saver.

After all, not only is time money, but "most of all, time is dreams. And computers give you time for dreams."

Yet some had more time on their hands than others. The technological advancements that spelled increased productivity and profit for those at the top of the corporate food chain also carried the specter of redundancy and job loss for those at the bottom. The point was made clear on the front page of *The New York Times* on July 4, 1982—almost exactly six months before *Time*'s "Machine of the Year" story—titled, "Worry Grows over Upheaval as Technology Reshapes Jobs: Job Turmoil Is Predicted with New Technologies," in which William Serrin writes of the potential for "wrenching change for many workers" caused by the widespread adoption of computers. According to Wassily Leontief, then director of New York University's Institute for Economic Analysis, the very purpose of the new technologies was "to reduce labor, and therefore . . . it should not be surprising if jobs are lost" (qtd. in Serrin 1982, "Worry Grows"). Indeed, the recession of the early 1980s hit not only blue-collar workers, but also white-collar employees in administrative, clerical, and technical positions, whose unemployment numbers rose 17.3 percent (Serrin 1982, "Recession and Spreading Layoffs").

In "Running on Ice," Joel's character refers to himself not only as a man, but as a "*modern* man" whose experience of the "rat race" is "breaking" him. The "rat race" refers to the daily commute into the city, which was only made possible by new highways and necessitated by new suburbs (see chapter 2). As anyone who has ever spent their rush hour on the Long Island Expressway knows, it can be a lengthy, frustrating slog.

Importantly, Joel also sings as a "modern *man.*" At the same time as the technological innovations just mentioned, the American workplace was undergoing another fundamental change as women held jobs in ever-greater numbers. A bevy of figures from the Bureau of Labor Statistics illustrate the trend. In 1970, for instance, 31,543,000 women participated in the American labor force, or 43.3 percent of all women over the age of sixteen. In 1980, the number of women at work rose to 45,487,000, or 51.5 percent, a ten-year gain of nearly fourteen million and an 8.2 percent increase, respectively. During the same decade, the number of men participating in the labor force increased only 10,315,000, from 51,228,000 to 61,543,000, while the percent of men participating fell 2.3 percent from 79.7 percent to 77.4 percent. The balance between men and women at work also shifted, from 61.9 percent and 38.1 percent in 1970 to 57.5 percent and 42.5 percent in 1980. During the 1970–1980 period, the growth rate for women at work averaged 3.7 percent annually, double that of men (Toossi 2002, 22–25). The rate of women's participation reached about 55 percent in 1985, an increase that can be attributed to several factors, including not only "changing attitudes regarding work" but also demographic shifts. According to the Census Bureau, the period 1970–1985 saw declines in women's fertility rates and family sizes (as well as delayed childbearing), increases in rates of divorce and numbers of women remaining unmarried, higher levels of education among women (which drive labor participation), and a smaller proportion of baby boomers of childbearing age (when women most often drop out of the workforce) compared to earlier periods (Lichter and Costanzo 1987).

Meanwhile, the disparity between men's and women's wages, and the question of whether laws should be passed to address it, became an increasingly hot topic. For example, a July 1984 article in *Newsweek* magazine described the debate in terms of "comparable worth" and observed how it had national political ramifications. In that year's presidential campaign, Democratic nominee Walter Mondale "embraced" the idea of "correcting pay imbalances." Ronald Reagan, the Republican who would win the contest, opposed the movement and reportedly threatened to veto any bill addressing it (Beck, Borger, and Weathers 1984).

Thus, Joel's character in "Running on Ice" works in an expanding world of rapidly changing technology, where one must compete vigorously for jobs that require skills in the use of machines nearly unimaginable just a few years earlier. At the same time, he faces a larger pool of female competitors, whose value in the workplace is in the national spotlight.

No wonder, then, that the anxieties expressed in the lyrics are matched by the frenetic synthesized piano line that introduces the song. The musical gesture is purposefully descriptive. "You're running through this urban jungle; it's almost a nightmarish kind of pattern," Joel says. "That's what I was trying to connotate with the music: you can't get your footing" (personal interview). The verses are accompanied by the piano, playing chords in between each beat. This rhythmic placement—one *and* two *and* three *and* four *and*—creates a feeling of imbalance. Rim shots, snare hits, machinelike synthesized percussion sounds, and syncopated drum fills constantly disrupt any sense of a stable groove despite the drum kit's hi-hats keeping a quiet, steady eighth-note pulse. Each syllable of Joel's lyrics gets its own discrete articulation, creating a steady stream of eighth notes, propelled along with few accents to offer any direction: "They say this highway's going my way, but I don't know where it's taking me."

The music does not seem to achieve a sense of stability until the chorus. Here, the offbeat piano chords remain, but the bass and drums assume steadier, rhythmically more prominent roles. Whereas in the verse the bass plays two longer notes per measure that do not provide a strong rhythmic underpinning, here the bass rhythm speeds up and the drums provide a regular kick-snare-kick-snare pattern typical of the rock style. Ironically, the sturdier-sounding chorus is where Joel's character gains just enough confidence to at least name the feeling he has, of "running on ice." Looking back, Joel did not like the way the song turned out, calling it "crap" (Schruers 2014, 183). But it nonetheless offers a window through which to glimpse the fast-changing, quick-paced lifestyle he tries to capture.

One thing uniting the songs discussed in this chapter is their expression of emotions incumbent upon working- and middle-class Americans in the third quarter of the twentieth century, what Schruers calls "the hopes and the heartbreaks at the center of the American dream" (2014, 8). "Prelude/Angry Young Man" is perhaps the most dramatic. "Ain't No Crime" is perhaps the simplest of these statements and also the most uplifting, with the communal implications of its gospel-inspired choir. "Allentown" and "The Downeaster 'Alexa'" are perhaps the most direct, naming specific industries, places, and historical events that prompted much concern in American manufacturing and commercial fishing. And "Pressure" and "Running on Ice" are a bit more general in the situations they describe—and the emotions of naïveté and anxiety that accompany them—while simultaneously maintaining a measure of specificity in the significant events in American culture they reference. The fact that "Allentown" and "Pressure" appeared together on *The Nylon Curtain* in the middle of Joel's recording career (1982), while "Running on Ice" and "The Downeaster 'Alexa'" appeared closer to its end (on *The Bridge* [1986] and *Storm Front* [1989], respectively) demonstrates that the concerns expressed through these songs persisted through Joel's compositional development.

Indeed, for Joel, the 1980s were an important decade. It closely coincided with his thirties, a time when many begin reassessing themselves and their lives. Careers are under way, young children are running around, parents are older and more frail. For Joel, the decade included career highlights such as his inclusion in the "We Are the World" project in 1985, which according to biographer Bill Smith signaled his acceptance by the music industry, as well as his groundbreaking tour of the Soviet Union (see chapter 3). Personally, the decade also saw the dissolution of his first marriage, the start of his second, and the birth of his first child.

In a broader sense, the 1980s saw several big trends in American culture come to a head. Environmental damage wrought by decades of chemical production combined with ecological damage to fish populations and legislative responses to deal a potential deathblow to the commercial fishing industry on the East Coast. Increasing international competition mixed with steadily rising pension costs spelled trouble for American heavy manufacturing. The good life, promised after World War II, was yanked off the horizon as recessions repeatedly rocked the American economy in the 1970s and 1980s (National Bureau of Economic Research). New technologies further troubled the waters, as older workers feared being made redundant by machines while administrators were eager for the increased productivity such devices promised. Meanwhile, feminist movements, having gained momentum for decades, saw tangible improvement in the status of women as participants in the American workforce, but this gendered rebalancing of the office also prompted great unease. Clearly, then, when looking to express what was on the minds of average Americans, Joel had much to draw on. That the results are so musically diverse is a testament to the great breadth of the American experience as it (was) steered through trying times.

Of the trends coinciding in this tumultuous decade, one in particular prompts further discussion. Many of Joel's songs address issues pertaining to gender in ways that go beyond just the expression of anxiety. The next chapter examines several other songs that deal with gender and relationships, a topic familiar to many songwriters and artists but nonetheless central to Joel's musical output.

5

"SHE'S ALWAYS A WOMAN"

Relationships and Gender

Many of Billy Joel's songs may be considered "love songs," yet rather few of them offer merely romantic adulation. Instead, this chapter groups Joel's songs about romantic relationships according to three themes: love and courtship, comfort amid separation, and cynicism and deception. While romantic songs are most prevalent, Joel's catalog also includes tracks about family and friends, as well as several that offer glimpses of changing attitudes in American society with regard to gender dynamics—the relative power of men and women in their relationships. A few songs on these topics are discussed later in the chapter. (Given the large number of songs in Joel's catalog that touch on relationships and gender, and the fact that this topic generated many of his hits, more songs are analyzed here than in previous chapters but each discussion is briefer.)

For Joel, love songs are rarely about just one emotion. He told biographer Fred Schruers that he does not

> think a love song is effective unless there's an element of anxiety in it, and an undercurrent of darkness. Love is not all glitter and wonderfulness and clouds and happiness forever—there are ups and downs in relationships. . . . There's always a bit of insecurity in love, if you truly love somebody. If you open yourself up, if you allow yourself to be hurt, there's potential vulnerability. That's real love. (qtd. in Schruers 2014, 130)

Thus, one conclusion to draw from Joel's songs about relationships is that even in moments of great happiness looms the potential for sadness. In Joel's personal and professional life, several of his deepest relationships ended in deception, betrayal, and anger, a fact that may explain the hint of gloom often found in these songs.

"I COULD NOT LOVE YOU ANY BETTER": SONGS OF LOVE AND COURTSHIP

Songs that feature Joel singing lovingly about or to a woman make up the first theme one hears in his love songs. The clearest example is "Just the Way You Are" (from *The Stranger*), probably his most well-known song aside from "Piano Man." Given the song's commercial success—it was Joel's first top-ten hit and won the Song of the Year Grammy Award in 1979—it may be surprising to learn that it was almost never recorded. While working on *The Stranger*, Joel and his band tried the song in a variety of styles, but none seemed satisfactory. (Liberty DeVitto is rumored to have thrown down his drumsticks in frustration, remarking with exasperation, "I'm no damn cocktail lounge drummer!") Producer Phil Ramone eventually suggested a samba beat, which seemed to work, but Joel remained unconvinced until singers Linda Ronstadt and Phoebe Snow, recording in a nearby studio, stopped by, heard the track, and insisted on keeping it. Despite Joel's concerns about how the song would affect the rock image he was trying to cultivate ("everyone thought it was too goofy and sappy"), the song made it onto the album (Smith 2007, 151; Schruers 2014, 130–31).

"Just the Way You Are" was intended as a birthday present for Joel's first wife, Elizabeth Weber. The first few verses impart his devotion by telling her she does not need to change—her clothes, hair, style of conversation, and so on—to keep him. "You always have my unspoken passion," Joel sings, before revealing why she might be concerned: "although I might not seem to care." Still, he is doing the best he can, as he sings, "I could not love you any better." The verses end with the comforting message: I'll want you, take you, and love you "just the way you are."

In the bridge, the spotlight moves to the singer, highlighting his needs and fears. He requires reassurance that she will not, in fact, change but will remain instead "the same old someone that I knew." Then, as the melody shifts up and a change in harmony adds new urgency, his voice becomes more insistent as he asks, "What will it take till you believe in me the way that I believe in you?" Thus Joel reveals, just before the song's final verse, that underneath the promises of love and fidelity lie deep concerns and disconnect; the two involved in the relationship do not, at least from Joel's perspective, view it in the same way. Therefore, "Just the Way You Are" is not just about love, but also about a hope for love amid troubling signs of doubt, just the sort of "undercurrent of darkness" he told Schruers about.

Joel's and DeVitto's fears about "Just the Way You Are" were not unfounded. It could easily fit in a lounge, as the samba beat makes for good dancing and Phil Woods's alto saxophone solo provides nice melodic interest without too much edge. Critics pounced. *Rolling Stone's* Ira Mayer called the track "forced and overly simplistic," while biographer Richard Scott later described it as "more like the 'powder-puff' material" of Joel's earlier works (2000, 33). Yet as a single release, the song has been credited with cementing Joel's success as a popular musician (Tamarkin). When Joel performed it the following year on *Saturday Night Live*, skipping his high school reunion to do so, he reached an audience of more than twenty million, further fueling album sales (Smith 2007, 157).

Of course, Joel has written many other songs about love and courtship. *An Innocent Man* contains two notable ones, "The Longest Time" and "This Night." Critic Stephen Holden (1983) called that album "a collection of affectionate imitations of early '60s urban rock fashions" due to the way it re-created the popular music styles of Joel's youth. These two songs exemplify that effort as they adopt the conventions of doo-wop. This "forgotten third of rock 'n roll" emerged in the 1950s among black amateur singers in cities such as New York, Philadelphia, and Chicago. It acquired the "doo-wop" moniker in the following decade. Five elements provided the style's musical conventions: vocal group harmony, a wide range of voices (including the lead soloist, the high-singing first tenor, and all the way down to the bass), frequent use of nonsense syllables (such as "doo-wop"), a simple beat combined with light instrumentation, and simple music and lyrics (Gribin and Schiff 1992).

"The Longest Time" draws on these musical features most directly. Joel performs all the vocal parts; the only instrument is an electric bass. Aside from passages where the background voices sing the lyrics along with the lead melody, they otherwise stick to vowels such as "ooo" and "ah." Simple finger snaps are heard on every other beat. And the words and music are straightforward, with innocently cast lyrics accompanied by a conventional pattern of doo-wop chords John Michael Runowicz (2010) calls "ice cream changes." The lyrics offer a tale of redemption, as Joel's character sings of how he had lost hope before meeting the woman he is serenading: "Once I thought my innocence was gone, now I know that happiness goes on." The song is ultimately about his need for her, as he expresses several times the positive impact her presence has had on him.

The tone of innocently cast courtship heard in "The Longest Time" is clearly based in the doo-wop tradition, which has a long history of songs about love sung from an adolescent perspective (Gribin and Schiff 1992, 54). Yet that tone is also subtly tempered by Joel's recognition that every new romantic venture carries the potential for crushing disaster: "Who knows how much further we'll go on?" he sings. "Maybe I'll be sorry when you're gone." Thus, despite the song's stylistic roots in a genre born in high school hallways and urban street corners, the perspective it embodies is more mature. Along with many of the other tracks on *An Innocent Man*, "The Longest Time" can be interpreted as being about Joel's personal relationships after the end of his first marriage. In that context, the youthful joy and excitement of newfound love amid a fear of repeated emotional pain makes sense.

The doo-wop influence is less overt but nonetheless evident on "This Night," where Joel's piano, Doug Stegmeyer's bass, DeVitto's drums, Mark Rivera's saxophone, and other instruments provide a full accompaniment. Yet the emphasis on voices remains. The first sounds one hears are of the bass singer, who provides a characteristic four-note introduction setting up the song's initial downbeat. During the verses, backup singers accompany Joel's lead melody with classic doo-wop syllable combinations, such as "shoop shoo-wah." The choruses feature soaring background vocals and harmony lines that parallel the melody. Joel has stated that the song's towering lead was inspired by the doo-wop group Little Anthony and the Imperials (WNYC 2012).

The verses of "This Night" speak of Joel's reluctance to engage in romance ("Didn't we promise we would only be friends?") and his ultimate inability to resist the woman's charms ("Suddenly I don't remember the rules anymore"). During the chorus, which draws its melody from the second movement of Beethoven's Piano Sonata No. 8 in C minor, op. 13 ("*Pathétique*"), Joel relents and embraces the attraction: "It's only you and I." ("This Night" and Joel's classical borrowings are discussed in the next chapter.) While Joel knows that his stay in paradise is temporary, he nonetheless seeks to hold onto the moment, as the chorus concludes: "Tomorrow is such a long time away; this night can last forever."

If "The Longest Time" and "This Night" situate themselves in the excitement of the moment of romantic discovery at the beginning of love affairs, "Shameless" (from *Storm Front*) focuses more closely on the devotion to the relationship under way, as the lyrics describe the lengths to which a man will go to prove his love to a woman. He will get down on his knees, admit his mistakes, and give up his hard-won control: "I've never lost anything I ever missed, but I've never been in love like this."

While Joel's recording peaked at number forty on the American *Billboard* Adult Contemporary charts, a 1991 cover by country singer Garth Brooks reached the top of the country charts, bringing "Shameless" to a new, wide audience. As Kevin C. Johnson (2000) of the St. Louis *Post-Dispatch* put it, Brooks "single-handedly rejuvenated the country music industry," drawing in fans of pop and rock by mixing those styles with his "blend of contemporary country." Musically, "Shameless" lends itself to Brooks's pop country style. The primary instrument is the guitar, a central sound in the country genre. The song also fits into country's long tradition of sentimental love songs stretching back at least to Jimmie Rodgers (see Malone 1985, 86–88).

What one finds in these four examples are pieces that praise their subjects while revealing the inadequacies of the character doing the praising. They maintain links to genres and styles long associated with love songs. And they pledge and plead for love while illuminating how much it is not only desired but needed. The sense of comfort resulting from the satisfaction of that need can be heard in several other songs, including "C'Etait Toi (You Were the One)" and "State of Grace."

"HOLDING YOU HERE IS SO HARD TO DO": SONGS OF COMFORT AMID SEPARATION

"C'Etait Toi (You Were the One)" is distinctive in Joel's catalog in two ways. It is his only song to prominently feature a language other than English (in this case, French) and also the song Joel considers the worst he ever wrote (Scaggs 2005; Sinclair 2002). Yet it is not only a good example of the trends found in the love songs already discussed, but also demonstrates the second recurring theme in Joel's songs about relationships: offering and seeking comfort amid separation.

A guitar accompanies Joel's voice as he sings of sitting alone, drinking and feeling lonely. Bielen claims that the accordion lends the song a "continental flair" (2011, 55). The singer's desire is plainly stated in the first chorus, sung in English: "I'm looking for comfort that I can take from someone else." He looks in vain for his lover's face. After all, he continues, she is the only one "who can save me from myself. You were the only one." As he sings the last two words in three long syllables, the melody descends from B to A to G, the song's tonic pitch, musically signaling a point of arrival, a conclusion. Two verses follow in French before Joel sings the chorus one last time in English.

The tense in which Joel's lyrics describe his feelings reveals the separation he feels. His lover is the only one who *can* save" him—present tense—but the conclusion that that ability is unique to her is stated in the past tense: "You *were* the only one." In fact, all of the song's lyrics employ the present tense except for this telling line. Thus, "C'Etait Toi" reveals this sad and lonely lover's emotional state in the active terms of the present, as if listeners are sitting at the table with him, but that present also contains the crushing realization that the love he seeks is now a thing of the past.

Comfort and separation are equally evident in "State of Grace," which differs from "C'Etait Toi" in that the protagonist's lover is present—but only sort of. She may be in the room but her head is somewhere else, in the state named by the song's title. The song thereby reveals that physical presence does not always mean emotional presence. Joel admits that reality is not always pleasant ("granted this world is not a perfect place"), but it is reality nonetheless ("still it's the world that I'm in"). While he is firmly rooted in real life, she is able to leave it behind, effecting separation and creating a distance between them that he cannot close. "Holding you here is so hard to do," he sings exasperat-edly. "I'm losing you."

Joel uses three musical elements to convey this sense of separation and the "state of grace" his lover escapes to: a delay effect, instrumenta-tion, and harmony. The song's opening melody is played in octaves on the piano and treated with a delay effect, so each note echoes a split second after it is initially played. This suggests a sense of distance, as only in large spaces do sound waves bounce back like that. The instru-mentation of the accompaniment features an organ, which implies the space may be a religious one, as a large church, built of hard and reflective materials like stone, would offer such acoustics. Given this aural context, the "state of grace" becomes a matter of clever wordplay, given the importance of grace as a concept in Christian theology. Such an interpretation is reinforced by the lyrics as Joel refers to that state of grace, in the song's final verse, as a "sacred place" where he has "never been." Though born Jewish and baptized Christian, Joel has never been especially religious.

The sequence of chords used in "State of Grace" also embodies this sense of distance. Written in the key of A-major, the introduction and the verses employ the same harmonic pattern, which begins with an A-major chord followed by an E-major chord (with G-sharp in the bass, enabling the bass line to descend stepwise). The relationship between these two chords is conventional; built on pitches five steps apart, they exploit one of the fundamental intervals of Western harmony for the past several hundred years. But as soon as the third chord arrives—right when, in the first verse, Joel sings the song's title—he switches to an F-major chord, well outside the key of A (F is not even part of an A-major scale). The fourth chord, built on D and played under the lyric, "I know the look," brings the bass line back into A, but in the support of a minor chord rather than the conventional major one.

The fifth chord, under "across your face," is built on B-flat, another pitch outside an A-major scale. Known as a "Neapolitan chord," it is a triad of pitches built on a lowered second scale degree; it usually serves as part of a cadence. The device has a history going back to at least the eighteenth century and was also a favorite of some of Joel's Romantic-era idols. Beethoven used it in the opening of his String Quartet in F Minor, Op. 95 (1810) (see Kerman 1979, 168–87), and Schubert em-ployed it in the end of his famous art song "Der Erlkönig" (1815, published in 1821) and in his String Quintet (1828) (Brown 1944). While uncommon, the Neapolitan has also been used in rock music, such as in The Beatles' "Do You Want to Know a Secret" (1963) (Everett 1999, 310). So it is not surprising that Joel uses the same technique here, raising the bass up to a B-natural, which leads (by five steps) to E and finally (by another five steps) back to A for the end of the phrase "it's so familiar to me." The result is an unusual sequence held together by a descending bass line and a melody line that cleverly exploits pitches that these seemingly unrelated chords have in common. Joel describes it as a "weird chord progression" whose unconventional quality is due to the fact that he never practiced his scales on the piano as a kid. "It's supposed to be about a jarring division. There you go, slipping away into that *place* I'm trying to write about.' That was the intention of those chords" (personal interview).

"THIS IS WHY MY EYES ARE CLOSED": SONGS OF CYNICISM AND DECEPTION

A third theme running through many of Joel's romantic songs is cynicism and deception. Here we find songs that, while mentioning or referencing lovers, nonetheless focus on the dark side of love. This category includes "Honesty" (from *52nd Street*), "All For Leyna" and "Sleeping with the Television On" (from *Glass Houses*), "Laura" (from *The Nylon Curtain*), and "This Is the Time" (from *The Bridge*), all of which depict relationships that suffer from some kind of deception, describe them in cynical terms, or both. The three songs discussed here, "Summer, Highland Falls" (from *Turnstiles*), "The Stranger" (from *The Stranger*), and "And So It Goes" (from *Storm Front*), illustrate this trend in albums from the beginning, middle, and end of Joel's pop career.

"Summer, Highland Falls" marks Joel's realizations after moving back to New York from Los Angeles and after the joy of "New York State of Mind" (described in chapter 2) receded. Living in the small New York town of Highland Falls, he felt a newfound sense of perilousness, professionally and personally. *Piano Man* had done respectably, but sales of the follow-up album, *Streetlife Serenade*, had been disappointing and he knew that another flop would effectively end his career.

At the same time, he was thrilled to have left Los Angeles, a move chronicled in "Say Goodbye to Hollywood" (discussed in chapter 2). Personally, his relationship with Elizabeth Weber was starting to crack under the pressure of his career and her increasing involvement in it. He described his self-assessment to an audience in Nuremberg in 1995: "That particular summer I felt that life wasn't as simple as it used to be. Things were changing for me. I was recognizing that I had faults that I needed to correct and I needed to work on, [and] the relationship I had with [Weber] wasn't as perfect as I wanted it to be" (Joel, "Q&A"). The tone is set from the opening lyric: "They say that these are not the best of times, but they're the only times I've ever known."

That sentiment carries through the rest of the piece, as Joel admits that he has "seen that sad surrender in [his] lover's eyes," yet he can do little but "stand apart and sympathize." After arguments and compromises, ultimately they "realize that nothing's ever changed." The honeymoon is over; loving someone in the real world means coming to terms with their needs while moderating your own. "How thoughtlessly we dissipate our energies," he sings with a poetic flourish that extends throughout the piece; "perhaps we don't fulfill each other's fantasies."

On several occasions Joel has described this song as a musical manifestation of the emotional extremes that artists often swing between, what he calls in "Summer, Highland Falls" as "either sadness or euphoria." Each phrase of the melody line ascends and then immediately descends. The sequence of chords underneath moves similarly. While Joel's right hand plays fast arpeggios, a sort of frenetic filigree, the left hand plays two notes at a time, spaced a fifth apart. First we hear the pair F and C, outlining the song's tonic chord. Then he moves up two steps to A and E. Next he moves down a step to G and D. Then up to B-flat and F, down to A and E, up to C and G, and down to B-flat and F before repeating the phrase. The result is an ascending-descending pattern that, despite the figuration on the surface above, physically and aurally evokes manic-depressive swings from high to low. Thomas MacFarlane points out that "in the interplay between the text and musical setting" of "Summer, Highland Falls," "happiness is layered on top of sadness, suggesting that the two states are always related." Yet the lyrics assert that one can only occupy one state: sadness or euphoria (2016).

"Summer, Highland Falls" illustrates Joel's ideal compositional process. After writing the music, he then asks what it is trying to say. The lyrics are based on the answer to that question. "What I try to do is decode what is inherent in the music. There's a mood, there's an emotion, there was a motivation to write those particular notes and use those chords in that rhythm. Even before I have a single word" (personal interview). When it comes to "Summer, Highland Falls," the procedure worked perfectly. "I'm particularly proud of that song," he says.

> I don't know if people know what they're hearing in the music. They're feeling it with the lyric, and I think it's pretty obvious I'm talking about a bipolar personality. It's *in the music*. It's one of the songs I just . . . I broke the code. Down, up, down, up—I want to be this but I'm going to always end up being that. . . . It's almost like a map, like I'm trying to draw a map for you. Here's what I mean with the music, and I'll show you how to get there with the words. (personal interview)

"The Stranger" engages the theme of deception as the lyrics of the verses describe it in several guises: the hidden, dark side of one's personality that is only revealed when the person is alone; the secrets that remain kept from one another despite close romantic relationships; and a man's romantic confidence that is destroyed by a woman immune to his charms. The bridge, sung twice, gives voice to another perspective, encouraging the song's subject to "try again" despite repeated failures.

The musical setting of "The Stranger" is quite different from "Summer, Highland Falls." It begins with a jazz-like trio of piano, bass, and drums. The piano plays a slow, meandering melody, which is then repeated in a whistle as the drums switch to a ride cymbal with a long sizzle. When the song proper begins, the tempo gets faster as the drums establish a tight rock beat and the distorted electric guitar provides the instrumental melody before Joel's voice enters. The piano is mixed rather quietly as the rhythm guitar, bass, and Joel's vocal delivery relish in the percussive texture. At the end, the more relaxed, detached mood of the introduction returns and the song fades out as Joel whistles and improvises on the piano.

Although "Summer, Highland Falls" remains high in Joel's vocal range and maintains a singular perspective, "The Stranger" offers contrasting registers and points of view. The verses sit rather low, which enables Joel to sound curt and matter-of-fact and combines with a punchy quality created by an extremely quick delay effect. However, during the bridges Joel slips into falsetto (quietly doubled in his voice an octave lower) and his vocal timbre becomes softer and purer, more like singing than the earnest, speechlike delivery of the verses. The difference between the two formal sections helps to underscore the track's two "voices," one bearing the warnings of danger and the other encouraging perseverance—an angel on each shoulder.

On "And So It Goes," released twelve years later, Joel returns to a purely piano-vocal combination. This forlorn ballad mourns love lost: he remains devoted; she does not: "I will share this room with you, and you can have this heart to break." The verses describe the relationship, beginning with his initial caution, wondering whether his self-conscious silence caused a rift, and ultimately pronouncing that, despite his choice to stay, she may go. In the bridges, Joel shifts focus from his lover to himself. He looks back sadly at a trail of romantic failures and wonders whether he has been the cause all along: "Every time I've held a rose, it seems I only felt the thorns." Resigned, he later concludes that this history of unsuccessful love is why his "eyes are closed." After all, he sings, "it's just as well for all I've seen."

With its slow and steady pace, "And So It Goes" evokes a solemn church hymn or chorale. Unlike "Summer, Highland Falls," Joel plays no manic piano figuration. Instead we hear a succession of chords, many of which contain among their consonant tones one pitch that creates a dissonance (a technique discussed in the analysis of "Allentown" in chapter 4). For example, take the first verse's initial phrase, "In every heart there is a room," the melody and harmony of which are reused throughout the composition. The first two words are a "pickup," arriving at the end of a measure and leading to the downbeat (under the word "heart") at the beginning of the next measure. "Heart" is accompanied by an F-major chord (F, A, and C) in a conventional manner. But as the melody moves from A down to G and back up to A again ("there is a"), the chords change with each word. "There" and "a," sung on a G, are accompanied by a C chord, but instead of the conventional collection of pitches (C, E, and G), Joel voices the chord as C, G, and B. The B is only a half-step from the chord's "root," C, so it creates a strong dissonance as the two pitches clash. When Joel finally arrives on the lyric "room," on the downbeat of the next measure, it too is accompanied by a chord, this time A-minor (A, C, and E), in which one of the conventional tones, C, is removed and a dissonant one, D, is added. The

D resolves down to C a beat later in what is known as a "suspension," but the impact of the D-against-E tension is heightened due to the fact that it falls on the downbeat, at the end of the phrase.

Similar clashes—between pitches that are "in" the harmony and those that are "not" but are played anyway—occur throughout the piece: the downbeat of the bridge ("and every *time*") features a C-major chord (C, E, G) with a B-flat in the bass, and the following phrase ("I've held a rose") sports an F-minor chord (F, A-flat, C), itself not naturally found in the song's overall C-major key, with an added D. These are heard again as the bridge is repeated after the piano solo and again as the song ends. Thus, the voicing of the chords aligns with the song's overall cynical message, that even in moments of joy (consonance) lies a hint of sadness (dissonance). Happiness, it would seem, is intrinsically deceptive.

"YOU'LL ALWAYS BE A PART OF ME": SONGS OF FAMILY AND FRIENDS

While not as common as those about romantic relationships, Joel's albums include several songs about family and friends. Like those discussed earlier, these songs also display a wide variety of styles and moods.

"Why Judy Why" (from *Cold Spring Harbor*) bears the name of Joel's cousin, with whom he had a close relationship as a child. After moving to Hicksville in 1950, Joel's mother welcomed Judy into their house, raising her as a daughter after her mother died. "She was raised like my sister," Joel said, "and I have always thought of her in that way. Together, back then, she and I were allies in the difficult life we all shared" (qtd. in Schruers 2014, 21).

In this song, a young Joel describes his turmoil following his rejection by a lover. He never thought she would leave, but now that she has he wants "to die." Turning to Judy, he asks the heartbroken question, why? He remarks how he feels old despite his youth and how he needs support despite his efforts to soothe himself. The lyrics about his lover are in the third person ("she" and "her"), while his words to Judy are in the second person (calling her "you" or using her name). This linguistic distinction makes it clear that Judy is not the lover who left, but the shoulder he wants to cry on. And while "Why Judy Why" reveals little about Judy herself, it positions her as a confidant not unlike Joel's actual cousin.

"Why Judy Why" is the first song from Joel's recorded solo repertory whose musical foundation is an acoustic guitar; all the others on *Cold Spring Harbor* are based on keyboards. Bielen describes this "rare production move" as adding to the "sad mood of the track," while Joel's vocal delivery has a "stiff, reserved character" (2011, 22). A heavy dose of vibrato, especially on long notes ("when I *cry*"), and a gentle falling off of pitches at the ends of phrases help convey a sense of emotional depth and exhaustion, as if he lacks the energy to hold out those notes any longer.

"Rosalinda's Eyes" (from *52nd Street*) takes on both a different familial subject and musical style. Joel sings as a young musician, struggling to get his career started. Rosalinda is his inspiration. No matter the challenges he faces, he will always return to her and her smile. The lyrics and music emphasize the Latin—specifically Cuban—aspect of their identity: he plays wedding gigs in "the Spanish part of town," he's been "searching for" Havana everywhere, and in Rosalinda's eyes he finds his "Cuban skies."

The lyrics of "Rosalinda's Eyes" are a fictionalized retelling of Joel's parents' early relationship. As DeVitto told biographer Mark Bego, "Listen to the lyrics; it is about his mother. Rosalinda is in reality Rosalind Joel" (2007, 137). Joel later explained: "Because my old man lived in Cuba for a couple of years" on his journey from Nazi Germany to the United States, "I just folded in some bits and pieces of what I knew about my family background and romanticized that situation" (qtd. in Schruers 2014, 140). In keeping with themes found elsewhere in his romantic songs, the narrative hinges on a sense of separation. The protagonist spends many nights away from Rosalinda, whom he encourages not to feel lonely. When he joins the wedding band and has steadier work, he still feels lonely, perhaps because it is a Puerto Rican band, not a Cuban outfit, so he does not fit in. And he continually searches for Havana because he has never found it (and likely never will, according to the lyrics). (As fate would have it, Joel played in a concert at the Karl Marx Theater in Havana called the "Havana Jam," sponsored by Columbia Records, in 1979. The performance received favorable notices, with John Rockwell writing in *The New York Times* that Joel's music was "stirring" and "drew the most fervent response of the entire festival" [1979].)

The Latin atmosphere Joel evokes in "Rosalinda's Eyes" is supported musically in Joel's vocal delivery and in the song's instrumentation and style. By the second verse, his singing begins to take on a Spanish affect similar to the one he adopted in "Los Angelenos" (see chapter 2), but this time more sustained. In that song he simply rolled his *r*'s on particular words, but here the accent is used through long lyrical passages.

"Rosalinda's Eyes" also includes several instruments often found in various Latin genres, such as the acoustic guitar, vibes, marimba, and flute. The percussion, too, adopts a rhythm typical of Latin styles, especially in the cowbell and snare drum, which play patterns more complex than rock's conventional backbeat. Early in the song one hears a shaker and a maraca, both common in Afro-Cuban (especially Yoruba) music. Toward the end of the flute solo, listeners may hear some drum fills played on congas, an instrument associated with Afro-Cuban *rumba*. And the marimba, played throughout the track by Mike Mainieri, has roots in the Cuban song genre *son*, where it is known as the *marímbula* (see Béhague and Moore; Moore 2009). As if to make the influence even clearer, approximately the final twenty-five seconds of the song feature only the drums and percussion as the rest of the band fades out. Yet one important marker of much Cuban music, and Latin music in general, is missing: the clave, a percussion instrument that usually plays a distinctive syncopated pattern often heard in salsa and related genres. Nonetheless, Joel uses not only the lyrics to connect "Rosalinda's Eyes" to his (imagined) family history, but also employs musical features to reinforce the link.

River of Dreams, Joel's final pop album, includes "Lullabye (Goodnight, My Angel)." Inspired by his young daughter Alexa's question about death, the lyrics at first instruct her to ask again another time but then assure her that in some way they will always be together: "You'll always be a part of me." As he sings her to sleep, he becomes increasingly emotional. He realizes how much he still wants to tell her, reminisces of their time together, and imagines her singing to her own daughter someday.

As a musical composition, "Lullabye" bears a distinctly classical tilt that differs markedly from the folksy guitar of "Why Judy Why" and the Cuban rhythms of "Rosalinda's Eyes." Like "Leningrad," another of his classically leaning songs, Joel's piano is the most prominent accompanying instrument. (For more on Joel's classical influence, see chapter 6.) After the first verse, an orchestra gradually fades in as well, but the piano remains louder in the mix, playing mostly chords with a few melodic passing tones connecting them. This accompaniment alternates major and minor chords, effecting a mood that is neither clearly happy nor clearly sad. And although the song begins and ends in the major, the persistent presence of such minor tonality suggests a dose of apprehension. Joel explains:

> It's almost like a dying man singing to his child. And he's trying to reassure his daughter, which is what the major key is, but he's also hinting at the fact that there will be separation. And that's where the minor key changes come in. Where there's not a minor, there are suspensions—chords that take longer to resolve—so you have the anxiety of the unresolved chord, then the release of the tension when it does resolve. (qtd. in Schuers 2014, 224)

Aside from the significance of Joel singing to his daughter, pledging the immortality of their love, the song's vocal line took on additional meaning as Joel realized, while recording it, that his singing echoed the way his mother sang to him during his childhood. When she forgot the lyrics to a song, she would simply sing "lu, lu, lu." In "Lullabye," these are exactly the sounds Joel puts to the wordless melody during the bridge (Schuers 2014, 224–25).

"Lullabye" demonstrates that, even on his last pop album and when the subject and topic of the song shifted from his sister to his mother to his daughter, separation remains a chief concern of Joel's songwriting. In this case, it may be simply a physical distance between father and daughter, since around the time this song was composed, Joel was often touring and away from his family. But it may also carry deeper meanings pertaining to distance created by aging, as Joel musically reenacts his mother's singing, and death, as Joel responds to Alexa's question.

The three songs discussed here convey markedly different moods yet remain united not only in their consideration of family but also in this anxiety of separation. "Why Judy Why" aches with heartbreak and desire for comfort from a distant confidant. "Rosalinda's Eyes" cheerfully addresses the physical gap between two lovers and a deeper nostalgia for an unreachable homeland. And "Lullabye" somberly assures un-

ending love between parent and child amid the reality that life is anything but eternal.

Joel's songs about friends are similarly varied in tone and musical
style and rich in meaning. From the introspective "James" (from *Turnstiles*, discussed in the next chapter) to the jubilant "Tell Her About It"
(from *An Innocent Man*) to the vindictive "The Great Wall of China"
(from *River of Dreams*), these pieces run the full gamut. "Tell Her
About It" and "The Great Wall of China" are discussed here.

Like many of the tracks on *An Innocent Man*, "Tell Her About It"
recalls one of the styles of popular music of Joel's youth, offering a
combination of the sounds of Detroit's Motown and Chicago's Soul.
Schruers reports that Joel had Diana Ross and the Supremes in mind
(2014, 174). *Rolling Stone* critic Parke Puterbaugh (1983) hears rever-
beration from the "Philly-soul district." It is a joyful tune with an infectious beat. The introduction features Joel's soaring falsetto, which helps
to set an energetic tone. The song includes a prominent horn section,
whose lines are often answered by a solo saxophone. Bielen hears
echoes of "blue-eyed soul" in Joel's vocal delivery, which bears traces of
Shades of Blue and the Young Rascals (2011, 65). Still, Joel warns
against hearing the song as a single, despite the fact that it reached
number one on the charts in that format. "To me," he says, "that [song]
sounds awful on its own. It sounds like Tony Orlando and Dawn. I hate
that single. But in the context of the album it makes sense, because the
Innocent Man album was sort of a tribute to old rock and roll influences" (qtd. in Bego 2007, 206).

"Tell Her About it" is an advice song, where one character offers
guidance to another. Joel plays the role of the older and wiser voice,
instructing his friend in the art of courtship. "I don't like watching
anybody make the same mistakes I made," he reveals in a moment one
might be tempted to interpret autobiographically. Of course, the song's
message is in the title, which begins the chorus: share your feelings with
her despite your insecurities. The bridge warns that inaction could be
costly: "Though you may not have done anything, will that be a consola-
tion when she's gone?"

Ultimately, "Tell Her About it" captures an echo of 1960s rhythm
and blues songs, recalling a time of youthful innocence for Joel and his
generation. The accompanying music video picks up this thread. It was
a big-budget production for the time, costing more than $100,000 ac-

cording to biographer Bill Smith (2007, 190–91), and included a simu-
lated live performance by "B.J. and the Affordables" on the *Ed Sullivan
Show*, a late-night standard of Joel's childhood on which major musical
acts often played. The program was "for millions of otherwise culturally
deprived Americans . . . the prime source of pure entertainment, television's most powerful, influential show for 23 years, between 1948 and
1971" (Nachman 2009, 1).

"The Great Wall of China" may be the most raucous and angry of
Joel's songs about friends, as well as one that levels a broadside of
critique. This fusillade takes aim at Frank Weber, Joel's manager from
1980 to 1989, without specifically mentioning his name. His onetime
brother-in-law (Frank's sister, Elizabeth, was Joel's first wife), Weber
presided over an important part of Joel's career but allegedly became
embroiled in a series of schemes and mismanaged investments that left
his client with little to show for nearly a decade of work. For example,
Smith writes that Weber and at least one associate "plundered Billy's
finances, often ending up with more money from Billy's tours and recordings than Billy himself had" (2007, 208–9). Weber reportedly in-
vested in racehorses, real estate, and oil wells. Some of the investments
paid him commissions, while others left Joel liable for losses. In the
end, Joel filed thirty-seven lawsuits in attempts to recoup his losses
(208–26). As Weber would be the subject of an FBI investigation a few
years later, biographer Richard Scott calls "The Great Wall of China" a
"lawsuit song" (2000, 79).

In this context, the vitriol of "The Great Wall of China" is understandable. Joel does not pull any punches, as even the first verse ac-
cuses, "Your soul was too defective." In the second verse, he warns,
"You take a piece of whatever you touch"; however, "too many pieces
means you're touching too much." False friends will quickly abandon
you once deceit is made plain. Just look at the distance you fell, Joel
taunts. The chorus makes direct reference to the 5,500-mile line of
defensive fortifications running across China (see Rojas 2010; Waldron
1989). As the world's largest man-made structure, the Great Wall is
undoubtedly a crowning achievement. Joel uses it metaphorically to
refer to his own career success, which Weber could have enjoyed too
were it not for his transgressions.

The song announces itself loudly. The introduction begins with a
large chorus of men singing an ascending melody on the syllable "ah,"

while Joel vocalizes in a similar wordless fashion. Distorted electric guitars, punchy bass, and a busy drum kit with crashing cymbals are joined by a string section playing a taunting, sliding melody. All in all, it makes for a startling and strong "wall" of sound (perhaps comparable to the effect achieved by Phil Spector; see chapter 2). When the introduction's final chord begins to fade, Joel's piano can finally be heard, pounding out octaves as if marking seconds on a clock. The verse begins with a sparser accompaniment as the guitar and bass play short notes, leaving space between them for Joel's lead, which in parts is as much rhythmic as it is melodic, avoiding downbeats and beginning each line just after the kick drum, bass, and guitar mark the start of each measure. The result is a straighter pattern emphasizing beats one and three.

Each verse has two sections. The first is sung, sitting squarely in the middle of Joel's range and featuring added harmonies (also performed by Joel). After four lines, the percussion and bass grow busier while the lyrics become shorter, enabling Joel to issue brief sneers that require little in the way of melodic singing. After all, the point of the song is not beauty but the clarity of its menacing message. The chorus returns to the volume and intensity of the introduction. In his analysis of the song, MacFarlane writes that "the use of these contrasting textures accesses the perceived rivalry between the Beatles and the Rolling Stones, and thus underscores the combative stance of the lyric" (2016).

Aside from musical references to The Beatles and the Rolling Stones, Joel makes several extramusical references within "The Great Wall of China." The first appears in the song's third line: "Nobody knows 'bout the troubles I've seen," a quotation from the African American spiritual of the same name. In the song's chorus, Joel sings, "All the king's men and all the king's horses can't put you together the way you used to be," a reference to the English nursery rhyme, Humpty Dumpty, where the verse reads, "All the king's horses and all the king's men couldn't put Humpty together again." The title character, commonly portrayed as an egg, falls off of a high wall and breaks into pieces; all efforts to reassemble him fail (see Opie and Opie 1997). Certainly, both the wall and the fall stand as points of intersection between this cautionary tale and Joel's song: do not climb too high.

Finally, in the second chorus of "The Great Wall of China," Joel sings, "You coulda had class; you coulda been a contender," a reference to the commercially and critically successful film *On the Waterfront*

(1954). This crime drama includes an iconic scene in which the character Terry laments to his brother, Charley, using the line Joel sings, that his life's deterioration began the night Charley convinced him to lose a boxing match. It captures the desperation and disappointment that results when partners—here, brothers—advise each other poorly (at best) or deceive each other (at worst). Certainly this allusion can be read in relation to Joel's situation with Weber, who once was his business partner and his brother(-in-law) but whose poor advice and deception ultimately led to his own ruin.

"THE POWER OF LOVE AND THE POWER OF HEALING": GENDER AND GENDER DYNAMICS

Joel's songs about relationships do more than just profess love, lament distance, or bemoan deception. Many can also be read as indications of more general attitudes toward gender and gender dynamics in American society, the final theme this chapter addresses. Two approaches are evident here: songs that describe and challenge the roles of lover and spouse, and those that depict women as baffling and dangerous. Both of these not only tell us about the subjects of the songs, but also demonstrate Joel's consistent tendency to portray himself, or at least his male characters, as stricken with fears of insufficiency, career anxieties, and a trail of failed relationships.

One of the earliest examples of a song about the role of lover or spouse in Joel's catalog is "You're My Home," written for Elizabeth Weber as a Valentine's Day gift and included on the *Piano Man* album. In the lyrics, Joel describes himself as a "crazy gypsy," no doubt due to his almost-nomadic lifestyle of touring to support his fledgling career in the early 1970s. He recognizes that this may not make him the most appealing, but he is thankful for his lover's affection because, despite his travels, his home is where she is. The acoustic guitar provides most of the accompaniment, playing a finger-picking pattern rather than strummed chords. Pedal steel creates a vague country-western tinge, which Bielen attributes to the influence of other emerging singer-songwriters in California at the time, such as Linda Ronstadt and the Eagles (2011, 24).

Listening to "You're My Home," one is left with the impression of Joel's lover as warm and comforting ("everything will be all right") as well as inviting ("use my body for your bed"). She is his "home" in both the physical sense (he names her as his castle, his cabin, and his "instant pleasure dome") and in an emotional sense. Above all else, she is his support. The music helps to make this clear, too. Joel's voice is calm and never strained. On the long notes, he adds a dose of vibrato. The sequence of chords features brief and somewhat predictable moments of musical tension, all of which are quickly resolved, delivering the listener to the song's "home key," or tonic, at all the expected times. These compositional choices convey a sense of stability, as if the lover were a stereotypical 1950s housewife who, to paraphrase Tammy Wynette's 1968 chart-topping hit, stands by her man.

"She's Right on Time" (from *The Nylon Curtain*) illustrates a different approach. On this track, Joel is the one at home, not his lover, busy preparing for her return, shuffling around the house to set the mood. He turns on the Christmas lights and choral music while keeping the fire alight. He reveals that he is "a man with so much tension," which will be effectively ignored once she returns—and he has "torn out all [his] telephones" to insure no interruptions.

Musically, "She's Right on Time" is more ambitious than "You're My Home." The harpsichord introduction is tonally ambiguous, forcing the listener to wait before learning which key the song is in. Joel likens it to an M. C. Escher painting, admitting that the sequence of chords was challenging to write ("I don't know how I got there; I can't even tell you what half those chords are—I don't know how I got away with that") and remains challenging to play (personal interview). The verses and choruses are supported primarily by electric guitars, whose harmonies shift subtly over an unchanging bass note for long stretches. This creates some tension as the guitar pitches occasionally clash with those of the bass, a musical anxiety that is eventually resolved.

What does "She's Right on Time" say about gender and gender dynamics? One fact that cannot be overlooked is the domestic aspect of Joel's character. It is he, not she, whose sphere is the home. Another is the anxiety simmering just beneath the song's surface. The musical anxiety created in the accompaniment is matched by lyrics, such as "far too many sins to mention, she don't have to take it anymore," that cast doubt on his own worth and value. He wonders why she sticks with him when he is the difficult, damaged one without a "normal" job. The reversal of gender roles described in "She's Right on Time" may ultimately be interpreted to reveal Joel's character's discomfort with the new gender landscape.

The music video for "She's Right on Time" aims for humor as Joel plays the hapless man who, despite the best of intentions, finds his efforts to prepare the house for his lover's return met with "Buster Keaton–style" failure and destruction (Bielen 2011, 117). The wood he adds to the fire covers his face and suit in soot, an attempt to clean the apartment causes a shelf of LPs to collapse, his bid to decorate the Christmas tree ends up knocking it over, and his struggle to remove the telephone winds up tearing a large hole in the wall. When she finally arrives, just before the song's bridge, a brief embrace is immediately followed by synchronized slapstick left-and-right glances around the apartment as they watch lights and faucets explode in showers of sparks and water. Joel knew it was over the top: "If I'd done [the music video] literally, [it] would've been too cornball. So I tried to do it funny, which was even worse" (qtd. in Bego 2007, 213). But the basis for the humor is revealing: for the video to make sense, viewers must link the ineptitude of Joel's male character to the fact that he cannot manage the home. Had it been a female character instead, the video would likely not offer an inflated attempt at humor but instead cause confusion. One wonders whether the true message of the video is to point out the absurdity of unconventional gender roles, a conclusion the song itself does not necessarily support.

In the final verse of "She's Right on Time," the lover's role is reframed in terms similar to the more conventional: "Every time I lost the meter," Joel sings, using a musical metaphor, "there she was when I would need her." In the end, then, her role is ultimately to meet his needs, though at least he, in his domesticity, is presumably also meeting hers. (This give-and-take is the topic of the next song on the album, "A Room of Our Own.") Thus, "She's Right on Time" can be said to challenge gender roles, albeit gently.

"All About Soul" (from *River of Dreams*) finds Joel singing about his relationship with Christie Brinkley. He praises her, once again describing himself as the misfit, difficult, or wounded one and her as the supporter and savior: "She gives me all her tenderness and takes away my pain." He is relieved she has not yet left him, despite "so many things getting out of control." Indeed, tough times lie ahead ("it's gonna get dark; it's gonna get cold"), but she has "the power of love and the power of healing" to keep their course true. By the song's end, he concludes, "she gives me all the love I need to keep my faith alive."

Joel's voice is more weary in "All About Soul" than in the earlier tracks. While it had been about twenty years since he recorded "You're My Home" and about a decade since "She's Right on Time," the edge in Joel's vocal delivery also suits the lyrics, which cast his character as one with a history rather than struck with a more innocent case of young, puppy love. The straight-ahead rock beat and instrumentation offer the song a sense of purpose—listeners are not distracted by any attempts to recapture other or older styles of popular music—while the strings and gospel choir lend a sense of gravity. The clap-along, wordless ("na na na") bridge featuring Joel and the choir, which repeats during the song's fade-out, invites the listener to sing along with the musical testimony to a love deeper than any he has previously described.

The generally positive portrayals of women found in "You're My Home," "She's Right on Time," and "All About Soul" are counterbalanced by other songs in which Joel takes a different approach, singing from perspectives ranging from cautious to outright angry. Perhaps his best known song of this type is "She's Always a Woman" (from *The Stranger*). Despite media reports suggesting the lyrics were misogynistic—the song was sometimes misquoted as "She *Only* a Woman"—Joel maintains that it, too, is a love song. Written for Elizabeth Weber, who was known for her tough negotiating skills that could be perceived as unfeminine, Joel's lyrics defend her. They explain that he loves all facets of her personality, even those that might strike others as unlovable, such as a smile that could kill, eyes that could wound, and her contrasting moods (Sheff and Sheff 1982).

In "She's Always a Woman," Joel's love song is certainly unconventional as he focuses almost exclusively on the woman's threatening aspects. Were it not for the song's underlying message of devotion, one might also sense a contrast between the menacing qualities detailed in the lyrics and the gentle guitar-like piano figures and flute melody of the accompaniment. She seems to have a strong grip on him and he loves it.

That grip is far less enjoyable in "Laura" (from *The Nylon Curtain*). Here, Joel's character sings of how Laura has him "caught in her vise."

She is whiny and needy (calling "in the middle of the night" to pass on "her painful information"), but he cannot let her go: "Laura loves me even if I don't care," he concludes in the final verse; "that's my problem." While some have speculated that Laura is based on one of Joel's love interests, he maintains it is based on his relationship with his mother. "There's a complete giveaway line where I sing, 'How can she hold an umbilical cord [for] so long?'" he told Chuck Klosterman (2004, 51).

The musical features of "Laura" help convey the frustration Joel's character feels. For example, as with several tracks on *The Nylon Curtain*, double-tracked vocals appear throughout the song. This effect is created when two recordings of the same voice, singing the same melody and lyrics, are played simultaneously. Because no two performances are exactly alike, the imperceptible variations between them generate a tone that may be perceived as menacing, mechanistic, and cold (Zak 2001, 70–76). While the entire lead vocal is double-tracked in "Laura," certain lyrics receive a more severe application of the effect, such as "then she tells me she *suddenly believes* she's seen a very good sign." This stronger double-tracking appears in analogous places in the melody of each verse and more frequently later in the song. Although sometimes it emphasizes the semantic meaning of the lyrics, the reason for its use is more clearly melodic, since it occurs when Joel's melody oscillates between the sixth step of the key's scale, which creates a moderate dissonance, and the fifth, which offers consonance (Duchan 2015, 180).

"Laura" paints a picture of a calculating and manipulative woman. She wakes the narrator at night, slams doors in his face, and disingenuously offers him platitudes while literally drawing his blood. Yet he is helpless to resist her. "I've done everything I can; what else am I supposed to do?" he asks in desperation.

Similar portraits of women may be found in "Stiletto" (from *52nd Street*) and "All for Leyna" (from *Glass Houses*), both of which came before *The Nylon Curtain*. In "Stiletto," Joel sings of a woman who will "cut you" repeatedly but "still you believe." She is so captivating that he will endure any pain for her. In "All for Leyna," the title character leads the narrator to similar pain—a dangerous loss of sleep and appetite, an electric shock from touching a train track's third rail, and nearly drowning amid a rocky undertow—and yet he is hopelessly entranced. "There's nothing else I can do," he sings; "I'm doing it all for Leyna."

Both songs feature strong rhythmic components. "Stiletto" may begin with a languorous saxophone solo, but the interplay between Joel's piano and DeVitto's drums, which include a heavy dose of syncopation and off-beat hits, gives the song propulsive momentum. The accompaniment of "All for Leyna" is built around steady chords on the keyboard and electric guitar, which offer a foil for the rhythmically evasive melody that emphasizes the off-beats (placing lyrics in between the piano and guitar chords) as much as the beats themselves.

Clearly, then, many of Joel's songs about women depict them as strong and dangerous, to varying degrees. In "She's Always a Woman," the danger is not great enough to scare him away—in fact, her strength is what draws him to her in the first place. In "Laura," "Stiletto," and "All for Leyna," however, the female characters are so strong and dangerous that Joel's male characters cannot escape their grasp even when they try.

"Modern Woman" (from *The Bridge*), featured on the soundtrack of the film *Ruthless People* (1986), offers a slightly different approach to songs about women. In this piece, the unnamed woman is dangerous not just because of her seductive powers, but because of the ease with which she navigates the "modern" man's world, which baffles the more traditional man to whom Joel sings. She does not rely on him for financial support. She is a double-threat, with her beauty and her intellect. She "makes up her face while she makes up her mind." Even after the two settle down together, she departs for work each morning and leaves him at home; "it's a strange situation for an old-fashioned guy." The concerns with the changing demographics of the American workplace expressed in "Running on Ice," from the same album (discussed in chapter 4), are certainly present here as well.

The rhythmic elements of "Modern Woman," like the other songs discussed here, are intense. A shaker plays constantly, like an incessant second hand on a clock. Joel's melody is especially rhythmic, with a limited range in the verses but a vast amount of lyrics, which are telegraphed with precision. And the heavily synthesized horn hits, which offer syncopated punctuation, consistently threaten to upend the straight-ahead beat. The production is "big," typical for 1980s pop. Bego describes it as Joel's only song that is "100 percent welded into the 'big eighties' mode" in an era that also valued "big shoulder pads, big jewelry, and big and boisterous synthesizer sounds" (2007, 224).

Several conclusions can be drawn from this discussion of Joel's songs about relationships and gender. First, within the broad category of "love songs," for which Joel is known, one finds a variety of topics, ranging from adoration and courtship, to comfort amid separation, to cynicism and deception. There is also a consistent undercurrent of anxiety. Even in their brightest and warmest moments, Joel's songs about relationships almost always carry a hint—sometimes subtle, sometimes not—of darker, colder days ahead. Second, the variety of themes populating Joel's love songs is also replicated in his songs about friends and family, which similarly run the gamut from reverence to concern to hatred.

Finally, when reading Joel's songs for what they say about gender and gender roles, we learn that women are portrayed not only as supportive lovers, but also as especially strong characters—for better and for worse. That strength can be attractive, captivating, baffling, and dangerous. "A lot of things about women baffle me," he says. "They do. But it intrigues me, and it's attractive to me" (personal interview). Importantly, Joel's songs about strong (and dangerous or baffling) women reveal a deeper power dynamic in which the men are not clearly superior and, in many cases, are clearly inferior. This trend aligns with the changing gender dynamics of the late twentieth century, in which women increasingly assumed public and professional personae, a shift that, as described in the previous chapter, was met with a measure of concern from their male colleagues.

6

"THE ENTERTAINER"

Stylistic Authenticity and the Entertainment Industry

For a significant part of his recording career, Billy Joel had a rocky relationship with music critics, who claimed that his music was nothing more than a rehash of older styles, reflecting a lack of compositional skill. Such an accusation reveals much about the values and assumptions of the critics; they sought a sense of authenticity requiring a style so distinctive as to obscure any connection with the musical past. Siding with Joel, music theorist Walter Everett observes that the "complex mix of stylistic markers" found in Joel's music was "too complex, in fact, for the rock press" and placed it "on a very different plane from that of most of his fellow artists and critics" (2000, 107), a disjuncture that critics may have found challenging. This chapter argues that Joel's work is not derivative or inauthentic due to its "complex mix" of connections with historical and contemporaneous musical styles. Instead, it is that very mix of "stylistic markers," whether references to another composer's or band's sound generally or to a specific song or piece, that makes it distinctive.

The first part of this chapter examines the critiques the rock press made of Joel's music, showing how critics drew on a concept of "authenticity" with deep historical and cultural roots. The next section describes traditions of borrowing and influence in classical and popular musics, which undermine a search for purity or originality. The third part takes a closer look at two of Joel's most frequent sources, classical music and The Beatles, by examining several of his songs that bear their influences. For classical music, "Nocturne" (from *Cold Spring Harbor*), "James" (from *Turnstiles*), "This Night" (from *An Innocent Man*), and "Invention in C-Minor" (from *Fantasies & Delusions*) are discussed; for The Beatles, "Through the Long Night" (from *Glass Houses*), "Laura" (from *The Nylon Curtain*), and "Scandinavian Skies" (also from *The Nylon Curtain*). Finally, the last section considers Joel's musical responses to his critics and to the mechanisms of the entertainment industry, which can be heard in songs like "Everybody Loves You Now" (from *Cold Spring Harbor*), "The Entertainer" (from *Streetlife Serenade*), "It's Still Rock and Roll to Me" (from *Glass Houses*), and "Getting Closer" (from *The Bridge*).

"I'M ON THE OUTSIDE; I DON'T FIT INTO THE GROOVE": THE CHARGE OF INAUTHENTICITY

Joel's music was compared to that of other musicians early in his career. While praising the "seriousness and musical flexibility" of *Piano Man*, *Rolling Stone*'s Jack Breschard (1974) immediately likened the production to Elton John and the "show-tune ambiance" to David Ackles. "Despite Joel's facility at portraying others," he concluded, "he seems unable to come to terms with himself." Reviewing the next album, *Streetlife Serenade*, Stephen Holden was even more critical, remarking, Joel's "pop schmaltz occupies a stylistic no man's land where musical and lyrical truisms borrowed from disparate sources"—which remain unnamed—"are forced together" (1974).

Perhaps the most stinging critique appeared in the December 14, 1978, issue of *Rolling Stone*, where Holden reviewed *52nd Street*. Joel is called a "a vaudevillian piano man and mimic who, having come of age in the late Sixties, has the grasp of rock and the technical know-how to be able to caricature both Bob Dylan and the Beatles as well as 'do' an updated Anthony Newley, all in the same Las Vegas format." Holden's criticism addresses both Joel's live performance and recordings:

> Joel works audiences into a lather of adulation with the snappy calculation of a borsch-belt ham. . . . He lards his performances with schtick that usually includes impersonations. . . .

Neither a great singer nor a great writer, Billy Joel is a great show-business personality in the tradition of Al Jolson. The same qualities that distinguish his schtick also distinguish his singing— bluntness, brashness, a middle- to lower-middle-class fringe urbanity and plenty of heart. . . . His complete lack of vocal subtlety, though an artistic limitation, is still one of his charms. . . .

Joel's songwriting forte is pop pastiche. . . . Both lyrically and musically, Joel's compositions tend to be very direct (there's not much beneath the surface), a little awkward, somewhat overstated and extremely melodic. Billy Joel's best pop songs . . . are closer to the old-fashioned, tub-thumping, Tin Pan Alley razzle-dazzle of George M. Cohan and Irving Berlin than to the polite theatrical tradition of George Gershwin, Cole Porter or Richard Rodgers and Lorenz Hart. . . . Recently, Joel has mastered Beatlesque pop- rock . . . a jittery note-to-syllable diction reminiscent of Paul McCart- ney's playful rockers. (Holden 1978)

Breschard's and Holden's reviews are just three samples of increas- ingly detailed and critical treatments of Joel's music. In fairness, they all come from the same publication, though an unquestionably important one. These critiques feature frequent comparisons of Joel to other con- temporaneous and historical composers and performers, as well as ob- servations of his impersonation skills. These trends can be read as back- handed compliments: they seem to imply that Joel's music is good inas- much as it sounds like that of others; what's missing is Joel's own com- positional voice. His style, the reviews suggest, is merely derivative, the songs derived from the works of others.

Joel fought back, criticizing the press and destroying copies of re- views on stage during performances. The 1983 release of *An Innocent Man* may not have helped either, as that album unabashedly adopted popular music styles from his youth in the 1960s—although a retreat into this feel-good era may have been exactly what he was going for. Listing the album's tracks and pairing each with its stylistic inspiration, Parke Puterbaugh writes:

Without missing a bomp, Joel manages to swing from the Wilson Pickett/James Brown and the Famous Flames-type raunch of "Easy Money" to the overdubbed Frankie Lymon and the Teenagers-style acapella [*sic*] of "The Longest Time" to, most uncanny of all, a per- fectly realized mimicry of the Four Seasons' unfathomable falsetto pop-soul, entitled "Uptown Girl." Along the way, he passes under the boardwalk to the Drifters' loping gait ("An Innocent Man"), takes a figurative spin through the Philly-soul district ("Tell Her About It") and turns his gaze southward, tipping his hat to various personages in Atlantic Records' Soul Clan, particularly Ben E. King. (Puterbaugh 1983)

But when Joel stops embracing older styles on *An Innocent Man*'s closer, "Keeping the Faith," Puterbaugh cries foul, calling it the album's "only wrong note." Again, when Joel is imitating others his work is good, but when he is perceived as trying to sound like himself, critics find him lacking in authenticity.

Why was authenticity so important? To answer that question, one needs to understand how the concept entered American popular music discourse by way of folk music in the middle of the twentieth century. According to Simon Frith, the "ideology of folk" developed at the end of the nineteenth century from a strong and widespread sense of nostalgia. For centuries, folk songs had been collected and published. In fact, Joel's mother owned such a collection, Margaret Bradford Boni's *Fireside Book of Folk Songs*, first published in 1947, which he still holds onto and claims influenced "The Downeaster 'Alexa'" (from *Storm Front*, see chapter 4). These songs were viewed as the genuine expression of the people to which they were attributed, arising spontaneously out of their experiences. Plantation songs were thought to express something true about working on an old plantation, likewise with sea shanties. Ethnic and national songs were perceived as sincere articulations of their groups or countries long ago. For those who wanted to cling to a memory of the past and also maintain and embody a connection to one's identity (vocational, ethnic, national, or otherwise), folk songs were an appealing way to do so.

These folk songs thus stood in contrast to pop songs, which were seen to be created purely for monetary gain. The American folk revival of the 1940s and 1950s rested in part on this ideology, which valorized the perceived purity of rural music in opposition to the commerce and alleged corruption of the city (itself a long-standing trope in American popular culture) and its music. From there, the idea entered the rock world, whose music was positioned as truer, more genuine than pop music; it was imagined and described as less "produced," less commercially oriented. "Armed with this ideology," Frith writes, "it was easy enough for 1960s rock fans to hear their music as more authentic than pop [and] to even claim that even if their music was commercial, it nevertheless symbolized a community" (1981, 161), in this case one centered around youth—the baby boomers.

This ideology was easily applied to the emerging genre of singer-songwriters, too. After all, if authentic music was the genuine expression of some people's collective experiences, then music made by singer-songwriters could be heard as the true expression of their individual, personal experiences (Shumway 2016). The genre was thus sometimes called "confessional," and to a great degree audiences expected that the stories of love, hope, and disappointment often sung by singer-songwriters like Bob Dylan, Joni Mitchell, Carly Simon, and James Taylor were actually drawn from the musicians' lives—which in many cases was true, as, for example, Taylor's "Fire and Rain" (from *Sweet Baby James*, 1970) referenced the suicide of one of his friends, his own drug addiction, and the dissolution of his first band (Crouse 1971). The fact that singer-songwriters typically wrote, played, and sang their own material helped reinforce the idea that whatever the songs expressed came from the voices heard on the recordings, while also distinguishing the genre from other forms of pop music in which songwriters wrote songs for other performers to perform. Although Joel began his solo career intending to be a songwriter, he ended up performing his compositions and is therefore often considered a singer-songwriter. His working-class upbringing can be heard through this singer-songwriter lens in several of his songs, including "Ain't No Crime" (from *Piano Man*), "Allentown" (from *The Nylon Curtain*), and "The Downeaster 'Alexa'" (Duchan 2016).

So whether one is considering rock music or songs by singer-songwriters, one of the main assumptions underpinning the listening experience is that what one hears is not a contrived amalgam of sounds designed for the purpose of optimizing profit, but rather the exact music and lyrics that the musician desired in order to express something about his or her experience in the world. Allan Moore calls this the "authenticity of expression," or "first person authenticity," in which the musician "succeeds in conveying the impression that his/her utterance [i.e. music] is one of integrity, that it represents an attempt to communicate in an unmediated form to the audience" (2002, 214). A lack of mediation is important, as scholars have repeatedly identified this value of popular music as one based on the fear that, in a capitalist society, people's distinctiveness—and, by extension, their agency—is threatened by mass culture (including music), whose producers homogenize their products in order to appeal to as many consumers as possible in the pursuit of maximum profit. In the process, whatever genuine expression the products had is co-opted by the dominant class and used for their benefit (Hamm 1995, 23). In other words, because people fear that the sound or message of popular music has been altered to serve those at the top of the corporate ladder, often making all popular music sound basically the same, they value that music they think is the least affected, the least interfered with. Often, critics are the arbiters.

All of this matters for Joel because it helps to explain some of the critical negativity toward his work. The variety of influences that could be heard in his music made it different from much popular music at the time and therefore difficult to categorize and, ultimately, understand. "There's a lot of things in my stuff that is not rock," Joel says. "It's antithetical to rock or just shouldn't happen in rock or hasn't happened in rock. . . . Rock is very orthodox. . . . You go outside of [critics'] parameters and you ain't the real deal no more" (personal interview). Everett explains in more technical terms:

> [Joel's] strong sense of melodic fluency in both vocal and bass lines, his preference of a balanced ensemble over individual virtuosity, his persistent election of the major diatonic scale over the minor pentatonic, his unifying command of both diatonic and chromatic harmonic direction, his taste for varied rhythms and tempos, and his often inquisitive nature in exploring poetic themes—all sharply distinct from rock norms may have led to a judgmental pegging of his work as an overly crafted pop that (for that reason alone) lacks the direct "sincerity" of good ol' physical rock 'n' roll. (2000, 107)

Listeners have different expectations of music depending on how it is categorized. Good rock is different from good jazz, good country, and so on. Because many aspects of Joel's music made it difficult to categorize, critics did not always know how to understand it and how to convey that understanding to readers. One could attempt understanding through comparisons, as critics did. But if critics' primary mode of understanding Joel's songs was to link them to those of others, then it is understandable that they were disappointed by, or simply could not find, a style of Joel's own. And a musician without a style of his own could not, by definition, be authentic—in Joel's words, "the real deal"—one of the chief criteria by which the music of rock musicians and singer-songwriters were judged. Therefore, the critiques of Joel's alleged inauthenticity actually reveal as much about the expectations of the critical establishment as they do about the sound or quality of the songs themselves.

When asked about this charge of inauthenticity, Joel theorized that one cause was his suburban roots:

> A lot of the critics from the music publications were urban. There was kind of an attitude of, "okay, if you're from the country, you're a country artist. If you're from the city, you're an urban artist. But if you're from the suburbs, you're *nothing*. You're vanilla. You don't mean shit. You don't represent anything. . . . You're from nowhere." And I used to kind of feel bad about that. "Oh, I guess I don't have an identity, I'm suburban." . . . I eventually came to terms with it. I said, "Wait a minute. That's who I am. And there's a lot of people like me. There's a lot of kids from the suburbs. They didn't grow up in the city." That doesn't mean they're inauthentic. It doesn't mean they don't have a point of view. (personal interview)

The New York Times' John Rockwell identifies Joel just this way, calling him "an archetypal New York suburbanite" (1978).

Indeed, the concept of suburbia, discussed in chapter 2, is a twentieth-century invention, added to American culture well after the ideas of "city" and "country." The fact that the first suburbs were preplanned and constructed as massive numbers of essentially indistinguishable structures by a single corporation only added to the sense of suburbia as inorganic, imposed from above, and ultimately fake. Moreover, from a music history perspective, critics knew which kinds of music came from the city or sounded like it (Tin Pan Alley, urban blues, rhythm and blues, etc.) and which came from the country or sounded like it (country-western, country, bluegrass, etc.). Rock and roll has been explained as a combination of urban and rural genres (Ennis 1992), but at the time there was no clear idea of what kind of music was germane to these new suburban towns. So it was easy to find a lack of authenticity in a kid from the suburbs, like Joel, whose "vanilla" perspective was neither urban nor rural. With roots in this manufactured, in-between place, what sort of genuine experience could he possibly have to sing about?

"NEXT PHASE, NEW WAVE, DANCE CRAZE, ANYWAYS": MUSICAL BORROWINGS

Plenty, it turns out. As Joel observes, there were many people in the suburbs forging their own life experiences in the 1950s and 1960s. Even as a child, his own included classical piano lessons, trips into Manhattan to take in arts and culture events, lots of books to read (especially after the family television broke), and plenty of records and radio to listen to. As expected, these can all be heard in his music one way or another. Unfortunately for Joel, the degree to which these influences come through is exactly what some writers criticized so harshly.

Joel is not shy about his penchant for drawing on the work of other artists in his own compositions. Everett finds this tendency "unsurprising given Joel's journeyman experience in 1964–68 covering Top 40 hits as a member of the Echoes, the Lost Souls, the Commandos, the Emerald Lords and the Hassles—all Long Island bar bands" whose repertoire included plenty of covers (2000, 105). When asked about his influences, Joel highlights Ray Charles but points out that, in his view, diverse influences are part of what makes American music distinctive.

> No one grows up in a test tube. You know, like Ray Charles was a product of Nat King Cole—he wanted to *be* Nat King Cole. I wanted to be Ray Charles. We're all an amalgam of our influences, and I'm proud of that. I think that's a very *American* trait. We've absorbed so many different historical art forms and we made it our own, which is what makes it unique. Our style is . . . American; it is a combination of influences in music: classical music, marching music, gospel, church music, blues. (personal interview)

Joel's admiration of Charles is evident in his choice of "Ray" for his first daughter's middle name. But it is also expressed musically, perhaps best in "Baby Grand" (from *The Bridge*). This "melancholy blues," a duet with Charles performed on two pianos with a jazz-like accompaniment of bass, light drums, and strings, anthropomorphizes the baby grand piano as a stand-in for a partner or soul mate. "When I'm blue, when

I'm lonely, she comes through," Joel sings in the first verse. Charles chimes in on the second, which describes the itinerant nature of a musician's life, where the instrument is a comforting constant, a touchstone.

The track gives about equal time to Joel and Charles, vocally and pianistically. But making a record with one of his idols made Joel "a bit petrified." Phil Ramone, who produced the recording, reportedly instructed Joel to "go after him," to "get Ray to sing like *Ray*" (Schruers 2014, 184). Indeed, Charles's voice had always impressed Joel. In *Rolling Stone*'s 2008 list of the one hundred greatest singers, he described it as "the most unique voice in popular music. . . . His joy was infectious. . . . When he sings, he's not just singing soulfully. He is imparting his soul. You are hearing something deep within the man" (Joel 2007).

Joel's skill at impressions helped him to follow Ramone's cue, to "get Ray to sing like *Ray*," and one hears some of Charles's inflections in Joel's vocal performance on "Baby Grand." But he was doing impersonations long before that. Biographer Hank Bordowitz writes that Joel developed his ability to mimic others "as a defense against his lack of confidence as a performer." Aside from Charles, Joel's renditions of Paul McCartney and Stevie Wonder "were so spot on that people often found themselves doing a double check to make sure it wasn't really them" (2005, 59). In fact, it was his impression of Joe Cocker that drew out the rain-soaked crowd at the Mar Y Sol festival in Puerto Rico in April 1972, creating what the *New York Times* called the event's "first real excitement" (Heckman 1972). Biographers have identified this as a turning point in Joel's career, when the generally shy piano player came into his own as a performer (Bordowitz 2005, 59–60; Schruers 2014, 82–83; Smith 2007, 99–100).

Frith writes that we all unthinkingly make associations between sounds and meaning that affect our future listening or, in the case of a composer, composing: "No sort of popular musician can make music from scratch" (1987, 148). Thus, Joel is certainly not the first or only popular musician to draw on the work of others. Much of The Beatles' early records, for example, draw explicitly on American rhythm and blues, including covers Chuck Berry's "Roll Over Beethoven," Little Richard's "Long Tall Sally," and the Isley Brothers' "Twist and Shout." Even as the Quarry Men (the name of a pre-Beatles skiffle group that included John Lennon, Paul McCartney, and George Harrison), they were playing American country and western songs by Hank Williams and rockabilly songs by Carl Perkins. The group also covered songs by Jerry Lee Lewis, Fats Domino, Les Paul and Mary Ford, Peggy Lee, and Big Joe Turner (Everett 2001, 16, 40). Later in their career, The Beatles continued to embrace diverse styles. For example, "Lennon and McCartney wished to have a soul arrangement for the horns" on "Got to Get You into My Life," writes Everett. "The brass sonority . . . rings of a Muscle Shoals production, but the lines . . . lean more toward Motown slickness," as does the rhythm McCartney plays on the bass (1999, 39).

Popular music traditions before rock and roll also leaned on other styles, contemporaneous and older. George Gershwin's Tin Pan Alley song "Swanee" (1919) quoted from Stephen Foster's minstrel hit "Old Folks at Home" (1851), in both lyrics and melody. Gershwin's pop music was then borrowed by musicians in the jazz world, where any piece using the sequence of chords from his "I've Got Rhythm" (1930) is called a "rhythm changes tune." Examples include Duke Ellington's "Cotton Tail" (1940) and Dizzy Gillespie's "Salt Peanuts" (1945).

By midcentury, one of the primary business models of the popular music industry involved copying songs that were already hits. For example, the Chords' March 1954 recording of the song "Sh-Boom," which reached number two on the R&B chart and number nine on the pop chart, helped launch the doo-wop craze (an a cappella vocal style that Joel would later embrace on "The Longest Time," from *An Innocent Man*). The black group from the Bronx recorded the song for Cat Records, a subsidiary of Atlantic Records. Toward the end of that same summer, the Crew Cuts, a white group from Toronto, recorded the same song for Mercury Records. That version also reached the top of the charts. In cases like this, the fact that a song had been previously recorded—and successful—was not cause for concern. Instead, it was evidence of the song's appeal and motivation for its embrace (Miller 1999, 73–79). A similar approach can be found in hip-hop music in the decades around the turn of the twenty-first century, where musicians routinely used sounds from earlier records in the process of composing their own songs, a technique called sampling. The practice led Neil Strauss (1997) of *The New York Times* to ask, "Sampling Is (a) Creative or (b) Theft?" So whether coping specific songs or recordings (or parts thereof), or styles in a more general sense, imitation is integral to the history of popular music.

The classical world is full of stylistic imitations too. The composers Joel often mentions in interviews—including J. S. Bach, Beethoven, Brahms, Chopin, Haydn, and Schumann—regularly borrowed from each other, as has been well documented by music historians. Schumann's *Fantasie* in C Major, op. 17 (1836) draws on two of Beethoven's works, *An die ferne Geliebte* (1816) and the Symphony No. 7 in A Major (1811–1812). And in Schumann's song cycle *Dichterliebe*, op. 48 (1840), one can hear the influence of Beethoven's late String Quartet in C-sharp Minor, op. 131 (1826) (Marston 1991, 248, 252–63). The finale of Brahms's last symphony, No. 4 (1884–1885), features a bass line taken almost directly from the final part of an early Bach cantata, *Nach dir, Herr, verlanget mich*, BWV 150 (c. 1707) (Frisch 2003, 130–40). Indeed, in a detailed article on musical borrowing, quotation, and adaptation in the classical and Romantic eras, Charles Rosen illuminates the musical relationships between many of the works of Beethoven, Brahms, Chopin, Haydn, and Mozart. Ultimately, the term "influence" seems the most useful for describing these connections (Rosen 1980).

All these examples show that what Joel did, in drawing on the styles and from the songs that influenced him, was something that many composers and songwriters had already done. To discount Joel's music because of the influence others have had on it—which the composer himself acknowledges—but not do the same thing for The Beatles or some of the most significant names in the classical canon is problematic. Indeed, one could argue (as this book does) that it is these very connections to the past that make Joel's music important to the history of popular music. They illustrate the varied lines of influence that converge in this musician's body of work. So for Joel to have borrowed from or been influenced by classical music or other popular music indicates not a lack of compositional skill, but instead that he is merely in good company.

"WHEN WILL YOU WRITE YOUR MASTERPIECE?": BACH, THE BEATLES, AND BILLY JOEL

Music from the classical and Romantic eras and the music of The Beatles are the strongest influences on Joel. From the most overt borrowing (like the Beethoven melody found in "This Night") to more subtle uses of The Beatles' style (such as instrumental choices and vocal techniques in "Through the Long Night" and "Laura"), Joel has described his use of classical and British-invasion rock and roll as a lifelong pursuit. "I was always writing classical music," he told Bill DeMain, "even the popular songs I wrote" (qtd. in Everett 2000, 111). Meanwhile, he "started writing ersatz Beatles songs" at age thirteen, when The Beatles came to the United States, he remarked in a 2012 interview (WNEW). Thomas MacFarlane hears Joel's efforts to blend The Beatles with other influences as a kind of "musical alchemy" that "resulted in a unique and highly original compositional voice" (2016).

These were certainly not the only styles he embraced. Ken Bielen likens "Until the Night" (from *52nd Street*) to the Righteous Brothers, observing how that song was "a precursor to the ground Joel would cover on the *An Innocent Man* album," where he describes the hit, "Tell Her About It" (discussed in chapter 5) as a tribute to mid-1960s Chicago and Detroit soul productions (2011, 136, 65). But, by Joel's own admission, classical music and The Beatles inspire much of his work, justifying the focus here. Everett's 2000 article, "The Learned vs. The Vernacular in the Songs of Billy Joel," is the most thorough study of these influences and provides much of the background to this discussion.

"Nocturne," an instrumental from *Cold Spring Harbor*, is one of the earliest of Joel's classically infused compositions. Indeed, *nocturne* is a genre of classical piano music, suggestive of night, which is usually "quiet and meditative in character" (Brown and Hamilton) and exhibits a "slow and dreamy nature in which a graceful, highly embellished melody in the right hand is accompanied by a broken-chord pattern in the left" (Bellingham). Bielen also invokes the night as he describes the song as a "respite from the glare of day," when "Joel's piano glides through the night" (2011, 23). Intending to stoke excitement for the album, the original Family Productions press release describes the song as "a subtle knockout."

The first to write nocturnes was the Irish composer and pianist John Field (1782–1827). Later in the nineteenth century, many composers, including pianists Franz Liszt and Schumann, embraced the genre, but "one composer stands out as having made a truly significant contribution to the genre: Chopin" (Rowland 1992, 49). Like many of Chopin's character pieces, Joel's "Nocturne" is brief and contains a minimal number of musical ideas organized in three formal sections, ABA. During each, Joel's piano adopts the procedure Jane Bellingham identifies: melody in the right hand, broken accompanimental chords in the left. The B section, starting about a minute and a half into the track, is more stirring, featuring right-hand chords, a faster tempo, and a louder dynamic. The excitement dissipates when the main melody, the A section, returns about twenty seconds later. But while Everett identifies "hints of Chopin" in "Why Judy Why" (from *Cold Spring Harbor*), "I've Loved These Days" (from *Turnstiles*), "Honesty" (from *52nd Street*), and "Lullabye (Goodnight My Angel)" (from *River of Dreams*), he does not hear the influence of the composer in "Nocturne," whose figuration he attributes to Henry Mancini and whose harmony he hears as reminiscent of André Popp (2000, 112–13).

Still, Joel's "Nocturne" may be identifiable to some listeners as classical music because it is a purely instrumental piece. After all, within pop and rock, those are uncommon (although it is not the only one Joel recorded; see *Streetlife Serenade*'s "The Mexican Connection" and "Root Beer Rag"). Like much Romantic piano music, it also contains a flexible approach to tempo called *rubato*, which involves subtly speeding up and slowing down for expressivity. (By contrast, most mid- and late-twentieth-century popular music tends to maintain a steady tempo.) Finally, the ABA form of "Nocturne" is also common to many classical works.

The relationship between Joel's style and classical music is subtler in "James." The song opens with the soft timbre of the Fender Rhodes, on which Joel plays three iterations of the opening phrase. Although the first comprises mostly block chords, the repetitions add more elaborate ornamentations to the melody, played in the right hand. The electric bass and drums, played using brushes for a gentler sound, enter at the verse; later, Richie Cannata offers a solo on the soprano saxophone. "James" does not adopt the character of a Romantic piano piece. It eschews *rubato* and its form is closer to a conventional song, with its clearly identifiable verses, refrains, and bridges.

In Everett's analysis, there are two styles at work in "James." On one hand, the more "learned" style of the title character is portrayed through classical elements. Joel's keyboard and Doug Stegmeyer's bass line are highly contrapuntal—their melodic movement is coordinated with and plays off of the melodic movement of the other instrumental parts—and "highly reminiscent of Bach." The lines are also ornamented in a Baroque fashion, with anticipations (notes played before the listener expects them), suspensions (noted held longer to clash against the underlying harmony, then resolved), and sequences (combinations of notes that are repeated higher or lower). On the other hand, the more down-to-earth "vernacular" style of Joel's narrator is communicated through jazz elements, especially in the song's chorus, where Joel's singing is a bit less formal and the accompanying chords are used in more modern combinations (Everett 2000, 120). Joel agrees with Everett's findings, joking "it's almost Pachelbel's Canon" (personal interview), in reference to the well-known Canon and Gigue in D by the seventeenth-century German organist and composer Johann Pachelbel that almost any piano student in the latter twentieth century learned at some point. Joel's remark is not meant literally, as Pachelbel's piece was scored for three violins accompanied by harpsichord, organ, or a small ensemble of similar instruments. Rather, he is using Pachelbel's piece, and its ubiquity, as a symbol for classical music writ large, adding that he too hears Baroque elements in "James."

The contrast between learned and vernacular matches the song's setting, where Joel's narrator contrasts his own life choices with those of his friend, whom Fred Schruers identifies as Jim Bosse, one of Joel's high-school bandmates in the Echoes (2014, 40). "I went on the road," Joel sings. "You pursued an education." He wonders whether that path was ultimately satisfying: is James happy? Does he "find release"? Looking back, he questions the wisdom of James's choices in lines like, "Are you still in school living up to expectations?" and "Will you always stay someone else's dream of who you are?" Although James dutifully follows the rules and meets his family's expectations, such obedience has not yet led him to success, leading the singer to ask, "When will you write your masterpiece?" Ultimately, Joel's narrator imparts his own wisdom, presumably learned from years "on the road": "Do what's good for you or you're not good for anybody."

As it questions life choices, "James" avoids outright critique—even if the Beatles-like background vocals offer a musical sigh, "head shaking with disappointment," during the chorus as Joel sings the title lyric (Everett 2000, 120). The irony, as Everett points out, is that while "the writer's innocence is the singer's target," the singer himself "is essentially advising James to ignore the advice of others." Some have interpreted such advice as an indication that the singer himself was also questioning his own career choices (Jones 2011, 11). In hindsight, Joel has his regrets about the song—not about its message, but the way it is conveyed: "I wanted to be empathetic and I found myself being preachy" (personal interview).

If "James" is subtle in its use of classical elements, "This Night" is not. That song does not evoke a classical style as much as it borrows, wholesale, a melody directly from the second movement of Beethoven's Piano Sonata No. 8 in C Minor, op. 13 (1797–1799), known as the Sonata Pathétique. Joel is upfront about the source of the melody, listing "L.V. Beethoven" in the credits to *An Innocent Man*. Yet stylistically, the song also bears a strong doo-wop influence, with typical background lyrics (such as "shoo-wop"), a deep vocal bass sound, and what Bielen calls "vocal histrionics [that] reflect the doo-wop aesthetic" (2011, 66).

Since Beethoven's melody only appears in the song's chorus, one might make a similar argument about "This Night" as Everett did with "James": that the distinction in musical elements mirrors a distinction within the world created by the song. The doo-wop elements are clearest in the verses, where the narrator describes how he did not expect to fall in love and resists the notion ("Didn't I say I wasn't ready for romance? Didn't we promise we would only be friends?"), bringing an amateurish quality to the music that might suggest innocence and youthfulness. But when the chorus arrives and Joel sings Beethoven's soaring melody over a more active accompaniment, the lyrics transport the dancing couple to a distant nirvana where time stands still ("Tomorrow is such a long time away; this night can last forever"). Perhaps the temporal distance between the song's mid-twentieth-century setting and the late-eighteenth-century origin of Beethoven's melody is a sonic embodiment of the perceptual distance these unexpected lovers put between themselves and the rest of the world during their moments together. It would not be the only time Joel used musical elements to connote distance (see the discussion of "State of Grace" in chapter 5).

No discussion of classical influences on Joel's music would be complete without mention of *Fantasies & Delusions: Music for Solo Piano*, Joel's last album of original music. Consisting entirely of solo piano pieces in the Romantic style, it was composed by Joel and performed by pianist Richard Joo. That the album contains only instrumental music should come as no surprise, considering the last track on Joel's previous album, *River of Dreams*—his final collection of songs in the popular style—was "Famous Last Words."

Joel clearly frames *Fantasies & Delusions* in classical terms. The cover art uses, with permission, the green border and lettering against a khaki background that graces many of the classical scores published by G. Schirmer. The names of the pieces are fitting as well. Each contains an opus number, just like how works by Beethoven, Chopin, and other composers are numbered. Moreover, many of the tracks bear names invoking classical genres, such as waltz ("Opus 2, Waltz No. 1 (Nunley's Carousel)"), aria ("Opus 7, Aria (Grand Canal)"), and invention ("Opus 6, Invention in C Minor"). Recognizing the classical underpinnings of many of Joel's earlier songs, James Hunter (2005) calls *Fantasies & Delusions* "in essence, Joel's roots album."

If Joel intended *Fantasies & Delusions* to be classical music, was it heard that way? According to critics, yes. Writing in the *Philadelphia Inquirer*, Peter Dorbin (2001) called the album a "reworking of the romantics: Schumann, Chopin, Scriabin, Tchaikovsky, Rachmaninoff." Tim Page of the *Washington Post* ventures that Joel's pieces would be accepted by audiences of classical music, whether listening in "a London palm court or Parisian salon in 1901" or to Washington's local classical radio station a hundred years later (2001). The album reached number 83 on the *Billboard* 200 chart, a feat for a classical work without a single vocal track. More impressive, however, was its performance on the classical chart, where it spent sixty weeks after its debut at number one.

Certainly the styles of the Romantic era strongly influence *Fantasies & Delusions*. That period in the history of Western classical music is remarkable for the explosion in compositional activity focusing on the piano. No wonder, then, that many of the composers of the day rank among Joel's favorites, whom critics often name in their reviews. Page contends that the "piano waltzes bear the mark of Chopin," while "the ghost of Franz Liszt dominates 'Reverie.'" Geoff Brown (2001), writing in the *Times* of London, hears evocations of "Schumann's spirit of fantasy," while the "harmonies drift toward Debussy and Satie." (Other influences include J.S. Bach in "Invention in C Minor," discussed below.)

Aside from just writing for piano, many Romantic composers also embraced program music, the term for pieces that paint a picture or tell a story using music (usually without lyrics). The actual programs ranged in specificity from detailed plots to mere impressions or suggestions. As noted in chapter 2, composers of this era also embraced the idea of music representing places, a kind of program music. In many cases, the titles composers give their pieces offer clues to the program. On *Fantasies & Delusions*, Joel does the same. "Opus 2, Waltz No. 1 (Nunley's Carousel)" is, according to Bielen, "a lively, carefree, and playful interpretation of the amusement park ride"; "Opus 7, Aria (Grand Canal)" evokes an image of Venice, Italy; and "Opus 1, Soliloquy (On a Separation)" conveys a "conversation . . . that Joel has with himself about love and romance" (2011, 89), an interpretation with which Joel does not agree (personal interview).

Bach lived from 1685 to 1750, before the idea of program music was popularized by the nineteenth-century Romantics, so it comes as no surprise that Joel's piece most strongly bearing his influence, "Invention in C Minor," lacks the sort of descriptive title that would hint at the scene or plot conveyed by the music. Instead, Joel relies on the term "invention" to guide listeners' expectations. Bach wrote many of these kinds of pieces, which usually featured two melodic lines that played off of each other contrapuntally, imitating melodic and rhythmic gestures in a carefully articulated duet. Joel's invention follows suit, featuring a pair of melodic lines, one in each hand. They move quickly at times, weaving about so that a melodic rise in one is echoed shortly thereafter by the other. The pitches do not necessarily match exactly, but the repetition of musical ideas is clear. About halfway through the minute-long piece, after a cadence on the tonic (C-minor) chord, the melody from the song's beginning, which in its first phrase outlined a C-minor chord's three pitches (C, E-flat, and G) starts again, this time five steps higher and sketching a G-minor chord (G, B-flat, and D). This kind of transposition is common in Baroque music. In essence, one hears the same musical idea as before but expressed in a new way, using new pitches. The journey from G-minor back to C-minor constitutes the second half of the piece, which concludes simply but satisfyingly with both hands ending on C.

Unlike the rest of the album's compositions, "Invention in C Minor" features no chords, no harmonic moments when three or more piano keys are played simultaneously. Instead, all one hears are the two complementary melody lines. In addition to being a staple of much Romantic piano composition, chords also underpin nearly all of Joel's popular-style songs. So although "James" bears some moments of Baroque-style counterpoint, "Invention in C Minor" marks the furthest Joel ever ventures from his more common and comfortable melody-and-accompaniment compositional style.

Although it attained commercial success, *Fantasies & Delusions* was not a critical darling. While faring better than other pop songwriters' attempts at classical music—Page contrasts it with "the bloated, embarrassing claptrap" of McCartney's "classical excursions" (2001)—reviews of the work frequently fall back on the familiar trope of authenticity, sometimes dressed up in terms of originality, or a lack thereof. "Joel has not yet begun to transcend his influences," Page remarks, ultimately composing "a garland of homages to some important masters." In a similar vein, Dorbin writes, "There's nothing original here, no discernable compositional voice," just adaptations, mimicry, copies—choose your term—of late nineteenth-century styles (2001). Joel is at his best, Page claims, when sticking to his pop songs, which "are at least specifically and recognizably his." In contrast, "the music on *Fantasies & Delusions* could be anybody at all." He concludes with his hope that, should there be a next time, Joel "will not so fiercely suppress his pop background."

These critiques not only rehash the arguments made about Joel's earlier songs, but come remarkably close to the discourse Timothy Taylor observes in "world music" criticism. There too, reviewers have difficulty when musicians depart from their roots and embrace new styles, as did Senegalese musician Youssou N'Dour when he used Western musical elements, such as a string quartet and rapping, on his album *The Guide (Wommat)* (1994). In response, one critic wrote that N'Dour's music "is at its most spectacular when soaring over the rhythms of his native country, in his native language, over his native rhythms" (qtd. in Taylor 1997, 135), an argument that grants the existence of N'Dour's Senegalese culture but simultaneously reprimands him for leaving it behind and adopting aspects of Western culture. In the case of Joel's record, the tension lies not between Western and non-Western musical cultures, but instead between two strains *within* Western musical culture; defenders of the classical tradition acknowledge the influence of classical composers on Joel's pieces, but at the same time discursively keep him in his place in the pop(ular) sphere. "Take away his Chopin and Schumann," Dorbin concludes, "and Joel would be little more than scales and arpeggios." "He is still an apprentice," Page writes, "one so determined to do nothing wrong that he has hardly a chance of making anything new." Yet Ben Folds, a piano-rocker of the generation following Joel's, disagrees colorfully: *"Fantasies & Delusions* . . . is very underrated and unfairly dismissed. . . . We should applaud it and not discourage one of our great 20th century composers to get back to the 'Uptown Girl' box and shut up. It makes me want to cut a bitch" (qtd. in Bacher 2015).

Aside from classical music, The Beatles have influenced Joel's music most profoundly. Lennon, McCartney, Harrison, and Ringo Starr (along with producer George Martin) together formed the English group that has been called "the greatest and most influential act of the rock era" (Unterberger). Beginning with *Please Please Me* (1963), through their arrival in the United States in 1964, to their final release, *Let It Be* (1970), the group enjoyed record-breaking sales, critical successes, and myriad artistic innovations. Within the field of popular music studies, they are canonical, with countless research articles (e.g., Platoff 2005; Price 1997; Wagner 2004), an entire issue of the journal *Popular Music* (1987), book-length studies (e.g., Everett 1999, 2001; Lewisohn 2010; Womack 2007), and even a collection of detailed transcriptions of their recordings intended for study (Beatles et al. 1993).

Joel first encountered The Beatles on television on the evening of February 9, 1964. "I saw them on *The Ed Sullivan Show* and that just knocked me out. . . . That's when it all took shape. I said, 'That's what I want to do!'" (qtd. in Sheff and Sheff 1982). Until that time, he had been primarily exposed to classical music in piano lessons, plus some Elvis and rhythm and blues on records and radio. "By the time of the British Invasion, I'd been defining my musical personality *against* rather than within classical music," he told Schruers (2014, 32). Throughout his career, The Beatles' influence has been observed by critics (e.g., Holden 1978; Nelson 1980; Cioe 1982) and scholars (Everett 2000). Joel himself admits it:

> I really liked *Magical Mystery Tour* [1967] and *Sgt. Pepper's Lonely Hearts Club Band* [1967] and all the crazy stuff they were doing. *Abbey Road* [1969]—I mean, *Abbey Road* is just a bunch of song fragments sewn together by George Martin, but brilliantly done.

"What does it mean?" Who gives a shit what it means! It *sounds* great! . . . It gets me and it intrigues me and compels me. (personal interview)

Although the Beatles' influence appears early in Joel's catalog—Bielen hears a "McCartney-like" vocal on *Cold Spring Harbor*'s "You Can Make Me Free" (2011, 21) and MacFarlane perceives echoes of "For No One," from The Beatles' *Revolver* (1966), and the title track of *Let It Be* (1970) on *Cold Spring Harbor*'s "She's Got A Way" (2016)—it can perhaps be best heard in three tracks from the middle of his career: "Through the Long Night," "Laura," and "Scandinavian Skies."

"Through the Long Night" features a plucked acoustic guitar, which creates a more intimate feeling—perhaps of a "peaceful lullaby" (Scott 2000, 40)—than the arena-oriented numbers of the rest of *Glass Houses*. Many of the song's musical aspects seem drawn from mid-1960s Beatles cues. Thickly harmonized vocals recall passages in Lennon's "I'm Only Sleeping," from *Revolver*, during which several layers of voices sing with and behind his lead, using lyrics or an "ooo" vowel sound. Joel's background vocal tracks do the same, with even greater emphasis on moving lines than the Beatles song.

The piano, bass, drums, and a French horn fill out the accompaniment on "Through the Long Night," much like on "For No One," where a clavichord can be heard instead of the acoustic guitar. In both songs, the choice of instruments is appropriate. The clavichord/guitar and piano provide the background chords, supported by the bass; the drums help to keep the beat but avoid an overpowering effect by sticking to the kick drum, rimshots, and light cymbal work; and the horn offers a tender timbre (as opposed to, say, a sharp stab on a trumpet) with plenty of dynamics to lead listeners gently into and out of melodic phrases. Additionally, both songs consist of two formal sections: a verse, which sits lower in Joel's and McCartney's ranges and largely tells the story, and a bridge, when the accompaniment is more active and the vocal melody is more reaching and dramatic.

The lyrics to "For No One" relate the sad story of a romantic relationship maintained beyond its expiration: the male character's feelings for his lover are unrequited. Performed in the key of C, the song's final chord conveys a lack of closure as it is not the expected tonic chord but instead one conventionally used to prepare for the tonic, along with a suspension that is "the musical equivalent of a sigh" (Riley 1988, 194, qtd. in Everett 1999, 56). "Through the Long Night" does not feature the same kind of uneven commitment amid its promises of comfort. It is sung from the perspective of a male character that clearly cares for his partner ("it's all right; sleep tight through the long night with me") and is satisfied that she cares for him too, even if she does not say so ("the way you hold me is all that I need to know"). The source of her nightmares is unclear, although their romantic nature is implied ("I didn't start it; you're brokenhearted from a long, long time ago"). Finally, Joel's song ends on a satisfying tonic chord, musically conveying calm and a sense of closure. Thus, although heartbreak is a central motivator in both "For No One" and "Through the Long Night," the Beatles' song is premised on estrangement, expressed in both lyrics and music, whereas Joel's is one of embrace.

The use of background voices is a distinctive feature of *The Nylon Curtain*'s "Laura" (also discussed in the previous chapter). Joel has remarked that that album in particular was intended to "go back and pick up" where *Sgt. Pepper's Lonely Hearts Club Band* left off musically (DeCurtis 1986, "Rolling Stone Interview," 78). On *Sgt. Pepper's* "Getting Better," one hears the kind of background voices Joel previously adopted on "Through the Long Night," but with an important difference. Whereas on "Through the Long Night" (and also "I'm Only Sleeping"), those voices sang with or behind the lead vocal, supporting it but not distracting the listener from the main melody line, on "Getting Better" and "Laura" the background voices are more active. They sing discernible words, echoing lyrics or providing their own in what seems like a response to or comment on the principal melody. About half a minute into "Getting Better," for example, as McCartney's lead vocal cheerily proclaims, "It's getting better all the time," Lennon and Harrison remark smartly, "Can't get no worse!" In the final verse to "Laura," Joel's character sings angrily, "Laura loves me even if I don't care." The background voices, also sung by Joel, echo the title lyric immediately after the lead sings it and then parrots "loves me" two beats later. At the end of the phrase, they taunt, "If I don't care ah-ah," holding out the open vowels with rather Beatle-esque inflection and executing a sighing gesture ("ah-ah") that would be at home on a Beatles record. The fact that the lead vocal is double-tracked for the entire song is itself a Beatle-esque move, heard on numbers like "I Want to

Hold Your Hand" (1963), "We Can Work It Out" (1965), and "Across the Universe" (1970), as well as much of *Sgt. Pepper's*. On "Laura," it lends Joel's voice a menacing, angry, and frustrated quality (Duchan 2015, 180).

Most biographies of Joel use *The Nylon Curtain*'s "Scandinavian Skies" to illustrate how The Beatles, especially Lennon, influenced his style. The song has been compared to "A Day in the Life" (1967) and "I Am the Walrus" (1967) (Scott 2000, 48; Holden 1982). Bielen likens the string parts to those used by Martin, Joel's vocal delivery to Lennon, and the percussion to Starr (2011, 62). Schruers mentions how, at the time Joel began recording *The Nylon Curtain*, he "came to the realization that the Beatles had begun using the studio as an instrument around the time of the *Revolver* album" (2014, 155); "we played the recording studio" while making *The Nylon Curtain*, Joel later remarked (personal interview).

Indeed, many of the songs on *Revolver* and *Sgt. Pepper's* employed new or distinctive studio techniques, such as playing a recorded sound backward (a trick Martin and The Beatles did not invent, but which was uncommon in popular music at the time). The same technique is used on the strings of "Scandinavian Skies." And while Joel uses the sound of jet aircraft and an airport announcement to help set the scene, the announcement is muffled to the point of unintelligibility as if to emphasize the song's abstruse nature—not unlike "I Am the Walrus" and "All You Need Is Love" (1967). The psychedelic atmosphere cultivated in the accompaniment to "Scandinavian Skies," for example through the meandering string line against the piano's tolling Cs, can be compared with "Strawberry Fields Forever" (1967) and may suggest a drug-induced haze similar to other musical expressions of psychedelia. After all, by his own admission, "Scandinavian Skies" "was a drug trip," a metaphor congruent with the song's theme of grueling travel. "[It] scared the crap out of me. . . . It was all very surrealistic and macabre and bizarre." Without skipping a beat, he immediately links that thought with The Beatles' "A Day in the Life," singing "I'd love to turn you on," complete with Lennon's eerie, extended trill that, in his view, communicated a sense of chilly morbidity. "I took a page from them for that, I think: this is so nightmarish and so bizarre and so surrealistic." The angular string line and marshal snare drum, introduced at the beginning of "Scandinavian Skies" and heard throughout the track, aim for the same effect: "There's something weird—it's not bad yet—but there's something a little weird going on. . . . And the drums are marching. . . . You're inevitably going into the drum cesspool" (personal interview).

Of course, as significant as The Beatles were, they were part of larger trends in mid-twentieth-century popular music. Thus, beyond studio techniques, Joel's use of word play, for example, can be traced to late-1960s rock more broadly. For instance, in "Scandinavian Skies," the line, "Who could say what was left and where was right?" bears poetic similarities to lyrics by the Young Rascals and the Beach Boys (Bielen 2011, 61–62). So the song can interpreted not only as an homage to The Beatles in particular, but also to the more general milieu of the 1960s, a decade of increasing political complexity—which Joel's lyrics encapsulate—as the Cold War accelerated, the Cuban Missile Crisis unfolded, and American involvement in Vietnam escalated.

"THOUGH I'VE LOST QUITE A LOT I AM STILL IN CONTROL": BILLY JOEL RESPONDS

So far this chapter has explored the critiques often made of Joel's music—that he channeled contemporaneous and older artists and styles—and the ideological background and historical context behind them. It then took a look at the traditions of borrowing and influence in popular and classical musics before examining the ways Joel borrowed from and was influenced by those styles. This section returns to the tension between Joel and his critics, as well as between Joel and other actors within the larger entertainment industry (agents, managers, record companies, etc.). As the short biographical sketch in chapter 1 describes, Joel has certainly had his troubles with those parts of what Joni Mitchell once called, in "Free Man in Paris" (1974), "the star-maker machinery behind the popular song." Although his first record deal was less than favorable, the worst was his discovery of Frank Weber's alleged theft and mismanagement, a betrayal that would surface on "The Great Wall of China" (from *River of Dreams*, see chapter 5). The chapter then concludes by placing Joel's musical borrowings and responses in a wider theoretical context, showing how they can be understood as examples of "intertextuality" and that, by doing so, his compositions can be better seen as part of broader trends in music history rather than an exception to them.

Several of Joel's songs reveal his attitude toward the music industry and the expectations the critics had for his music. One early example is "Everybody Loves You Now," which is described in the original Family Productions press release announcing *Cold Spring Harbor* as "simply an honest statement of love, with an easily accessible depth and meaning." The modified strophic song features Joel singing to someone who has achieved fame. Yet that kind of success changes people, he warns: "You have lost your innocence somehow, but" at least "everybody loves you now." The title lyric thus serves as a stinging reminder to be careful what you wish for.

On the original recording, Joel's piano part includes fast alternations between pitches, a musical embodiment of the frenetic excitement of the rising star to whom he sings. On *Songs in the Attic*, a quickly strummed acoustic guitar adds to this effect. The pace of the song slows in only two moments, the cadences ending the two bridge sections. In the first, Joel complains that his "friend" scarcely has time for him. In the second, he laments that his "friend" never seems to return home. In both, the band holds out longer notes—a sharp contrast to the verses full of fast piano work and strumming—while Joel sings the punchlines: "They await your reply, but between you and me and the Staten Island Ferry . . . so do I" in the first bridge and "But you ain't got the time to go to Cold Spring Harbor . . . no more" in the second.

Joel's treatment of the entertainment industry continues on "The Entertainer." The lyrics describe a musician as he builds his career, recognizing the fickle taste of the public and the potentially fleeting quality of fame. He understands the landscape: he is just "another serenader" who today may have "won your hearts," but he knows that he may be easily forgotten if his music fails to "stay on the charts." Subsequent verses discuss learning from his mistakes, the way the excitement of touring fades into monotony, the pressure to meet the expectations of the companies backing him, and the futility of seeing his hard work (mis)handled on its way to radio airplay (the line about his song being cut "down to 3:05" in length for the radio is a direct reference to the fate of "Piano Man" and therefore an expression of Joel's personal experience of corporate manipulation). The penultimate verse juxtaposes his status as "the idol of my age" with the realization that such status is tenuous: "If I go cold, I won't get sold; I get put in the back in the discount rack like another can of beans."

"The Entertainer" begins with a strummed acoustic guitar, which plays throughout, and a synthesizer, whose jumpy melody appears in the introduction and the interludes between verses. As the song progresses, more instruments are added: drums and pedal steel in the second verse, more guitars in the third, banjo in the fourth, a more active piano part in the fifth, and so on. This has the effect of a gradual crescendo, of increasing energy as the character's career gains momentum. Yet beneath the growing excitement of the music, "The Entertainer" remains a cautionary tale. In fact, both "Everybody Loves You Now" and "The Entertainer" are musical fables, revealing the dark underside of the entertainment industry.

"It's Still Rock and Roll to Me" demonstrates Joel's continued concern with the industry and its obsession with all things new and also shows him responding to his critics in his music. The lyrics are structured as a back-and-forth exchange between Joel and another character, although he sings both; the voice responding to him is double-tracked. Joel laments changing public taste in fashion ("your tie's too wide"), cars ("it's out of style"), and social circles ("they're out of touch"). In each case, he returns to the tried-and-true, preferring an older version to the newest thing. In musical terms, it is rock and roll over whatever the latest trend is (which he names as new wave, a 1980s outgrowth of 1970s punk). The accompaniment is spare, with a muted rhythm guitar, an electric bass, and the drums providing much of the musical backing. A saxophone takes a solo before the last verse.

The song's bridge opens up a bit, adding a more active off-beat guitar line and abandoning the back-and-forth lyrical pattern in favor of more direct commentary. Here, Joel remarks on the music press rather obliquely: "It doesn't matter what they say in the papers," he declares, "'cause it's always been the same old scene." He also makes what Bill Smith describes as a jab at *Rolling Stone* (2007, 171–72), as he sings, "You can't get the sound from a story in a magazine."

Later in Joel's catalog, "Getting Closer" heralds his efforts to move beyond the frustrations the industry has visited upon him. He calls out the "con men and their acrobats" who duped him when he was younger and more innocent, and although "if you count up their percentages" they may be "getting rich," they "haven't taken everything" from him.

Indeed, much of the song is devoted to a resurrection of the soul, where worldly losses matter little in a bigger philosophical equation. "What was ripped off by professionals was not all that it seems," he sings in the second verse. "While I must live up to contracts, I did not give up my dreams." He chooses to see these events not as moments of failure but as "experience." Ultimately, though he may not have figured it all out, he is "getting closer" to contentment. Steve Winwood appears on the Hammond organ on "Getting Closer," lending the track an "upbeat, Traffic-like swing" that gives the recording a sense of optimism not often found in Joel's songs (DeCurtis 1986, "The Bridge"). It is a more balanced perspective that acknowledges challenges, mistakes, and regrets, but maintains a generally positive outlook that stands in contrast to the tone of much of his earlier songs about the music business.

These four examples of Joel's songs about the entertainment business illustrate some level of consistency in his perspective, as audience tastes are constantly changing (and not always in predictable or comprehensible ways) and the multiple parts of the industry all take their cut. Yet the change in tone evident in "Getting Closer" also shows how, by the mid-1980s, Joel's viewpoint was shifting—or at least he was trying to shift it himself. Still, the rage of "The Great Wall of China" indicates that the sting of Joel's experiences with the industry had not completely faded.

If there is a conclusion to be drawn from this examination of Joel's influences and musical statements about the entertainment industry, it is that no one escapes their historical context; no one's voice is purely original, free from the effect of other earlier and contemporaneous voices. Such a view fits nicely with the literary concept of dialogism, which refers to the way earlier texts affect later ones—namely, that an interaction with what has come before is unavoidable. (Here, "texts," or "utterances," mean not only things people say, but any kind of expression, including music.) The theory was developed by the Russian philosopher Mikhail Bakhtin, who writes: "In the makeup of almost every utterance spoken by a social person . . . a significant number of words can be identified that are implicitly or explicitly admitted as someone else's. . . . Within the arena of almost every utterance an intense interaction and struggle between one's own and another's word is being waged" (1981, 354). Later thinkers, such as Julia Kristeva, have applied Bakhtin's dialogism to the idea of intertextuality to demonstrate that, in essence, no text exists in a vacuum. It has also been applied to music, specifically in the case of jazz, where Ingrid Monson calls it "intermusicality," referring to "the particular ways in which music and, more generally, sound itself can refer to the past and offer social commentary" (1996, 97). Joel would probably understand. He told Schruers:

> I love to play around with genres—blues, doo-wop, a waltz—and because of that, I've often been accused of being derivative. You know what? Hell *yes*, I'm derivative. Nobody grows up in a test tube. We're all influenced by what's come before us. But what is it that you're always drawn back to? What is it that speaks to your soul? (qtd. in Schruers 2014, 326)

If one accepts intermusicality as a foundation of musical-artistic creation, then the fact that Joel acknowledges his influences so overtly, musically and in interviews, is not a problem. If all music is intermusical and no music is truly pure or wholly original, then an insistence on authenticity makes little sense. Perhaps one can question the *degree* to which any given piece is intermusical, but to dismiss it outright due to its intermusicality would be illogical. Yet, as Joel observes in "Everybody Loves You Now," "The Entertainer," "It's Still Rock and Roll to Me," and "Getting Closer," the music industry (and the entertainment industry more generally) values certain things over others. One is commercial appeal, which was, at certain times in music history and in American (and Western) culture, explained in terms of authenticity. Thus, the tension created by the intermusical nature of Joel's music places it at odds with the prevailing paradigm of twentieth-century popular music criticism.

Ultimately, understanding the intermusicality of Joel's music may not mollify critical arguments about it, but it does offer a more nuanced way of seeing his compositions in the broader scope of music history. And it is to an appreciation of history that the next chapter turns.

7

"THIS IS THE TIME"

A Historically Conscious Composer

One of Billy Joel's distinctions is that he is a particularly historically conscious composer. He is keenly aware of history—musical and otherwise—and incorporates it into his works. Evidence for this thesis has been mounting throughout this book. He incorporates into his songs the sounds and histories of American geography and places, national and international political and social history, social class, relationships in his personal history and historically changing gender roles, as well as compositional styles from across the continuum of music history.

In a way, this is nothing new. There is a long history of music about historical events. One famous example is "The Ballad of Chevy Chase," first printed in approximately 1540 but possibly dating back a hundred years (or more) earlier. It describes a bloody conflict near the English-Scottish border in which the Scottish Earl of Douglas attacked a hunting party, led by Percy, the English Earl of Northumberland, whom he believed was launching an invasion of Scotland. There are also plenty of songs about historic disasters, such as those about the sinking of the *Titanic* in 1912 (see Scanlon, Vandervalk, and Chadwich-Shubat 2011) or about various incidents of violence, including Neil Young's "Ohio" (1970), about the shootings at Kent State University.

Many of Joel's peers also composed songs about important historical events. Bob Dylan's "Hurricane" (1975) addresses the 1967 murder trial and conviction of boxer Rubin "Hurricane" Carter, which Dylan describes as racially motivated and unfair (it was retried in 1976 and dismissed in 1988) (Boehlert 2000). The Police's "Invisible Sun" (1981), about the hunger strikes in Belfast, Northern Ireland, in the 1980s, during the period of conflict with Britain known as "the troubles," is one of several "socially conscious" songs the band would record (see West 2015, 82). While purposely steering clear of a pro-republican stance, U2's "Sunday Bloody Sunday" (1983) also deals with the troubles, describing the 1972 Bloody Sunday incident in which British troops killed civil rights protesters in Derry, Northern Ireland (Rolston 2001, 56–57). The group's similarly successful song, "Pride (In the Name of Love)" (1984), refers to the assassination of Martin Luther King Jr. And while often interpreted as a nationalistic celebration of the United States, the lyrics to Bruce Springsteen's hit "Born in the U.S.A." (1984) in fact critique American involvement in the Vietnam War and the harsh treatment some veterans received upon their return. The tension between the song's anthemic chorus and more desperate narrative verses captures the growing sense of working-class anxiety—which Joel's music also tapped into—in the 1970s and early 1980s (Cowie and Boehm 2006).

So Joel's songs about historical events, such as "Allentown" and "Goodnight Saigon" (from *The Nylon Curtain*) and "Leningrad" and "We Didn't Start the Fire" (from *Storm Front*), do not make him unique as a composer, but instead place him in the good company of his peers, who themselves join a long line of musical reporters of and commenters on significant events in the broad sweep of music history. Looking closer, however, a further distinction can be made, one that does add to Joel's exceptional position within popular music: he writes not only about particular events in history, but about history itself. All the songs mentioned so far are about specific historical events or periods; in fact, such songs are rather common in popular music. However, as will be discussed later, songs about history itself, such as "Two Thousand Years" (from *River of Dreams*) and, of course, "We Didn't Start the Fire," are much more rare. These attempt to engage not with a particular point in time but instead adopt a more comprehensive approach, raising questions about what is to be remembered, how history is created from the string of events that mark time's passing.

The term "historical consciousness" has been used in scholarship for some time. Hayden White (1973), for example, used it to describe "the dominant modes of historical thinking" (38) and "the deep structure of historical imagination" (40). For Peter Seixas (2004), historical consciousness pertains to the role of historical education in democracy. More recently, John Paul Meyers (2015) has applied the concept directly to popular music in his study of tribute bands, where he uses it to mean the way "the past in popular music is a proper subject matter for historical thinking and historical study" (68). While in Meyers's work the members of tribute bands deal most directly with the sounds and styles of popular music's past, here the term "historical consciousness" refers to the presence of the past more generally—its stories, personages, symbols, and lessons—as it is evoked, invoked, and woven into the fabric of a piece of music.

Joel's biographers remind readers that he is, in Fred Schruer's words, "a history buff" (2014, 73) and of his frequent claim that, had he not been a successful musician, he would have been a history teacher (Marcano 1990; Scott 2000, 70; Smith 2007, 218). He told Steve Morse of *The Boston Globe* in 1989, "I was going to be a high school history teacher, you know, but I didn't graduate from high school." And he remarked the following year: "I'm very interested in why things are the way they are today, why are we here, why are we like this, why is the world the way it is, and it's because of what happened before. . . . I find the truth is much more interesting than fiction" (qtd. in Marcano 1990). According to his mother, Joel's interest in history started early: "By the time he was seven, Billy was a bookworm . . . history books, picture books, storybooks, anything" (qtd. in Smith 2007, 33).

While many of Joel's songs contain implicit connections to various historical trends, this chapter makes those connections explicit by examining three pieces that illustrate different approaches to the use of history in song: "The Ballad of Billy the Kid" (from *Piano Man*), "We Didn't Start the Fire," and "Two Thousand Years." The first, from near the beginning of Joel's career, is largely fictional yet constructed in ways that give it a historical sensibility. The second, from closer to the end of his pop catalog yet at the height of his commercial success, is strictly factual but offers almost no narrative linking its facts together. And the third, the penultimate statement on his final pop album, attempts a grand tour through human history in the broadest possible terms. These approaches exemplify some of the ways that Joel has incorporated history most directly into his musical works while at the same time showing how his songwriting developed over the course of his pop career: he started off writing about particular historical events (fictionalized or not) and gradually widened his scope until he was writing about history itself.

"A LEGEND IN HIS TIME": CONSTRUCTING "THE BALLAD OF BILLY THE KID"

"The Ballad of Billy the Kid" was discussed in chapter 2 as an example of the western theme on Joel's *Piano Man* album. The title character is indeed drawn from the Wild West. However, as Joel himself has said, there is little historical truth to the song's lyrics. Still, the song uses enough references to the general idea of the Wild West, in combination with some specific musical elements, to cultivate a sense of the legendary. In other words, it may not be factually true, but it sure *sounds* like it could be.

William H. Bonney (born Henry McCarty, aka Billy the Kid) was born in New York City on September 17, 1859. His criminal exploits, primarily in the Arizona and New Mexico territories, were well publicized at the time, especially after New Mexico governor Lew Wallace put a bounty on his head (Utley 1989, 145–46). Bonney was tried and convicted of murder, escaped custody, and became an outlaw and fugitive. Sherriff Pat Garrett ultimately gunned him down on July 14, 1881, at Fort Sumner, New Mexico.

Joel's song tells a somewhat different story. Bonney, who is simply called "Billy" or "Billy the Kid," is said to come from "a town known as Wheeling, West Virginia." The lyrics also mention how he "robbed his way from Utah to Oklahoma," contrary to historical accounts, which do not place him in those territories. Joel sings how Bonney "always rode alone," while in fact he was at one point a member of the Lincoln County Regulators, a deputized posse in Lincoln, New Mexico, that participated in the conflict that became known as the Lincoln County War in 1878 (Nolan 1992).

Although the narrative told in the lyrics is largely fabricated, there are some truthful moments. While describing a fictitious bank robbery, Joel sings, "His age and his size took the teller by surprise," a reference to Bonney's youthfulness and slight build (Wallis 2007, 110–11). And while describing Bonney's end, Joel succeeds in the broad strokes, singing, "One cold day a posse captured Billy, and the judge said, 'String him up for what he did.'" Bonney was in fact apprehended by a group of lawmen, led by Garrett, and tried and convicted in Mesilla, New Mexico. Judge Warren Bristol did, indeed, sentence him to be hanged in May 1881—although he escaped before the sentence could be carried out (Wallis 2007, 242).

The final verse of "The Ballad of Billy Kid" relocates the narrative. Rather than a western setting, the action is transported to Oyster Bay, New York, along the north shore of Long Island about forty miles from Manhattan. The song also moves from the late nineteenth century to the twentieth, as a "boy" carries not a six-shooter pistol but a six-pack of beer. Ken Bielen interprets this unnamed boy as Billy, the song's composer (2011, 25). After all, Oyster Bay is only about eight miles north of Joel's childhood home in Hicksville. But Joel has also said that the verse is about a bartender at an Oyster Bay restaurant (which Bielen acknowledges). In discussing the song, he remarked, "We all ended up at the pub at the end of the day and were entertained by the bartender. He was a very personable guy" (Gamboa 2012). Joel concludes the verse with allusions to Bonney, connecting the ending with the beginning, by reprising the earlier line, "His daring life of crime made him a legend in his time east and west of the Rio Grande."

Thus, while not strictly history, the story Joel tells in "The Ballad of Billy the Kid" has enough historical-sounding bits that it might come off as convincing, at least to those not steeped in American criminal history. Aiding that interpretation are musical choices. The most obvious is Joel's use of chords, played in the song's introduction using a string sound, in which each pitch is spaced widely from the others. This device is distinctive of the music of American classical composer Aaron Copland, whose works are often described as evocative of the United States and Americana in general, and in the case of his ballet, *Billy the Kid* (1938), Bonney and the Wild West in particular (Everett 2000, 111). Indeed, Copland's *Billy the Kid* weaves several cowboy tunes and American folk songs into its musical fabric, although they are often melodically and rhythmically altered (Crist 2009, 127). The opening to "The Ballad of Billy the Kid" and later orchestral passages, which employ instruments such as strings, horns, and timpani, also recall the soundtrack to *The Magnificent Seven* (1960), a western film popular during Joel's childhood. The film's composer, Elmer Bernstein, was a student of Copland's (Bielen 2011, 26) and his teacher's style certainly influenced his score in, at the very least, its pastoral elements (Lerner 2001, 499). Bernstein's style then left its mark on Joel. "I used to love the music of Elmer Bernstein and . . . soundtracks like *The Magnificent Seven*," Joel says. "I loved stuff like that" (personal interview).

Set in the Old West, *The Magnificent Seven* (a remake of the 1954 Japanese film *Seven Samurai*) is the story of seven gunfighters hired to protect a Mexican village from marauding bandits. The film's stars, including Charles Bronson, Yul Brynner, Steve McQueen, and Eli Wallach, went on to successful careers whose filmographies include other westerns. Bernstein's score, which was nominated for an Oscar, was later used in television commercials for Marlboro cigarettes, further adding to the widespread associations between the music, the West, and masculinity as personified by smoking cowboys and gunslingers.

So for a song with a western setting and a well-known gun-toting main character, it made sense for Joel to use musical elements that were already established in American culture as viscerally connected to the Wild West, such as Coplandesque chord spacing. Joel also adds a trotting figure in piano's left hand, the clopping of horse hooves, and the lonely whine of the harmonica. The latter is common in musical representations of cowboys and also features prominently in the title track from *Piano Man*, where the loneliness of cowboy life that the instrument seems to connote is put to use in a piano bar, perhaps to suggest the piano player's loneliness in that setting. On "The Ballad of Billy the Kid," Joel says that he tried "to couch the song itself in cinematic terms" (personal interview), an effort Thomas MacFarlane credits for pushing "song form into the realm of the symphonic" (2016). With this composition, Joel thus not only satisfied his own desire to write a film soundtrack ("I wanted to write the soundtrack to a movie but nobody ever offered me the opportunity") but also enabled him to use music to evoke a storytelling experience—film—that for many is an indelible and important part of their engagement with history.

"SINCE THE WORLD'S BEEN TURNING": THE NARRATIVELESSNESS OF "WE DIDN'T START THE FIRE"

Engaging with history is the point of "We Didn't Start the Fire," a number-one hit that was nominated for Grammys for Record of the Year, Song of the Year, and Best Pop Vocal Performance, Male, in 1990. According to biographer Bill Smith, the song originated in "a conversation that Billy had briefly with a twenty-something student who told Billy that he felt sorry for him because 'no history' had happened during his lifetime" (2007, 217). Schruers identifies Joel's partner in the conversation as Sean Lennon, who was in school with Joel's stepbrother, Alexander. Feeling down about events in 1989—war in Chechnya, terror attacks in London, building up armaments in Iraq, and skirmishes in Africa and the Middle East—Lennon reportedly said to Joel, "At least when you were a kid, you grew up in the fifties, when nothing happened" (2014, 199–200). Joel had just turned forty, so he was already in the mood for retrospection, asking himself, "What's happened in my life?" (DeMain 2004, 119). So in response to Lennon, Joel began writing lyrics that night, naming significant people and events each year from 1949, the year he was born, until the late 1980s.

"We Didn't Start the Fire" is unusual in Joel's catalog because he wrote the words before the music. During the verses, he recites a list of 118 events and people. The sixty-six events named include the 1952 succession of Queen Elizabeth II of England upon the death of her father, King George VI ("England's got a new queen"); the 1953 uprising in East Germany, which was crushed by the Volkspolizei and Soviet troops ("Communist bloc"); the Watergate scandal of the early 1970s, which began in June 1972 when the Democratic National Headquarters in the Watergate office complex in Washington, D.C., was broken into and ended in August 1974 with the resignation of President Richard Nixon ("Watergate"); and the early 1980s detection and recognition of AIDS ("AIDS"). The fifty-two people mentioned include Joe DiMaggio, who helped the New York Yankees go to the baseball's World Series five times in the 1940s, winning four; Albert Einstein, the scientist who died on April 18, 1955; Adolf Eichmann, a Nazi war criminal who was arrested and convicted for crimes against humanity in 1961; and Sally Ride, the first American woman to travel into space, on the *Challenger* shuttle, on June 18, 1983. The final item named before each chorus is a troublesome or dangerous one, such as "trouble in the Suez," a reference to the crisis in the Suez Canal that eventually led to its nationalization by Egypt in October 1956, and "JFK blown away," a reference to the assassination of President John F. Kennedy in Dallas on November 22, 1963.

The chorus includes the title, describing the "fire" as continuous and permanent: "It was always burning since the world's been turning." Whatever the "fire" is, we are ultimately powerless to stop it. Writing in *Rolling Stone*, John McAlley (1989) hears "We Didn't Start the Fire" as "sound[ing] the alarm on a society that has lost its moral center and is spinning out of control." Joel's own comments support McAlley's reading: "Is it an apologia for the baby boomers? No, it's not. It's just a song that says the world's a mess. It's always been a mess; it's always going to be a mess" (qtd. in Schruers 2014, 201).

"We Didn't Start the Fire" went through several musical iterations before Joel settled on its final form. He had been working on the chords to a country tune but lacked words (Schruers 2014, 200; personal interview). Lennon's inspiration solved that problem. According to biographer Richard Scott, Joel also toyed with the idea of a rap song (2000, 70). In the end, the song may be satisfying to its composer lyrically—he told Bill DeMain, "I kind of like the lyric. . . . I thought it was a clever one" (qtd. in Bego 2007, 252)—but not musically. Joel sees the melody to the verse as the song's weakest aspect. "I hated the melody," he said. "It was horrendous . . . like a droning mosquito" (qtd. in Schruers 2014, 201). Indeed, with its emphasis on the lyrics, sung in a rapid-fire, syllabic manner, there is not much room for melodic gesture or creativity. Most of the melody stays within a few pitches and moves stepwise. The result is a melodic line that is easy to sing but not adventurous. The challenge lies in the delivery of the lyrics. "It's a nightmare to perform live, because if I miss one word, it's a trainwreck" (qtd. in Smith 2007, 217). The melody to the chorus fares slightly better, in Joel's view: at least "there was a hook" (personal interview), a catchy melodic idea.

Perhaps more than any of Joel's other songs, "We Didn't Start the Fire" had a life and a purpose beyond the record store and concert stage. It quickly became a favorite of teachers in the United States and elsewhere, who used it in their world or modern history classes. In January 1990, the educational publisher Scholastic distributed a special cassette tape with the song, plus a ten-minute address from Joel, to

40,000 junior and senior high school classrooms nationwide. Joel reportedly endorsed the idea after receiving "a ton of letters" from teachers who were using the song as the basis for their lesson plans (Marcano 1990), although certainly not all teachers were so inclined (Baird 1990).

British educator Scott Allsop describes using the song in classrooms in the United Kingdom and in Egypt to teach students not only about history but also about how history is written. "The lesson sequence that I devised was . . . built upon my view that 'We Didn't Start the Fire' provides a snapshot of Billy Joel's implicit values concerning historical significance. It ought to be possible to study the song in order to infer his implicit criteria for judging events to be historically significant" (2009, 53). In other words, by not only understanding the events and people Joel mentions but trying to figure out why he sings about them in the first place, students gain a better understanding of the role historians play in the inscription of history itself.

Aside from its commercial—and classroom—success, one of the distinctive things about "We Didn't Start the Fire" is not just that it contains a litany of historical references, but that it offers so little context within which they are meant to be understood. The chorus may be as close as listeners get, but its message is limited: the march of history, it argues, has and always will go on. In that light, the accomplishment of "We Didn't Start the Fire" is in the way it shifts the narrative burden from the song (or songwriter) to the audience: Joel does not tell the story; the listener has to figure it out. That may be why it was such an effective teaching tool. It is also an unusual method of songwriting.

The song's musical structure supports this storytelling shift. The verses consist of repetitions of a harmonically stable sequence of four chords that are satisfyingly circular, leading listeners away—but not far—from the tonic chord (G-major) and setting up its return at the start of the following phrase. Each chord is held for four beats before moving predictably onto the next: G-major, D-major, E-minor, and C-major. The cadence at the end of the phrase, from C back to G, is what is known as a "plagal" cadence (often used under "Amen" in church). While bringing about resolution to the tension wrought by the phrase's journey a short distance away from tonic, the "finality" of this kind of cadence is limited. Had Joel used a "perfect" cadence, which would have entailed D-to-G movement, the resolution would have felt more final (Nagley and Whittall). Thus, Joel uses a chord progression that offers a modicum of release without offering much drama to the musical structure. And the way the chords repeat themselves supports the idea of the chorus, that history is an unending stream.

Although Joel does not really like the song's melody, its static nature—in the verse he often goes long stretches singing only few pitches repeatedly—accentuates the overall lack of forward motion. The chorus melody offers a little more excitement, with its ascending pitches ("we didn't start the fire") balanced by a brief descent ("always burning since the world's been turning"). Background singers join in too. Yet the pitches mostly outline a tonic G-major chord, albeit in inversion: "We," the first lyric of the chorus, is sung on a D; "the" falls on a G; and the second syllable of "fire" lands on a B. The second of each pair of phrases in the chorus ends fittingly on the tonic pitch. In other words, despite some slightly more exciting trappings, there is little melodic tension to be resolved: again, no drama in the musical structure, no big musical "story" to follow.

While the chorus of "We Didn't Start the Fire" uses the same chord progression as the verses, the bridge ("Little Rock, Pasternak, Mickey Mantle, Kerouac") is different. It starts on C-major, then moves through A-minor to E-minor, and ends each phrase on D-major; the chords continue to change every four beats, as they did in the verses and chorus. This pattern, which is repeated once ("Lebanon, Charles de Gaulle, California baseball"), not only introduces more minor chords into the song, but also sets up the kind of perfect cadence lacking in the rest of the composition. For example, as Joel sings "children of Thalidomide" (a reference to birth defects afflicting children born to mothers who had taken the drug during pregnancy), the transition into the following verse ("Buddy Holly, *Ben-Hur*, space monkey, Mafia") may sound more final. Yet, the ear quickly realizes that the song's original four-chord sequence has resumed. Thus, even a resolution with more "finality" only leads back to more of the same.

Ultimately, this musical analysis points to the conclusion that, while following well established patterns of tension and release, "We Didn't Start the Fire" does not offer any particularly dramatic musical moments in its harmony or melody. In fact, in this song these foundational musical elements are circular: phrases tend to lead listeners away and bring them back with functional-but-not-rousing gestures. This is not to say that the musical material of "We Didn't Start the Fire" is weak—

although Joel may think so—but instead to argue that, to hear narrative or drama in the song, listeners must help to create it. They have to imagine the story for themselves. They have to meet Joel halfway.

For members of Joel's generation, who lived through each item mentioned in the lyrics, that narrative may be constructed from their own memories. As Joel mentions the character, Davy Crockett, a baby boomer may ask himself or herself, "Where was I when Disney's *Davy Crockett* miniseries was broadcast in 1954–1955, sparking a brief 'coonskin cap' fad?" (The faux-raccoon headwear sold 5,000 caps a day, driving the price of raccoon fur from twenty-five cents to eight dollars per pound [Johnson 2002].) Or "Where was I when John Glenn became the first American to orbit the Earth in 1962?" (Soviet cosmonaut Yuri Gagarin was the first human in space the year before.) For younger audiences, the process of narrative construction, familiarizing themselves with the events and people Joel mentions, required more effort. Thankfully, teachers were eager to help.

"TIME IS RELENTLESS": HISTORY FROM THE BEGINNING OF/IN "TWO THOUSAND YEARS"

On *River of Dreams*, Joel offers perhaps his most expansive yet least specific song about history. "Two Thousand Years" treads a path somewhere between the overt storytelling of "The Ballad of Billy the Kid" and the narrativeless approach of "We Didn't Start the Fire." It begins simply: Joel sings the opening phrase, "in the beginning," by himself before the piano joins in. The piano remains the only accompaniment through the first verse; the band enters at the start of the second ("too many kingdoms"), featuring acoustic guitar, bass, drums, and, in passages between verses, an accordion.

In sweeping gestures, Joel's lyrics trace human history using a strophic structure. The first verse describes the importance of fire while the second alludes to factional conflicts. In the third, the narrator focuses on the present ("here at the crossroads of time"), expressing his hope that future generations ("our children," who "are the vintage") will carry on the dreams of their ancestors. Joel, whose parental instinct shone through earlier on the album with "Lullabye (Goodnight My Angel)," wonders: "Is this a curse or a blessing that we give?" The next verse finds him pondering whether mankind will ever triumph over its fears, which have caused much hate and sorrow, and "learn from all we've been through." In the fifth verse, Joel imagines "a new world to come," in which science and poetry "rule" and there is no more war. The final verse returns to the ideas of the first, noting again how "time is relentless" and cannot be stopped. The song ends on a hopeful note of possibility: "We're on the verge of all things new; we are two thousand years."

The lyrics to "Two Thousand Years" offer a mixture of biblical imagery and a love story. Of course, beginning the song's story "in the beginning" would mean, to many listeners, glancing back much farther than two thousand years. Still, the reference to Genesis in the first few words is unmistakable, and the appearance of Joel's voice a cappella may suggest a pre-Creation emptiness. Later, he mentions "prophets and angels," important biblical personages who serve as guides and protectors. Yet he does not name any in particular, a choice that keeps the song on a general level, not too specific.

Other lines offer glimpses of the romantic element. Despite the challenges of human history, Joel sings, "only true love perseveres," a theme he touched on earlier on the album in "All About Soul" (the power of perseverance: "the power of love and the power of healing") and "Lullabye" (love transcends death: "someday we'll all be gone but lullabies go on and on"). In fact, one could argue that this theme helps to tie *River of Dreams* together as a concept album. It begins, in "No Man's Land" and "The Great Wall of China," with destruction and treachery, both cultural and personal, but slowly resolves to make peace with the world and its past in these tracks (as well as "The River of Dreams" and "Famous Last Words"). Joel explains:

> The transition goes from a complete disillusionment [with] everything—I lost faith in everything: I got divorced from my wife, my kid got taken away from me, they moved to another state, my manager cleaned me out of my money, the music business has just fucked me again and I should have known better. I was angry, so angry. And there's a whole evolution that goes on throughout the album, where I reunite with my child and I start regaining faith again. It's like a reclamation of faith. And at the end—what was the last thing?— "Two Thousand Years": "Okay. I'm back; it's okay. Everything's going to be okay." (personal interview)

Thus, the use of "we" in the final couplet of "Two Thousand Years" can be interpreted as encompassing the lovers, who are finally, at the end of the epic story, able to embark on their journey together: "We're on the verge of all things new; we are two thousand years." Or the love can be familial, as the listener can imagine the father and daughter of "Lullaby" looking out on the world she will inherit. But it can also be heard as encompassing the entirety of humanity, as seen through the eyes of a songwriter who has been to hell and back. Unlike "We Didn't Start the Fire," where Joel provided no story at all, in "Two Thousand Years," he offers multiple ways to understand the song's story.

There are several reasons why Joel might feel inclined to write a song encompassing thousands of years of history in five and a half minutes. In the early 1990s, the new millennium, less than a decade away, occupied a special place in the American imagination. On one hand, fear of the "Y2K Bug"—the much-anticipated error resulting from the common practice of using two digits to indicate a year, so the "00" of "2000" would be misinterpreted (primarily by computers) as "1900"—was widespread, with transportation and information networks, utilities, governments, and militaries all thought to be at risk (Webster 1999). Government panels and commissions were appointed around the world to prepare for and deal with the problem, which, in the end, turned out to be far less damaging than anticipated.

On the other hand, there was a sense of hope and progress. The United States was entering what would be an unusually long period of peacetime economic expansion. The Cold War had recently ended, with the dismantling of the Berlin Wall in 1989 and the Soviet Union in 1991. Nelson Mandela, who had led the fight against apartheid in South Africa, was released in 1990 after thirty years in prison. And the increasing accessibility of personal computers, along with the advent of the Internet, brought greater numbers of American consumers into the information age, becoming a symbol of progress. Indeed, the "amazing future" Joel sings about seemed tantalizingly close. "I was being philosophical in that song," he recalls.

> [I was] trying to sum up the history of the world in a couple of verses in a song. But it was before the year 2000—'93, this was—and [there was a sense that] there is, out there, the millennium, the change of the millennium. "God, this is such a big thing! I'm going to see the

onset of that millennium!" And I was very optimistic about it. (personal interview)

While both "We Didn't Start the Fire" and "Two Thousand Years" argue for the "relentlessness" of time and history, Joel's musical choices mean they do so in rather different ways. The aggressiveness of the electric guitars on "We Didn't Start the Fire," which worked well for live performances in large arenas, is replaced on "Two Thousand Years" with the gentler strumming of Danny Kortchmar's acoustic guitar. When combined with the accordion, the instrumental forces in the later song seem to connote a folk element not unlike Joel's efforts in "The Downeaster 'Alexa'" (from *Storm Front*, see chapter 4).

Moreover, the harmony of "Two Thousand Years" creates a stronger musical narrative than "We Didn't Start the Fire." The chord progression, in the key of F-major, is lengthier and encompasses a much wider variety of sonorities due to the more active movement of the bass line. Whereas in the earlier song the bass usually played the "root" of each chord—for a G-major chord, the root is G, for example—here it is more independent. In the first verse, under the lyric "there was the cold," Joel plays a tonic chord, F-major, under "cold" but instead of the root (F), the bass features another chord tone, A. This has the effect of maintaining the sense of stability inherent in the tonic chord but also setting up the movement to come, which arrives under the next lyric as the bass line moves up to B-flat, the root of the next chord. Later, when Joel sings, "Man was triumphant," he offers a tonic F-major chord, but the bass plays an E-flat, which adds considerable tension to the harmony because it is not usually part of an F-major scale (and is therefore not in the song's key) and thus necessitates resolution, which arrives when the bass moves down to D, the root of the next chord. The idea of a bass line moving underneath a song's chords is not new on "Two Thousand Years"; Joel points to his use of the compositional device on many of his songs, ranging from "Captain Jack" (from *Piano Man*) to "All for Leyna" (from *Glass Houses*) to "No Man's Land," as well as on other popular songs (e.g., The Beach Boys' "Good Vibrations" [1966]) and his classical favorites (e.g., passages in Beethoven's Symphony No. 3, Op. 55 "Eroica" [1803]) (personal interview).

Thus, in "Two Thousand Years" Joel's longer musical phrases afford him the room to write a more expansive harmonic progression, which reflects the expansiveness of the story told in the lyrics. At the same time, his more active bass line helps him to construct chords that tug at the ear, requiring resolution and the sense of movement such resolution creates. The cumulative effect is one of progress, of forward motion, and it allows Joel not only to tell a story through lyrics, but to create a narrative in the music too. It is subtle, however.

> The magic of what's going on—whether it's pop music or classical music or standards—is underneath what's apparent. . . . Things that you don't really know you're hearing, but you hear them. . . . And you're not trying to enlist people to know this. It's better, it's more effective if it's really not pushed in your face. . . . You're trying to let people into the inside, but not banging them over the head with it. "If you want to go there, it's there." But that's the wonderful thing about music. (personal interview)

Although Joel tells a story in "Two Thousand Years," the song shares with "We Didn't Start the Fire" a focus on history—not just as a series of names and dates, but as the construction and representation of the past in the present. The lyrics are intentionally vague, mentioning biblical types without naming specific characters, referencing the "same endless fears" without explaining them, and allowing for multiple readings of the final lines. When combined with the relentlessness of time, the narrator's position at time's crossroads, and the imagination of a better future, these features enable the listener to understand the song not as a retelling of any particular (hi)story, but as an appreciation of history more generally.

Near the beginning of his biography, Schruers describes the library in Joel's house. It is filled with books, many of which are biographies and music and military histories (2014, 36). Elsewhere in his home one finds the trappings of history as well: *The Fireside Book of Folksongs* mentioned in the previous chapter, as well as an antique virginal, a kind of harpsichord popular in Europe in the sixteenth and seventeenth centuries. So it is easy to make the case that his music is infused with a sense of history.

More interesting, then, is a consideration of the *ways* history infuses Joel's music. This chapter has offered three. In "The Ballad of Billy the Kid," Joel admittedly took great creative license with the outlaw's story but provided a musical foundation that fit nicely with popular and cinematic representations of the Wild West. In "We Didn't Start the Fire," Joel sought to prove the consequential nature of events during his lifetime while also suggesting that history unfailingly precedes each generation and continues on after it. While providing only names or referential phrases, "We Didn't Start the Fire" avoided the lyrical or musical suggestion of narrative. Instead, listeners had to construct the song's story for themselves—and given its success, many did. Finally, "Two Thousand Years" offers Joel's most ambitious attempt at history-in-song, tracing mankind from "the beginning." In words and music, he offers a much clearer sense of narrative and purpose. Yet for all their differences, both "We Didn't Start the Fire" and "Two Thousand Years" do not simply reference elements of history, but engage with the concept of history itself.

8

"AND SO IT GOES"

The Lasting Significance of Billy Joel

This book's introduction offered a few ways the significance of Billy Joel's music could be demonstrated. One was through sales, an indication of commercial success that offers a clue to the widespread dissemination of Joel's songs. Another was through the awards he and his music have won, an indication of the high regard with which the awarding institutions and their members hold him and his work.

Yet Joel's music is significant because of its sound, too. His style was always a combination of styles, a fact that caused some confusion among critics but behind which he stands. His own remarks about how combinations of musical styles makes for a rather American approach to songwriting (quoted in chapter 6) were echoed in the words of President Barack Obama, who, while celebrating Joel's Kennedy Center Honors in 2013, called him "an artist whose songs are sung around the world but are thoroughly, wonderfully American" ("Remarks by the President"). Many of Joel's songs are notable for the way they deftly incorporate stylistic elements of jazz and The Beatles into cohesive musical statements (see MacFarlane 2016). Perhaps this stylistic diversity helped render his music appealing and enduring in the first place. He may not have pushed too hard at the edges of American popular music—he mostly rejected punk in 1970s, new wave in the 1980s, and grunge in 1990s—but his sound stood in the wide middle of popular taste, so its appeal can be seen as an indication of what many listeners enjoyed or found meaningful.

More tangibly, one could point to examples of the impact of Joel's music through specific songs. "Piano Man" (from *Piano Man*), a hit from early in his career, was recognized for its impact when, in 2015, it was inducted into the Library of Congress National Recording Registry (National Recording Preservation Board). "We Didn't Start the Fire" (from *Storm Front*), a later hit, prompted a surge in the use of music to teach schoolchildren about world history (see chapter 7). And while perhaps not the same kind of impact, "Just the Way You Are" (from *The Stranger*) became the musical centerpiece of countless weddings, etching Joel's voice into one of the most significant memories of many people's lives.

Joel's music kept alive an emphasis on well-crafted melody and harmony extending back, in the history of popular song through Tin Pan Alley and nineteenth-century Parlor Song. But it did so in contemporaneously relevant ways through its subject matter, to which listeners could clearly relate. To a certain degree, his music became the soundtrack of Long Island, where he grew up and where he continues to live. It also contributed powerfully to the soundtrack of his generation more generally, regardless of geography. His current residency at New York's Madison Square Garden, begun in 2014 and including monthly shows for as long as demand lasts, is built in part on his appeal to a local crowd. But it also goes beyond that, as audiences are filled not just with fans from New York and nearby states, but also people from across the country (and the world) who travel great distances to hear his music. "Billy at the Garden has the unique status of being a national, even global, destination gig," says *Billboard* senior editor Ray Waddell (qtd. in Gamboa 2015).

The impact and relevance of Joel's music can also be observed in its steady use in popular culture, especially on television and film (see Schruers 2014, 328–30). *Bosom Buddies*, a sitcom starring Tom Hanks and Peter Scolari (running 1980–1982 on ABC), used "My Life" (from *52nd Street*), although not Joel's recording, as its theme song during its initial run. A version of "You May Be Right" (from *Glass Houses*) served as the theme song for the sitcom *Dave's World* (airing 1993–1997 on CBS). Neil Patrick Harris covered "Piano Man" in a 2010 episode of the musical comedy *Glee* on Fox; "Only the Good Die Young" (from *The*

Stranger) was used in another episode later that year. During the same season, the CBS sitcom *Two and a Half Men* featured an episode titled, "The Immortal Mr. Billy Joel," in which a character does a rendition of "We Didn't Start the Fire." Meanwhile, the same year, Fyfe Dangerfield's cover of "She's Always a Woman" (from *The Stranger*) was used in a television advertisement for the British retail chain John Lewis, which spurred renewed interest in Joel's recording of the song. Joel's songs have also appeared in multiple episodes of NBC's *The Office*. On film, Zach Galifianakis's character, Alan, plays a dedicated fan in *The Hangover* (2009). In the sequel (2011), three Joel songs are featured: "The Downeaster 'Alexa,'" (from *Storm Front*), "Allentown" (from *The Nylon Curtain*), and "Just the Way You Are."

Another indication of the impact of Joel's music is the large number of other musicians who have recorded cover versions and by the variety of styles with which those versions are played (see Bielen 2011, 121–32). The list is extensive and only partly represented here: "New York State of Mind" (from *Turnstiles*) was covered by Barbara Streisand in 1977, Mel Tormé the same year, Carmen McRae in 1981, Oleta Adams in 1993, and Tony Bennett (with Joel joining on vocals) in 2001. "Say Goodbye to Hollywood" (also from *Turnstiles*) was recorded separately by Ronnie Spector and Bette Midler in 1977. "Just the Way You Are" was covered in separate recordings by Isaac Hayes, Barry White, and Johnny Mathis and Deniece Williams all in 1978. Frank Sinatra released his version of the song in 1980, and Gerry and the Pacemakers included it (along with "It's Still Rock and Roll to Me," from *Glass Houses*) on a live album in 1981. Diana Krall sang it on her 2002 album, *Live in Paris*, and Harry Connick Jr. included it on *Your Songs* (2009). Garth Brooks famously covered "Shameless" (from *Storm Front*) on his album *Ropin' the Wind* (1991), a recording arguably more famous than Joel's original. Folk singer Joan Baez included "Goodnight Saigon" (from *The Nylon Curtain*) on her album *Brothers in Arms* (1991). Dolly Parton offered her take on "Travelin' Prayer" (from *Piano Man*) on *The Grass is Blue* (1999). The Beastie Boys put their version of "Big Shot" (from *52nd Street*) as the B-side of their 1999 single "Alive." For his collection of covers, *Classic Songs, My Way* (2007), Paul Anka did "I Go to Extremes" (from *Storm Front*). And finally, Beyoncé covered "Honesty" (from *52nd Street*) on her album, *I Am . . . Sasha Fierce* (2009).

Other popular musicians have certainly been influenced by Joel's music even if they have not recorded versions of Joel's songs. Ben Folds, for example, came strongly to Joel's defense following *Fantasies & Delusions* (see chapter 6). The continued importance of the piano in rock music after Joel's career is exemplified in Folds's works, as well as those by Sara Bareilles, Vanessa Carlton, Gavin DeGraw, and John Legend.

The preceding chapters have shown another way Joel's songs were significant, by illustrating the connections between them and the context within which they were written. "Context" does not mean merely the "stuff" going on at the time, which the lyrics happen to mention. Instead it indicates the forces affecting people's lives on a daily basis and over time—the stuff people cared about because it affected them deeply. Maybe it was shifting demographics, as some noticed the ways their neighborhoods were changing. Or perhaps it was an acute sense of rising anxiety, prompted by the Cold War, Vietnam, technological advancements, or evolving ideas about the roles of men and women at home and in the world. In this way, Joel's music reflected people's concerns.

But Joel's music did more than just reflect concerns. It gave voice to them. It provided familiar characters in familiar situations: men working in dying industries, twenty-somethings facing the real danger of deployment, and the concerns of men and women as they navigated the complicated and often rough terrain of love and courtship, the pain of betrayal, and the enduring love between long-standing friends and parents and their children. As Stephen Holden wrote in his *New York Times* review of Joel's documentary film, *Last Play at Shea*: "Mr. Joel, who largely abandoned songwriting in the mid-1990s, sounds more and more like the rock 'n' roll answer to Irving Berlin and George M. Cohan. His blunt, irresistibly tuneful songs, however autobiographical, are also nuggets of American cultural history" (2010).

After a rough start with *Cold Spring Harbor*, the musical wandering of *Piano Man*, and the inability to fully realize his vision on *Streetlife Serenade*, Billy Joel hit his stride for the first time with *Turnstiles* and broke into the top echelon of pop music with *The Stranger* and *52nd Street*. He returned to the sounds of his (and his audience's) youth on

Glass Houses and *An Innocent Man*, aimed for a sustained sense of greater artistic depth on *The Nylon Curtain*, held it together while waxing autobiographical on *The Bridge*, and once again embraced different (in some cases, harder) styles on *Storm Front* and *River of Dreams*. Columbia Records continues to release new combinations of his recordings (something he does not have control over), an indication of the value it continues to see in the music, its ability to sell as well as its sustaining appeal.

This book aimed to add a new dimension to that appeal, placing some of Joel's music in a wider context. Perhaps future books will examine some of the songs not addressed in these pages. At the very least, this book has argued for the importance of Joel's music, which will hopefully lead to its more thorough inclusion in the history of American and popular music.

Because Joel continues to perform and compose—even if those compositions are rarely (if ever) heard—it is premature to claim the final word on his music. Hopefully a closing thought from the composer himself, with a characteristic long view and a touch of melancholy, will suffice. As he sings in "Getting Closer" (from *The Bridge*), he may "still have far to go, no doubt," yet is nonetheless "getting closer, getting closer."

FURTHER READING

Allsop, Scott. "'We Didn't Start the Fire': Using 1980s Popular Music to Explore Historical Significance by Stealth." *Teaching History* 137 (2009): 52–59.

Anderson, Terry H. "Vietnam Is Here: The Anti-War Movement." In *The War That Never Ends: New Perspectives on the Vietnam War*, ed. David L. Anderson and John Ernst, 245–64. Lexington: The University Press of Kentucky, 2007.

Atlantic States Marine Fisheries Commission (ASMFC). "Fisheries Management Report No. 1 of the Atlantic States Marine Fisheries Commission: Interstate Management Plan for the Striped Bass." October 1981. http://www.asmfc.org/species/atlantic-striped-bass. Accessed January 7, 2015.

Bacher, Danielle. "Ben Folds Talks New Orchestral L.P.: 'I Want to Piss in Your Yard With This Record," *Billboard* online, September 10, 2015.

Baird, Robert. "Teachers' Reactions Mixed to Billy Joel History Lesson." *The Pittsburgh Press*, January 20, 1990.

Bakhtin, Mikhail M. "Discourse in the Novel." In *The Dialogic Imagination*, ed. Michael Holquist, trans. Caryl Emerson and Michael Holquist. Austin: University of Texas Press, 1981.

Barnett, Lincoln. "Fred Astaire." *Life*, August 25, 1941, 73–85.

Barrie, J. M. *Peter Pan; or, The Boy Who Wouldn't Grow Up*. London: Hodder & Stoughton, 1911.

Barthes, Roland. "The Death of the Author" (1968). In *Image—Music—Text*, trans. Stephen Heath, 142–48. New York: Hill and Wang, 1977.

Basker, Emek, Shawn Klimek, and Pham Hoang Van. "Supersize It: The Growth of Retail Chains and the Rise of the 'Big-Box' Store." *Journal of Economics and Management Strategy* 21, no. 3 (2012): 541–82.

Beatles et al. *The Beatles: Complete Scores*. Milwaukee: Hal Leonard, 1993.

Beck, Melinda, Gloria Borger, and Diane Weathers. "Women's Work—And Wages." *Newsweek*, July 9, 1984, 22.

Bego, Mark. *Billy Joel: The Biography*. New York: Thunder's Mouth Press, 2007. Bego's book is a detailed, though not flawless, biography that draws on a variety of Joel's interviews and other media accounts for much of its information.

Béhague, Gerard, and Robin Moore. "Cuba." *Grove Music Online, Oxford Music Online*. Oxford University Press. http://www.oxfordmusiconline.com/subscriber/article/grove/music/06926. Accessed August 10, 2015.

Bell, John. "Disney's Times Square: The New American Community Theatre." *The Drama Review* 42, no. 1 (1998): 26–33.

Bellingam, Jane. "Nocturne." *The Oxford Companion to Music*, ed. Alison Latham. *Oxford Music Online*. Oxford University Press. http://www.oxfordmusiconline.com/subscriber/article/opr/t114/e4743. Accessed January 13, 2016.

Berman, Larry. *Lyndon Johnson's War*. New York: W.W. Norton, 1991.

Bielen, Ken. *The Words and Music of Billy Joel*. Santa Barbara, CA: Praeger, 2011. Bielen's valuable book is not a biography, per se, but is structured around Billy Joel's songs, offering brief descriptions of the music, analyses of the lyrics, and often commenting on variations between different recordings of each song.

"Billy Joel Blows His Cool, Upsets Piano in Moscow." *Los Angeles Times*, July 27, 1987.

"Billy Joel Has a Tantrum." *The New York Times*, July 28, 1987. Web.

Boehlert, Eric. "Dylan's 'Hurricane': A Look Back." *Rolling Stone*, January 21, 2000.

Boni, Margaret Bradford, ed. *The Fireside Book of Folk Songs*. New York: Simon & Schuster, 1947.

Bordowitz, Hank. *Billy Joel: The Life and Times of an Angry Young Man*. New York: Billboard Books, 2005. Bordowitz's biography is particularly strong on the earlier parts of Joel's career.

Borshuck, Michael. "The 'Professional' Singer-Songwriter in the 1970s." In *The Cambridge Companion to the Singer-Songwriter*, ed. Katherine Williams and Justin Williams, 86–99. New York: Cambridge University Press, 2016. Borshuck examines the idea of the "singer-songwriter" in 1970s, as musicians bearing the label sought more mainstream, commercial exposure; he includes specific references to Joel and his songs.

Boustan, Leah Platt. "Was Postwar Suburbanization 'White Flight'? Evidence from the Black Migration." *The Quarterly Journal of Economics* 125, no. 1 (2010): 417–43.

Bradford, David F., and Harry H. Kelejian. "An Econometric Model of the Flight to the Suburbs." *Journal of Political Economy* 81 (1973): 566–89.

Breschard, Jack. "Piano Man." *Rolling Stone*, March 14, 1974.

Brown, Geoff. "Sing Us a Song, Piano Man." *The Times* (London), November 27, 2001.

Brown, Maurice J. E. "Schubert and Neapolitan Relationships." *The Musical Times* 85, no. 1212 (1944): 43–44.

Brown, Maurice J. E., and Kenneth L. Hamilton. "Nocturne (i)." *Grove Music Online, Oxford Music Online*. Oxford University Press. http://www.oxfordmusiconline.com/subscriber/article/grove/music/20012. Accessed January 13, 2016.

Buchler, Michael. "Modulation as Dramatic Agent in Frank Loesser's Broadway Songs." *Music Theory Spectrum* 30, no. 1 (2008): 35–60.

Buzzanco, Robert. *Vietnam and the Transformation of American Life*. Malden, MA: Blackwell, 1999.

Charters, Samuel B., and Leonard Kunstadt. *Jazz: A History of the New York Scene*. New York: Doubleday, 1962.

Chevigny, Paul. *Gigs: Jazz and the Cabaret Laws in New York City*. New York: Routledge, 1991.

Cioe, Crispin. "Billy Joel: The Nylon Curtain." *Musician* 50 (1982): 101.

Cone, Edward T. *The Composer's Voice*. Berkeley: University of California Press, 1974.

Connelly, Christopher. "Billy Joel: Not as Bad as You Think." *Rolling Stone*, October 28, 1982.

Cowie, Jefferson R., and Lauren Boehm. "Dead Man's Town: 'Born in the U.S.A.,' Social History, and Working-Class Identity." *American Quarterly* 58, no. 2 (2006): 353–78.

Crawford, Richard. *America's Musical Life: A History*. New York: W.W. Norton, 2001.

Crist, Elizabeth Bergman. *Music for the Common Man: Aaron Copland during the Depression and the War*. New York: Oxford University Press, 2009.

Crocker, Michael. "Saving Striped Bass." *The New York Times*, May 11, 2014, SR6.

Crouse, Timothy. "The First Family of the New Rock." *Rolling Stone*, February 18, 1971.

Deardorff II, Doland L. *Bruce Springsteen: American Poet and Prophet*. Lanham, MD: Scarecrow, 2014.

DeCurtis, Anthony. "The Rolling Stone Interview: Billy Joel." *Rolling Stone*, November 6, 1986.

———. "The Bridge." *Rolling Stone*, September 11, 1986.

DeMain, Bill. "Billy Joel: Scenes from a Musical Life." *Performing Songwriter*, January/February 1996.

————. *In Their Own Words: Songwriters Talk About the Creative Process*. Santa Barbara, CA: Praeger, 2004.

Dobbs, Michael. *One Minute to Midnight: Kennedy, Khrushchev and Castro on the Brink of Nuclear War*. New York: Knopf, 2008.

Dolgon, Corey. *End of the Hamptons: Scenes from the Class Struggle in America's Paradise*. New York: New York University Press, 2005.

Dorbin, Peter. "Billy Joel Tries Classical with New CD." *The Philadelphia Inquirer*, October 3, 2001, E09.

Duchan, Joshua S. "Disappointment, Frustration, and Resignation in Billy Joel's *The Nylon Curtain*." *Rock Music Studies* 2, no. 2 (2015): 168–87. This article argues that *The Nylon Curtain* was a peak in Joel's compositional development due to his use of the classical device, the song cycle, and the confluence of recording techniques that he embraced on this record.

————. "Depicting the Working Class in the Music of Billy Joel." *The Cambridge Companion to the Singer-Songwriter*. Ed. Katherine Williams and Justin Williams. New York: Cambridge University Press, 2016. 137–43. This essay analyzes, compares, and contrasts three of Joel's songs that adopt a working-class perspective.

Dunstan, Roger. "Overview of New York City's Fiscal Crisis." California Research Bureau Note 3.1 (March 1, 1995). http://www.library.ca.gov/crb/95/notes/v3n1.pdf. Accessed August 4, 2014.

Edgar, Andrew, and Peter Sedgwick. *Key Concepts in Cultural Theory*. New York: Routledge, 1999.

Elliott, Susan. "Billy Joel: Up from Piano Man." *High Fidelity Magazine*, January 1978, 110–21.

Ennis, Philip H. *The Seventh Stream: The Emergence of Rocknroll in American Popular Music*. Hanover: Wesleyan University Press, 1992.

Erlewine, Stephen Thomas. "Bob Dylan." *Allmusic*. http://www.allmusic.com/artist/bob-dylan-mn0000066915/biography. Accessed February 3, 2016.

————. Review of *Cold Spring Harbor*, by Billy Joel. *Allmusic*. http://www.allmusic.com. Accessed July 28, 2014.

Ethington, Philip J., William H. Frey, and Dowell Myers. "The Racial Resegregation of Los Angeles County, 1940–2000." Race Contours 2000 Study, Public Research Report No. 2001-04, released May 12, 2001. http://www.usc.edu/schools/price/research/popdynamics/pdf/2001_Ethington-Frey-Myers_Racial-Resegregation.pdf. Accessed July 9, 2014.

Evans, David. "Blues: Chronological Overview." In *African American Music: An Introduction*. Ed. Melonee V. Burnim and Portia K. Maultsby. New York: Routledge, 2006.

Everett, Walter. *The Beatles as Musicians: Revolver through the Anthology*. New York: Oxford University Press, 1999.

————. "The Learned vs. the Vernacular in the Songs of Billy Joel." *Contemporary Music Review* 18, no. 4 (2000): 105–29. This article is one of the first scholarly considerations of Joel's music in a music journal, analyzing several of Joel's songs for their classical aspirations, poetic themes, and use of style, focusing on "James" and "Laura" in particular.

————. *The Beatles as Musicians: The Quarry Men through Rubber Soul*. New York: Oxford University Press, 2001.

Family Productions. Press release announcing *Cold Spring Harbor*, by Billy Joel. Undated (ca. 1971). Library and Archives, Rock and Roll Hall of Fame and Museum. Michael Ochs Collection, Series I: Business Papers, Subseries 1: Artist Files, Joel, Billy. Box 6, Folder 114.

Fetters, Ashley. "'We Didn't Start the Fire,' Billy Joel's Awful, Educational Hit Turns 25." *Entertainment Weekly*, September 27, 2014.

Fletcher, Tony. *All Hopped Up and Ready to Go: Music from the Streets of New York, 1927–77*. New York: W.W. Norton, 2009.

Fox, Aaron A. *Real Country: Music and Language in Working-Class Culture*. Durham, NC: Duke University Press, 2004.

Frey, William H. "Central City White Flight: Racial and Nonracial Causes." *American Sociological Review* 44 (1979): 425–48.

Frisch, Walter. *Brahms: The Four Symphonies*. New Haven, CT: Yale University Press, 2003.

Frith, Simon. "'The Magic That Can Set You Free': The Ideology of Folk and the Myth of the Rock Community." *Popular Music* 1 (1981): 159–68.

———. "Towards an Aesthetic of Popular Music." In *Music and Society: The Politics of Composition, Performance, and Reception*, ed. Richard Leppert and Susan McClary, 133–49. Cambridge: Cambridge University Press, 1987.

Fry, Joseph A. "Unpopular Messengers: Student Opposition to the Vietnam War." In *The War That Never Ends: New Perspectives on the Vietnam War*, ed. David L. Anderson and John Ernst, 219–43. Lexington: The University Press of Kentucky, 2007.

Gaines, Steven. *Philistines at the Hedgerow: Passion and Property in the Hamptons*. Boston: Little, Brown, 1988.

Gamboa, Glenn. "Billy Joel Talks About His Top Long Island Songs." *Newsday*, August 6, 2012.

———. "Billy Joel Talks Madison Square Garden Record-Breaking Residency, New Baby, and Rewriting the Industry Rules." *Newsday*, June 26, 2015.

Garrett, Charles Hiroshi. *Struggling to Define a Nation: American Music and the Twentieth Century*. Berkley: University of California Press, 2008.

George, Alice L. *Awaiting Armageddon: How Americans Faced the Cuban Missile Crisis*. Chapel Hill: University of North Carolina Press, 2003.

George, Arthur L. *St. Petersburg: Russia's Window to the Future—the First Three Centuries*. Lanham, MD: Taylor, 2003.

Gibson, Campbell, and Kay Jung. "Historical Census Statistics on Population Totals by Race, 1790 to 1990, and by Hispanic Origin, 1970 to 1990, for the United States, Regions, Divisions, and States." U.S. Census Bureau Working Paper No. 56, September 2002. https://www.census.gov/population/www/documentation/twps0056/twps0056.pdf. Accessed July 9, 2014.

Giddens, Gary, and Scott DeVeaux. *Jazz*. New York: W.W. Norton, 2009.

Gillett, Charlie. *The Sound of the City: The Rise of Rock and Roll*. New York: Da Capo, 1996.

Gracyk, Theodore. *Rhythm and Noise: An Aesthetics of Rock*. Durham, NC: Duke University Press, 1996.

Grazian, David. "The Production of Popular Music as a Confidence Game: The Case of the Chicago Blues." *Qualitative Sociology* 27, no. 2 (2004): 137–58.

Gribin, Anthony J., and Matthew M. Schiff. *Doo-Wop: The Forgotten Third of Rock 'n' Roll*. Iola, WI: Krause, 1992.

Grubb, W. Norton. "The Flight to the Suburbs of Population and Employment, 1960–1970." *Journal of Urban Economics* 11 (1982): 348–67.

Guterbock, Thomas M. "The Push Hypothesis: Minority Presence, Crime, and Urban Deconcentration." In *The Changing Face of the Suburbs*. Ed. Barry Schwartz. Chicago: University of Chicago Press, 1976.

Hamm, Charles. *Yesterdays: Popular Song in America*. New York: W.W. Norton, 1983.

———. *Putting Popular Music in Its Place*. New York: Cambridge University Press, 1995.

Harrison, Helen, and Constance Dryer Denne. *Hamptons Bohemia: Two Centuries of Writers and Artists at the Beach*. San Francisco: Chronicle, 2002.

Heckman, Don. "Pop Festival Excitement Grows as Night and the Stars Appear." *The New York Times*, April 4, 1972.

Hill, Constance Valis. *Tap Dancing America: A Cultural History*. New York: Oxford University Press, 2010.

Holden, Stephen. "Streetlife Serenade." *Rolling Stone*, December 5, 1974.

———. "52nd Street." *Rolling Stone*, December 14, 1978.

———. "The Nylon Curtain." *Rolling Stone*, October 14, 1982.

———. "Neil Young and Billy Joel Revisit the Roots of Rock." *The New York Times*, August 7, 1983, H19.

————. "Brenda, Eddie, Billy and Friends Bury a Ballpark." *The New York Times*, October 28, 2010.

Hunter, James. "Fantasies & Delusions (Music for Solo Piano)." *Rolling Stone*, October 17, 2005.

Hunter, Tea. *To 'Joy My Freedom: Southern Black Women's Lives and Labors after the Civil War*. Cambridge, MA: Harvard University Press, 1997.

Jackson, Jerma. *Singing in My Soul: Black Gospel Music in a Secular Age*. Chapel Hill: University of North Carolina Press, 2004.

Jackson, Travis A. *Blowin' the Blues Away: Performance and Meaning on the New York Jazz Scene*. Berkley: University of California Press, 2012.

Jacobson, Marion. *Squeeze This!: A Cultural History of the Accordion in America*. Urbana: University of Illinois Press, 2012.

James, David. "The Vietnam War and American Music." In *The Vietnam War and American Culture*, ed. John Carlos Rowe and Rick Berg, 226–54. New York: Columbia University Press, 1991.

Joel, Billy. Untitled letter accompanying the Family Productions press kit for *Cold Spring Harbor*. Undated (ca. 1971). Library and Archives, Rock and Roll Hall of Fame and Museum. Michael Ochs Collection, Series I: Business Papers, Subseries 1: Artist Files, Joel, Billy. Box 6, Folder 114.

————. "Ray Charles," in "100 Greatest Singers." *Rolling Stone*, November 27, 2007.

Johnson, John. "Coonskin Cap Clings to 'Crockett.'" *The Lost Angeles Times*, August 23, 2002.

Johnson, Kevin C. "Country Music May Survive A.G. (After Garth)." *St. Louis Post-Dispatch*, November 12, 2000, C3.

Jones, A. Morgan. "The Other Sides of Billy Joel: Six Case Studies Revealing the Sociologist, The Balladeer, and the Historian." Ph.D. diss., University of Western Ontario, 2011. This dissertation analyzes six of Joel's songs as examples of different modes of composition. It also pays close attention to music videos.

Keil, Charles, and Angeliki V. Keil. *Polka Happiness*. Philadelphia: Temple University Press, 1992.

Kelly, Barbara M. *Expanding the American Dream: Building and Rebuilding Levittown*. Albany: State University of New York Press, 1993.

Kerman, Joseph. *The Beethoven Quartets*. New York: W.W. Norton, 1979.

Klein, Christian. "A Multi-level Analysis of Billy Joel's 'Goodnight Saigon.'" *Popular Music and Society* 15, no. 3 (1991): 75–93. In one of the earliest scholarly articles on Joel's music, Klein surveys Vietnam veterans and college students to compare responses to Joel's song about the conflict.

Klosterman, Chuck. "The Stranger." *The New York Times Magazine*, September 15, 2002.

————. "Every Dog Must Have His Day, Every Drunk Must Have His Drink." In *Sex, Drugs, and Cocoa Puffs: A Low Culture Manifesto*, 42–54. New York: Scribner, 2004.

Knudson, Thomas J. "With Striped Bass Ban, A Way of Life Is Fading." *The New York Times*, May 9, 1986, B1–2.

Kristeva, Julia. *Desire in Language: A Semiotic Approach to Literature and Art*. New York: Columbia University Press, 1980.

Lankevich, George J. *New York City: A Short History*. New York: New York University Press, 2002.

Lerner, Neil. "Copland's Music of Wide Open Spaces: Surveying the Pastoral Trope in Hollywood." *The Musical Quarterly* 85, no. 3 (2001): 477–515.

Lewisohn, Mark. *The Complete Beatles Chronicle: The Definitive Day-by-Day Guide to the Beatles' Entire Career*, 2nd ed. Chicago: Chicago Review Press, 2010.

Lichter, Daniel T., and Janice A. Costanzo. "How Do Demographic Changes Affect Labor Force Participation of Women?" Bureau of Labor Statistics *Monthly Labor Review*, November 1987, 23–25. http://www.bls.gov/opub/mlr/1987/11/rpt2full.pdf. Accessed May 22, 2015.

Macaulay, Alastair. "Astaire the Artist, Even in Blackface." *The New York Times*, January 27, 2011.

MacFarlane, Thomas. *Experiencing Billy Joel: A Listener's Companion*. Lanham, MD: Rowman & Littlefield, 2016.

Malone, Bill C. *Country Music USA*, rev. ed. Austin: University of Texas Press, 1985.

"Man of the Year: Gen. Westmoreland, The Guardians at the Gate." *Time*, January 7, 1966.

Manning, Kara. "River of Dreams." *Rolling Stone*, August 19, 1993.

Marcano, Tony. "Teachers Fire Up History Students With Billy Joel Hit." the *Los Angeles Times*, February 11, 1990.

Marsh, Dave. "Billy Joel: The Miracle of 52nd Street." *Rolling Stone*, December 14, 1978.

Marshall, Harvey. "White Movement to the Suburbs: A Comparison of Explanations." *American Sociological Review* 44 (1979): 975–94.

Marston, Nicholas. "Schumann's Monument to Beethoven." *19th-Century Music* 14, no. 3 (1991): 247–64.

Massachusetts State Office of Energy and Environmental Affairs, Department of Fish and Game. http://www.mass.gov/eea/agencies/dfg/dmf/recreational-fishing/species-profiles-striped-bass.html. Accessed January 13, 2015.

Mayer, Ira. "The Stranger." *Rolling Stone*, December 15, 1977.

McAlley, John. "Billy Joel: Storm Front." *Rolling Stone*, November 30, 1989.

McCartney, Scott. *ENIAC: The Triumphs and Tragedies of the World's First Computer*. New York: Walker & Co., 1999.

Meyers, John Paul. "Still Like That Old Time Rock and Roll: Tribute Bands and Historical Consciousness in Popular Music." *Ethnomusicology* 59, no. 1 (2015): 61–81.

Mieszkowski, Peter, and Edwin S. Mills. "The Causes of Metropolitan Suburbanization." *Journal of Economic Perspectives* 7 (1993): 135–47.

Miller, James. *Flowers in the Dustbin: The Rise of Rock and Roll, 1947–1977*. New York: Fireside, 1999.

Mills, Edwin S., and Richard Price. "Metropolitan Suburbanization and Central City Problems." *Journal of Urban Economics* 15 (1984): 1–17.

Monson, Ingrid. *Saying Something: Jazz Improvisation and Interaction*. Chicago: University of Chicago Press, 1996.

Moore, Allan F. "Authenticity as Authentication." *Popular Music* 21, no. 2 (2002): 209–23.

———. *Song Means: Analysing and Interpreting Recorded Popular Song*. Burlington, VT: Ashgate, 2012.

Moore, Robin. *Music in the Hispanic Caribbean: Experiencing Music, Expressing Culture*. New York: Oxford University Press, 2009.

Morgan, Ted. *Reds: McCarthyism in Twentieth-Century America*. New York: Random House, 2004.

Morse, Steve. "Joel Comes Full Circle." *The Boston Globe*, October 17, 1989.

Nachman, Gerald. *Right Here on Our Stage Tonight!: Ed Sullivan's America*. Berkeley: University of California Press, 2009.

Nagley, Judith, and Arnold Whittall. "Cadence." *The Oxford Companion to Music*, ed. Alison Latham. *Oxford Music Online*. Oxford University Press. http://www.oxfordmusiconline.com/subscriber/article/opr/t114/e1072. Accessed February 8, 2016.

National Bureau of Economic Research. "US Business Cycle Expansions and Contractions." http://www.nber.org/cycles/cyclesmain.html. Accessed May 27, 2015.

National Oceanic and Atmospheric Association (NOAA). "FishWatch" page on the Atlantic striped bass. http://www.fishwatch.gov/seafood_profiles/species/bass/species_pages/atlantic_striped_bass.htm. Accessed January 13, 2015.

Negus, Keith. "Authorship and the Popular Song." *Music and Letters* 92, no. 4 (2011): 607–29.

Nelson, Paul. "Glass Houses." *Rolling Stone*, May 1, 1980.

"The New Miss, Near Misses." *Life*, September 15, 1961, 53.

Nolan, Frederick W. *The Lincoln County War: A Documentary History*. Norman: University of Oklahoma Press, 1992.

O'Donnell, Kevin. "Billy Joel Reflects on his Nearly 50-Year Career—and Breaking Records Today." *Entertainment Weekly*, July 24, 2015.

Opie, I., and P. Opie. *The Oxford Dictionary of Nursery Rhymes*, 2nd ed. Oxford: Oxford University Press, 1997[1951].

Page, Tim. "'Fantasies': Mr. Joel's Opus." The *Washington Post*, October 28, 2001, G02.

Palmer, Roy. "Shanty." *New Grove Dictionary of Music and Musicians. Grove Music Online, Oxford Music Online*. Oxford University Press. http://www.oxfordmusiconline.com/subscriber/article/grove/music/25583. Accessed January 27, 2015.

Platoff, John. "John Lennon, 'Revolution,' and the Politics of Musical Reception." *The Journal of Musicology* 22, no. 2 (2005): 241–67.

Plunkert, Lois M. "The 1980's: A Decade of Job Growth and Industry Shifts." Bureau of Labor Statistics *Monthly Labor Review*, September 1990, 3–16. http://www.bls.gov/mlr/1990/09/art1full.pdf. Accessed May 22, 2015.

Polizzotti, Mark. *Highway 61 Revisited*. New York: Bloomsbury, 2006.

Price, Charles Gower. "Sources of American Styles in the Music of the Beatles." *American Music* 15, no. 2 (1997): 208–32.

Puterbaugh, Parke. "An Innocent Man." *Rolling Stone*, August 18, 1983.

Rather, John. "A Way of Life Hinges on Bass." *The New York Times*, March 31, 1985, LI1.

Reitano, Joanne. *The Restless City: A Short History of New York from Colonial Times to the Present*. New York: Routledge, 2006.

"Remarks by the President at 2013 Kennedy Center Honors Reception." The White House, Office of the Press Secretary. December 8, 2013. https://www.whitehouse.gov/the-press-office/2013/12/08/remarks-president-2013-kennedy-center-honors-reception. Accessed March 11, 2016.

Righi, Len. "Billy Joel Revisits 'Allentown.'" *The Morning Call* (Allentown, PA), November 28, 2007.

Riley, Tim. *Tell Me Why: A Beatles Commentary*. New York: Knopf, 1988.

Roberts, Sam. "Infamous 'Drop Dead' Was Never Said By Ford." *The New York Times*, December 28, 2006.

Rockwell, John. "Billy Joel Sings the Praises of New York." *The New York Times*, December 10, 1978, B16–17.

———. "Billy Joel Brings Cuban Crowd to Its Feet." *The New York Times*, March 6, 1979, C11.

Rojas, Carlos. *The Great Wall: A Cultural History*. Cambridge, MA: Harvard University Press, 2010.

Rolston, Bill. "'This Is Not a Rebel Song': The Irish Conflict in Popular Music." *Race and Class* 42, no. 3 (2001): 49–67.

Root Beer Rag. "Live From Leningrad." Spring/Summer 1988. Library and Archives, Rock and Roll Hall of Fame and Museum. Michael Ochs Collection, Series 1, Subseries 2. Box 13, Folder 68.

Rosen, Charles. "Influence: Plagiarism and Inspiration." *19th-Century Music* 4, no. 2 (1980): 87–100.

Rosenbaum, Ron. "The Worst Pop Singer Ever: Why, Exactly, Is Billy Joel So Bad?" *Slate*, January 23, 2009.

Rosenblatt, Roger. "A New World Dawns." *Time*, January 3, 1983.

Rossi, Roberto. "Times Square and Potsdamer Platz: Packaging Development as Tourism." *The Drama Review* 42, no. 1 (1998): 43–48.

Rowland, David. "The Nocturne: Development of a New Style." In *The Cambridge Companion to Chopin*, ed. Jim Samson, 32–49. New York: Cambridge University Press, 1992.

Ruble, Blair A. *Leningrad: Shaping a Soviet City*. Berkeley: University of California Press, 1990.

Runowicz, John Michael. *Forever Doo-Wop: Race, Nostalgia, and Vocal Harmony*. Amherst: University of Massachusetts Press, 2010.

Scaggs, Austin. "Q and A: The Piano Man Hates to Love Britney's 'Toxic,' Dug the Cream Reunion and Wishes He Never Sang in French." *Rolling Stone*, December 15, 2005.

Scanlon, Joseph, Allison Vandervalk, and Mattea Chadwich-Shubat. "Challenge to the Lord: Folk Songs About the 'Unsinkable' Titanic." *Canadian Folk Music* 45, no. 3 (2011).

Schmidley, Dianne, and Arthur Cresce. "Tracking Hispanic Ethnicity: Evaluation of Current Population Survey Data Quality for the Question of Hispanic Origin, 1971 to 2004." U.S. Census Bureau Working Paper No. 80, December 2007. https://www.census.gov/population/www/documentation/twps0080/twps0080.pdf. Accessed July 9, 2014.

Schrecker, Ellen W. *The Age of McCarthyism: A Brief History with Documents*. Boston: St. Martin's, 1994.

Schruers, Fred. *Billy Joel: The Definitive Biography*. New York: Crown Archetype, 2014. This thoroughly detailed biography is the most recent and based on many hours of conversations with Joel himself.

Schultz, Robert D. "Three Analytical Essays in Twentieth-Century Music." MA Thesis, University of Washington, 2005. One of this thesis's three chapters examines classical constructions in Joel's compositions.

Scott, Richard. *Billy Joel: All About Soul*. New York: Vantage, 2000. Scott's relatively brief biography emphasizes Joel's recordings.

Seixas, Peter, ed. *Theorizing Historical Consciousness*. Toronto: University of Toronto Press, 2004.

Serrin, William. "Recession and Spreading Layoffs Hitting the White-Collar Worker." *The New York Times*, January 12, 1982, 1.

———. "Worry Grows over Upheaval as Technology Reshapes Jobs: Job Turmoil Is Predicted with New Technologies." *The New York Times*, July 4, 1982, 1.

Sheff, David, and Victoria Sheff. "Playboy Interview: Billy Joel." *Playboy*, May 1982. Republished at http://davidsheff.com/article/billy-joel/. Accessed February 16, 2016. One of the most extensive interviews with Joel, published as he completed a run of highly successful albums that made him a household name.

Shumway, David R. "The Emergence of the Singer-Songwriter." In *The Cambridge Companion to the Singer-Songwriter*, ed. Katherine Williams and Justin Williams, 11–20. New York: Cambridge University Press, 2016. Shumway provides a concise and instructive history of the term "singer-songwriter," including musical, economic, social, and cultural aspects.

Simonett, Helena. *The Accordion in the Americas: Klezmer, Polka, Zydeco, and More!* Urbana: University of Illinois Press, 2012.

Sinclair, Tom. "The Worst Song I Ever Wrote." *Entertainment Weekly*, August 16, 2002.

Smith, Bill. *I Go To Extremes: The Billy Joel Story*. London: Robson, 2007. In this biography, Smith is clearly a fan, but he had authorized access to Joel that many other biographers did not.

Stewart, Alex. *Making the Scene: Contemporary New York City Big Band Jazz*. Berkley: University of California Press, 2007.

Stokes, Martin. "Introduction: Ethnicity, Identity and Music." In *Ethnicity, Identity and Music: The Musical Construction of Place*, ed. Martin Stokes, 1–27. New York: Berg, 1994.

Strauss, Neil. "Sampling Is (a) Creative or (b) Theft?" *The New York Times*, September 14, 1997. In *The Pop, Rock, and Soul Reader: Histories and Debates*, ed. David Brackett, 422–23. New York: Oxford University Press, 2005.

Sussman, Mark. "New York's Facelift." *The Drama Review* 42, no. 1 (1998): 34–43.

Swain, Joseph P. *The Broadway Musical: A Critical and Musical Survey*. Lanham, MD: Scarecrow Press, 2002.

Tamarkin, Jeff. "Joel, Billy." *Grove Music Online, Oxford Music Online*. Oxford University Press. http://www.oxfordmusiconline.com/subscriber/article/grove/music/46857. Accessed July 27, 2015.

Tawa, Nicholas. *The Way to Tin Pan Alley: American Popular Song, 1866–1910*. New York: Schirmer, 1990.

Taylor, Timony D. *Global Pop: World Music, World Markets*. New York: Routledge, 1997.

Thomson, Liz. "Phil(ip Harvey) Spector." *Grove Music Online, Oxford Music Online*. Oxford University Press. http://www.oxfordmusiconline.com/subscriber/article/grove/music/47740. Accessed July 11, 2014.

Toossi, Mitra. "A Century of Change: the U.S. Labor Force, 1950–2050." Bureau of Labor Statistics *Monthly Labor Review*, May 2002, 15–28. http://www.bls.gov/opub/mlr/2002/05/art2full.pdf. Accessed May 22, 2015.

Unterberger, Richie. "The Beatles." *Allmusic*. http://www.allmusic.com/artist/the-beatles-mn0000754032/biography. Accessed January 27, 2016.

Utley, Robert M. *Billy the Kid: A Short and Violent Life*. Lincoln: University of Nebraska Press, 1989.

Van Riper, Frank. "Ford to City: Drop Dead." *Daily News* (New York), October 30, 1975.

von Clausewitz, Carl Phillip. *On War*. 1832. Ed. and trans. Michael Howard and Peter Paret. Princeton, NJ: Princeton University Press, 1989.

Wagner, Naphtali. "Fixing a Hole in the Scale: Suppressed Notes in the Beatles' Songs." *Popular Music* 23, no. 3 (2004): 257–69.

Waldron, Arthur. *The Great Wall of China: From History to Myth*. New York: Cambridge University Press, 1989.

Wallis, Michael. *Billy the Kid: The Endless Ride*. New York: W.W. Norton, 2007.

Wasko, Janet. *Understanding Disney: The Manufacture of Fantasy*. Malden, MA: Polity, 2001.

Webster, Bruce F. *The Y2K Survival Guide: Getting To, Getting Through, and Getting Past the Year 2000 Problem*. Upper Saddle River, NJ: Prentice Hall, 1999.

Weitzman, Steve. "Billy Joel Tickles the Phillies." *Rolling Stone*, June 20, 1974.

West, Aaron J. *Sting and The Police: Walking in Their Footsteps*. Lanham, MD: Rowman & Littlefield, 2015.

White, E. B. "This Is New York." 1949. Reprinted in *Empire City: New York Through the Centuries*, ed. Kenneth T. Jackson and David S. Dunbar, 695–711. New York: Columbia University Press, 2005.

White, Hayden. *Metahistory: The Historical Imagination in Nineteenth Century Europe*. Baltimore: Johns Hopkins University Press, 1973.

White, Timothy. *Rock Lives: Profiles and Interviews*. New York: Henry Holt and Company, 1990.

Wick, Steve. "Joel, Taking on His Neighbors' Cause." *Newsday*, October 4, 1992, 42.

Willibanks, James H. *The Tet Offensive: A Concise History*. New York: Columbia University Press, 2007.

Wollman, Elizabeth. "The Economic Development of the 'New' Times Square and Its Impact on the Broadway Musical." *American Music* 20, no. 4 (2002): 445–65.

WNEW. "Billy Joel" on *Here's the Thing*. July 30, 2012. Podcast. http://www.wnyc.org/story/225651-billy-joel/#transcript. Accessed August 4, 2015.

Womack, Kenneth. *Long and Winding Roads: The Evolving Artistry of the Beatles*. New York: Continuum, 2007.

Wright, Michael. "Maryland Tries to Save the Striped Bass." *The New York Times*, September 30, 1984, E8.

Wyatt, Clarence. "The Media and the Vietnam War." In *The War That Never Ends: New Perspectives on the Vietnam War*, ed. David L. Anderson and John Ernst, 265–87. Lexington: The University Press of Kentucky, 2007.

Zak, Albin. *The Poetics of Rock: Cutting Tracks, Making Records*. Berkley: University of California Press, 2001. In this book, Zak argues for the importance of sound in the study of rock music, providing detailed discussions of the various techniques and tools used to create and affect sound in rock recordings.

Zepp, Ira G. *The New Religious Image of Urban America: The Shopping Mall as Ceremonial Center*. Boulder: University Press of Colorado, 1997.

FURTHER LISTENING AND VIEWING

12-12-12: The Concert for Sandy Relief. PBS/WNET, December 12, 2012. Television.

Adams, Oleta. "New York State of Mind." Originally by Billy Joel. *Evolution*. Fontana, 1993. CD.

Anka, Paul. "I Go to Extremes." Originally by Billy Joel. *Classic Songs, My Way*. Decca, 2007. CD.

Attila. *Attila*. Epic, 1970. LP.

Baez, Joan. "Goodnight Saigon." Originally by Billy Joel. *Brothers in Arms*. Gold Castle, 1991. CD.

The Barkleys of Broadway. Dir. Charles Walters. Perf. Fred Astaire and Ginger Rogers. MGM, 1949. Film.

The Beach Boys. "Good Vibrations." By Brian Wilson and Mike Love. Capitol, 1966.

Beastie Boys. "Big Shot." Originally by Billy Joel. *Alive*. Capitol, 1999.

The Beatles. "Do You Want to Know a Secret." By John Lennon and Paul McCartney. *Please Please Me*. Parlophone, 1963.

———. *Please Please Me*. Parlophone, 1963. LP.

———. "I Want to Hold Your Hand." By John Lennon and Paul McCartney. *Meet the Beatles!* Capitol, 1963. LP.

———. "We Can Work It Out." By John Lennon and Paul McCartney. Capitol, 1965.

———. "For No One." By John Lennon and Paul McCartney. *Revolver*. Capitol, 1966. LP.

———. "I'm Only Sleeping." By John Lennon and Paul McCartney. *Revolver*. Capitol, 1966. LP.

———. *Sgt. Pepper's Lonely Hearts Club Band*. Capitol, 1967. LP. Joel cites this record as one of his chief influences, especially for his album *The Nylon Curtain*.

———. "A Day in the Life." By John Lennon and Paul McCartney. *Sgt. Pepper's Lonely Hearts Club Band*. Capitol, 1967. LP.

———. "Getting Better." By John Lennon and Paul McCartney. *Sgt. Pepper's Lonely Hearts Club Band*. Capitol, 1967. LP.

———. "All You Need Is Love." By John Lennon and Paul McCartney. *Magical Mystery Tour*. Capitol, 1967. LP.

———. "I Am the Walrus." By John Lennon and Paul McCartney. *Magical Mystery Tour*. Capitol, 1967. LP.

———. "Strawberry Fields Forever." By John Lennon and Paul McCartney. *Magical Mystery Tour*. Capitol, 1967. LP.

———. "Got To Get You Into My Life." By John Lennon and Paul McCartney. *Revolver*. Parlophone, 1966. LP.

———. *Let It Be*. Apple, 1970. LP.

————. "Across the Universe." By John Lennon and Paul McCartney. *Let It Be*. Apple, 1970. LP.

The Bell Telephone Hour. NBC, 1959–1968. Television.

Ben-Hur. Dir. William Wyler. Perf. Charlton Heston, Jack Hawkins, Haya Harareet, Stephen Boyd, and Hugh Griffith. MGM, 1959. Film.

Bennett, Tony. "New York State of Mind." Originally by Billy Joel. *Playin' with My Friends: Bennett Sings the Blues*. Sony, 2001. CD.

Berry, Chuck. "Roll Over Beethoven." Chess, 1956.

Beyoncé. "Honesty." Originally by Billy Joel. *I Am . . . Sasha Fierce*. Platinum edition. Columbia, 2009. CD.

Bosom Buddies. ABC, 1980–1982. Television.

Brooks, Garth. "Shameless." Originally by Billy Joel. *Ropin' the Wind*. Liberty, 1991. CD.

Charles, Ray. "Georgia on My Mind." By Hoagy Carmichael and Stuart Gorrell. *The Genius Hits the Road*. ABC-Paramount, 1960.

The Chords. "Sh-Boom (Life Could Be a Dream)." By James Keyes, Claude Feaster, Carl Feaster, Floyd F. McRae, and James Edwards. Cat, 1954.

The Concert for New York City. Sony, 2001. CD.

The Concert for New York City. Sony, 2002. DVD.

Connick Jr., Harry. "Just the Way You Are." Originally by Billy Joel. *Your Songs*. Columbia, 2009. CD.

the Crew Cuts. "Sh-Boom." By James Keyes, Claude Feaster, Carl Feaster, Floyd F. McRae, and James Edwards. 1954.

Crosby, Stills, Nash & Young. "Ohio." By Neil Young. *So Far*. Atlantic, 1970. LP.

the Crystals. "Then He Kissed Me." By Phil Spector, Ellie Greenwich, and Jeff Barry. London, 1963.

Dave's World. CBS, 1993–1997. Television.

Davy Crockett. Disney/ABC, 1954–1955. Television.

Dylan, Bob. "Hurricane." By Bob Dylan and Jacques Levy. *Desire*. Columbia, 1975. LP.

The Ed Sullivan Show. CBS, 1948–1971. Television. Arguably one of the most important television programs of the twentieth century. Joel was strongly influenced by The Beatles' appearance in 1964.

Flying Down to Rio. Dir. Thornton Freeland, George Nicholls Jr., and Ray Lissner. Perf. Dolores del Río, Gene Raymond, Ginger Rogers, Fred Astaire. RKO Radio Pictures, 1933. Film.

Frederick S. Boros Audio Recordings, Joel, Billy, Live at the Bottom, June 10, 1976. Library and Archives, Rock and Roll Hall of Fame and Museum. Box 6, Disks 61–62. CD.

Gerry & the Pacemakers. "It's Still Rock and Roll to Me." Originally by Billy Joel. *Ferry Across the Mersey*. United Artists, 1981. LP.

————. "Just the Way You Are." Originally by Billy Joel. *Ferry Across the Mersey*. United Artists, 1981. LP.

Glee. FOX, 2009–2015. Television.

Great Feats of Feet: A Video Portrait on Jazz and Tap Dance. Directed by Brenda Bufalino. Dancing Theater Productions, 1977. Film.

The Hangover. Dir. Todd Phillips. Perf. Bradley Cooper, Ed Helms, Zach Galifianakis, Heather Graham, Justin Bartha, Jeffrey Tambor. Warner Bros., 2009. Film.

The Hangover Part II. Dir. Todd Phillips. Perf. Bradley Cooper, Ed Helms, Zach Galifianakis, Ken Jeong, Jeffrey Tambor, Justin Bartha, Paul Giamatti. Warner Bros., 2011. Film.

The Hassles. *The Hassles*. United Artists, 1967. LP.

————. *Hour of the Wolf*. United Artists, 1969. LP.

Hayes, Isaac. "Just the Way You Are." Originally by Billy Joel. *For the Sake of Love*. Polydor, 1978. LP.

The Hunt for Red October. Dir. John McTiernan. Perf. Sean Connery, Alec Baldwin, Scott Glenn, James Earl Jones, Sam Neill. Paramount, 1990. Film.

"The Immortal Mr. Billy Joel." *Two and a Half Men*. Dir. James Widdoes. CBS, October 18, 2010. Television.

The Isley Brothers. "Twist and Shout." By Phil Medley and Bert Russell. *Twist & Shout.* Wand, 1962. LP.

Jackson, Michael. *Thriller.* Epic, 1982. LP.

Jazz Hoofer: The Legendary Baby Laurence. Directed by Bill Hancock. Rhapsody Films, 1986. Film.

Joel, Billy. *Cold Spring Harbor.* Family Productions, 1971. LP. Columbia, 1983. CD. Joel's first solo studio album.

———. *Piano Man.* Columbia, 1973. LP. Joel's second solo studio album and first to be released by Columbia Records.

———. *Streetlife Serenade.* Columbia, 1974. LP. Joel's third solo studio album.

———. *Turnstiles.* Columbia, 1976. LP. Joel's fourth solo studio album.

———. *The Stranger.* Columbia, 1977. LP. Joel's fifth solo studio album.

———. *52nd Street.* Columbia, 1978. LP. Joel's sixth solo studio album.

———. *Glass Houses.* Columbia, 1980. LP. Joel's seventh solo studio album.

———. *Songs in the Attic.* Columbia, 1981. LP. A live album featuring recordings of performances from the early part of Joel's career.

———. *The Nylon Curtain.* Columbia, 1982. LP. Joel's eighth solo studio album.

———. "Allentown" music video. Dir. Russell Mulcahy. 1982.

———. "She's Right On Time" music video. Dir. Russell Mulcahy. 1982.

———. *An Innocent Man.* Columbia, 1983. LP. Joel's ninth solo studio album.

———. "Tell Her About It" music video. Dir. Jay Dubin and Jon Small. 1983.

———. *Greatest Hits, Vol. I & Vol. II.* Columbia, 1985. CD.

———. *The Bridge.* Columbia, 1986. CD. Joel's tenth solo studio album.

———. *Kohuept.* Columbia, 1987. CD. A live album recorded during Joel's 1987 tour of the Soviet Union.

———. *Storm Front.* Columbia, 1989. CD. Joel's eleventh solo studio album.

———. *Live at Yankee Stadium.* Sony, 1990. VHS.

———. *River of Dreams.* Columbia, 1993. CD. Joel's twelfth solo studio album.

———. *Greatest Hits, Volume III.* Columbia, 1997. CD.

———. *Greatest Hits Volume III: The Video.* Dir. Andrew Morahan, Chris Blum, Derek Horne, Ernie Fritz, Howard Deutch. Perf. Billy Joel, Ray Charles. Sony, 1998. DVD.

———. *2000 Years: The Millennium Concert.* Columbia, 2000. CD. A live album recorded on December 31, 1999.

———. *Fantasies & Delusions: Music for Solo Piano.* Columbia/Sony Classical, 2001. CD. Joel's first album of classical compositions, performed by Richard Joo.

———. *My Lives.* Sony, 2005. CD.

———. *12 Gardens Live.* Columbia, 2006. CD.

———. *Live at Shea Stadium: The Concert.* Sony, 2011. CD, DVD.

———. "Q&A—Story of 'Summer, Highland Falls?' (Nuremberg 1995) Pt7." http://vevo.ly/qVSCSR (accessed July 29, 2015).

———. Personal interviews with the author. September 3, 2015, and October 15, 2015.

The Johnny Carson Show. CBS, 1955–1956. Television.

Kiss Me Kate. Dir. George Sidney. Perf. Kathryn Grayson, Howard Keel, and Ann Miller. MGM, 1953. Film.

Krall, Diana. "Just the Way You Are." Originally by Billy Joel. *Live in Paris.* Verve, 2002. CD.

The Lawrence Welk Show. KTLA/ABC, 1951–1971. Television.

Little Richard. "Long Tall Sally." By Enotris Johnson, Robert Blackwell, and Richard Penniman. Specialty, 1956.

The Magnificent Seven. Dir. John Sturges. Perf. Yul Brenner, Eli Wallach, Steve McQueen, Charles Bronson, Robert Vaughn, Horst Buchholz, and James Coburn. United Artists, 1960. Film.

Mathis, Johnny, and Deniece Williams. "Just the Way You Are." Originally by Billy Joel. *That's What Friends Are For.* Columbia, 1978. LP.

McRae, Carmen. "New York State of Mind." Originally by Billy Joel. *I'm Coming Home Again.* Buddah, 1981. LP.

Midler, Bette. "Say Goodbye to Hollywood." Originally by Billy Joel. *Broken Blossom*. Atlantic, 1977. LP.

Mitchell, Joni. "Free Man in Paris." *Court and Spark*. Asylum, 1974. LP.

N'Dour, Youssou. *The Guide (Wommat)*. Columbia, 1994. CD.

No Maps on my Taps: The Art of Jazz Tap Dancing. Directed by George T. Nierenberg. GTN Productions, 1979. Film.

The Office. NBC, 2005–2013. Television.

On the Waterfront. Dir. Elia Kazan. Perf. Marlon Brando. Columbia Pictures, 1954. Film.

Parton, Dolly. "Travelin' Prayer." Originally by Billy Joel. *The Grass is Blue*. Blue Eye/Sugar Hill, 1999. CD.

The Police. "Invisible Sun." By Sting. *Ghost in the Machine*. A&M, 1981. LP.

the Righteous Brothers. "You've Lost That Lovin' Feelin'." By Phil Spector, Barry Mann, and Cynthia Weil. Philles, 1964.

Ruthless People. Dir. Jim Abrahams, David Zucker, Jerry Zucker. Perf. Danny DeVito, Judge Reinhold, Helen Slater, Bette Midler. Touchstone Films, 1986. Film.

Saturday Night Live. NBC, 1975–present. Television.

Seven Samurai. Dir. Akira Kurosawa. Perf. Toshiro Mifune, Takashi Shimura, Keiko Tsushima, Isao Kimura, Daisuke Kato, Seiji Miyaguchi, Yoshio Inaba, Minoru Chiaki, Kamatari Fujiwara, Kokuten Kodo, Yoshio Tsuchiya, Yukiko Shimazaki, Eijiro Tono, and Bokuzen Hidari. Toho, 1954. Film.

Simon, Paul. *Still Crazy After All These Years*. Columbia, 1975. LP.

Sinatra, Frank. "Just the Way You Are." Originally by Billy Joel. *Trilogy: Past, Present, Future*. Reprise, 1980. LP.

Singin' in the Rain. Dir. Gene Kelly and Stanly Donen. Perf. Gene Kelly, Donald O'Connor, Debbie Reynolds, Jean Hagen, Millard Mitchell, and Cyd Charisse. MGM, 1952. Film.

Spector, Ronnie. "Say Goodbye to Hollywood." Originally by Billy Joel. Epic, 1977.

Springsteen, Bruce. "Born in the U.S.A." *Born in the U.S.A.* Columbia, 1984. LP.

Sting. "Russians." *The Dream of Blue Turtles*. A&M, 1985. LP.

Streisand, Barbra. "New York State of Mind." Originally by Billy Joel. *Superman*. Columbia, 1977. LP.

The Surfaris. "Wipe Out." By Bob Berryhill, Pat Connolly, Jim Fuller, and Ron Wilson. Dot, 1963.

Tormé, Mel. "New York State of Mind." Originally by Billy Joel. *Tormé: A New Album*. Gryphon, 1977. LP.

U2. "Sunday Bloody Sunday." *War*. Island, 1983. LP.

———. "Pride (In the Name of Love)." *The Unforgettable Fire*. Island, 1984. LP.

White, Barry. "Just the Way You Are." Originally by Billy Joel. *The Man*. 20th Century Fox Records, 1978. LP.

WNYC. "Here's the Thing: Billy Joel." July 30, 2012. http://www.wnyc.org/story/225651-billy-joel/ (accessed August 4, 2015).

Wynette, Tammy. "Stand By Your Man." By Billy Sherrill and Tammy Wynette. *Stand By Your Man*. Epic, 1968. LP.

INDEX

ABOUT THE AUTHOR

Joshua S. Duchan is an ethnomusicologist specializing in American popular music. He earned his PhD from the University of Michigan with a dissertation on collegiate a cappella groups, which led to the publication of his first book, *Powerful Voices: The Musical and Social World of Collegiate A Cappella* (2012). Dr. Duchan's other publications include essays in *American Music* (2007), the edited collection *Play It Again: Cover Songs in Popular Music* (2010), the *Journal of American Folklore* (2012), the *Journal on the Art of Record Production* (2013), *Rock Music Studies* (2015), the book *A Cappella* (2015), the *American Music Research Center Journal* (2015), and *The Cambridge Companion to the Singer-Songwriter* (2016). He has presented his work at meetings of the American Musicological Society, the Society for American Music, the Society for Ethnomusicology, the International Council for Traditional Music, the International Association for the Study of Popular Music, the international Art of Record Production conference, and at various conferences on and festivals of a cappella music. Dr. Duchan is on the faculty of the Department of Music at Wayne State University in Detroit, Michigan, where he serves as the department's director of graduate studies and teaches undergraduate and graduate courses in music history, world music, popular music, and ethnomusicology.